The Chalk Goddess

Conversations with a Witch

LOIS BOURNE

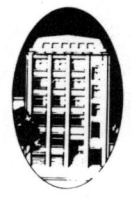

ROBERT HALE · LONDON

© Lois Bourne 1989
First published in Great Britain 1989

Robert Hale Limited
Clerkenwell House
Clerkenwell Green
London EC1R 0HT

British Library Cataloguing in Publication Data

Bourne, Lois
Conversations with a witch : a witch talks frankly about her work and beliefs.
1. England. Witchcraft. Bourne, Lois
I. Title
133.4'3'0924

ISBN 0-7090-3829-1

Photoset in North Wales by
Derek Doyle & Associates, Mold, Clwyd.
Printed in Great Britain by
St Edmundsbury Press Ltd, Bury St Edmunds, Suffolk.
Bound by WBC Bookbinders Limited.

Contents

Foreword		11
1	Letters to a Witch	13
2	A Vision, a Visitor and a Black Witch	24
3	Magic, Amulets and Black Magic	34
4	Money, Magic and Light Relief	43
5	A Family Affair	48
6	Encounters in Other Lands	56
7	Crystal Vision	65
8	Psychometry and Clairvoyance	77
9	Meditation	86
10	Shades of Jung and Stone Circles	93
11	Weather, Wedding and Familiars	102
12	Invocation and Artemis	111
13	The Goddess in the Ancient World	122
14	Hallowe'en	134
15	Major Festivals	144
16	Questions on Witchcraft	153
17	Healing and a Visitation	163
18	When an Animal Dies	172
19	On Reincarnation	182
20	Communion	191
21	Further Communion	200
22	Mediums and Mysticism	206
Bibliography		219

For
David and Gyll – Mark and Jan
Adam and Rosalind
and
To the memory of Sam

By the same author

Witch Amongst Us: The Autobiography of a Witch

I am whatever hath been, is, or ever will be,
and my veil, no man hath yet lifted.

> Inscription over the portal of the Temple of Isis

To disbelieve in witchcraft is the greatest of all heresies.

> Malleus Maleficarum, 1486

Hear O ye regions, the praise of Queen Nana: Magnify the Creatress; exalt the dignified; exalt the Glorious One; draw nigh to the Mighty Lady.

> Sumer, nineteenth century BC

The Beautiful Artemis from Ephesus

Foreword

Biologist John Randall has said –

> that we all have an internal model of the world which has developed as a result of years of practical experience, and which is perfectly adequate for everyday life. According to this model we live in a uniform space of three dimensions in which all objects behave in an orderly way, retain their shape and position unless acted on directly by some outside force, and are lawfully organised in a linear sequence which moves inevitably from the past, through the present and into the future.
>
> Our minds are strongly conditioned by this model, programmed and predisposed to look for explanations of each new event which will be consistent with it. The chances are that any event which does not fit and cannot be made to conform will be discounted, forgotten or rejected altogether.
>
> The effect of a confrontation with a bizarre fact on a balanced mind is to reject it and refuse to consider it. The more bizarre the fact, the stronger the reaction.

One would imagine that books on witchcraft and paranormal experience would fall into this category, but the thousands of letters I have received since the publication of my first book, *Witch Amongst Us* demonstrate a great interest in the mystical and magical elements of life. There is a growing awareness of the importance of psychic phenomena in the steady movement towards the search for alternative answers to the questions which mankind has asked since our ancient ancestors became capable of logical thought, shown by the desire of many people to explore their own personal spiritual potential.

This book in some respects, is a response to the questions asked by readers. I have called it *Conversations with a Witch* because it is ruminative and speculative as conversations often are, and covers the diverse themes referred to by my correspondents concerning my continuing spiritual and psychic experiences, their curiosity about my family life and how deeply my commitment to magical activity extends into this.

My search for kernels of truth in all religions has led me into pathways and experiences not directly associated with witchcraft, or the Old Religion as it is sometimes called. I have gained wisdom from all these diverse wanderings and encounters, and been gratified to discover elements of the ancient *Magna Mater* in even the most masculine-orientated faiths.

Maxim Gorky, the Russian author said, 'Generally speaking, there is nothing fantastic in life. All that seems mysterious has a very definite basis in reality ...', and Gautama the Buddha (563–483 BC) emphasized in addresses to his followers that they should not necessarily believe the word of others merely because they commanded higher authority, but to form one's own conclusions, from one's own studies, examinations and evaluations.

I welcome observations and opportunities to learn of the experiences of others. A stamped addressed envelope would be appreciated with letters requiring a reply (international reply coupons if abroad).

Finally, my thanks to Judy Billson for supplying the illustrations to this book.

1 *Letters to a Witch*

Answering the urgent summons of my doorbell one evening, I encountered the stern and stony faces of two detectives, one of whom unsmilingly enquired, 'Mrs Bourne, is it? We are from the CID and we are making enquiries regarding a murder, may we speak to you in private please?'

My heart missed a couple of beats, and suspecting a practical joke I replied, 'You're not serious, are you?'.

'I am afraid we are,' this uncompromising guardian of the Law asserted and I had little alternative but to invite them into my house.

After a frantic affectionate attack and enthusiastic licking from my dog, which did not amuse them, the story emerged of a young woman who was found murdered in the North of England, and among her effects was discovered either a letter from me, or my name and address in her address book, and they required to know the basis of my association with her. I did not recognize her name, nor any of the several aliases that she frequently used, nor did her photograph strike any chord of remembrance. The previous week, whilst on holiday in the Lake District, I had seen a programme called 'Crimewatch' on television which had included a re-enactment of this particular murder and I recalled the case. The detectives were clearly highly suspicious of me and I found their cold appraisal rather unnerving.

It suddenly dawned on me that perhaps this poor woman was one of the thousands of people who had written to me since the publication of a book called *Witch Amongst Us* and I had replied to her; perhaps she had kept my letter or my address for future reference. Almost immediately on revealing this information to the two detectives, the tension in the atmosphere evaporated, their features relaxed, almost into smiles, and they asked me in an avuncular manner if I possessed her letter. Unfortunately I did not. At that time I destroyed correspondence after I had replied to it, and I was unable to give them any further assistance despite repeated probing of my memory. They wrote out a statement which was read to me, I signed it, and after some casual conversation unrelated to their visit, they departed.

I very much regretted that I had not kept all my correspondence, perhaps this woman's letter had referred to a recalcitrant lover or an enemy who was her murderer and I could have helped with his identity, always presuming it was a male; this incident served to reinforce the sense of responsibility I feel towards people who take the trouble to write to me after reading my book.

People write to me for a variety of reasons. Why to a witch? What is a witch? The stereotype of the wrinkled old hag crouching over a cauldron, pointing a bony finger and muttering incantations is the picture which would most clearly come to mind, but it is actually likely to be the furthest from the truth. The witch today has become, as well as the weaver of mankind's fabled dreams of magic spells, the adviser and counsellor; she gives strength to the weak, comfort and consolation to the bereaved and hope to the despairing. She is Samaritan, Social Worker and Marjorie Proops; her prescient abilities are always in demand. 'Will an impending court case be successful for the enquirer?' 'If the crystal ball or the Tarot say 'no', can a magic spell be worked to reverse the portents?' 'Should a woman bored with her life and her husband, fly into the willing arms of her lover?' – She is usually advised that her lover is as likely to become as boring as her husband in time, and she should stay where she is, nurturing her security and making some attempt to revive the magic in her marriage.

The brave men who write complaining of impotence are invariably advised in the first instance to consult their doctor, since this is a condition which can often easily be cured by medicine or referral to a sex therapist. If all else fails, a certain herb can be suggested or a magic spell invoked.

Dear old ladies are attracted to witches; in their youth many were likely to have lived in a village where there was a local wise woman, the dispenser of all wisdom and knowledge. A woefully unhappy elderly lady wrote to me that the house next door was being used as a workshop and a concrete-mixer rumbled all night long disturbing her sleep. The police and the local environmental officer had all investigated and found the premises empty. Her solicitor had suggested wearily, 'Why don't you move house?' It was all in her mind but she could not be convinced and with the best will in the world, I could not spirit away a non-existent cement-mixer.

Requests for a talisman to increase sex appeal and encourage a love affair are a recurring theme in my postbag, but requests for healing of mind or body receive priority of attention and I often refer them to other healers if I have more than I can successfully handle.

Perhaps troubled people turn to witches because they feel a sense of alienation in a world of such advanced technology, there is a desperate need for someone with time, patience and compassion to listen and understand. Family units are often separated by distance, the witch with her long history of magic, spells and mystery from the distant past, calls to the atavism in our natures, and provides a sense of continuity with a calmer and more spacious age; she is the last link with Mother Nature and the ancient gods of these islands, they who held the destinies of mankind in their hands, perhaps these gods can be called upon for aid through the intercession of the witch.

The problems of people today are not so different from those of our ancestors. I am no longer asked to work a spell for strong sons to till the land, for good crops at harvest time and fertile cattle, but difficulties in human relationships still obtain. The need for stability, for love and companionship is still overwhelming, modern science cannot cure all the diseases of mind and body, and the witch, with her powers and psychic ability, is often the last hope of a despairing cry for healing and the relief of pain.

Trouble is endemic to the human species; everyone encounters problems, but not all have the courage or strength of mind to cope constructively and so mature and grow spiritually. A witch, if she is wise, does not always provide a solution and so deprive a person of initiative, instead she may suggest a path where illumination may be found, counselling patience and endurance and the precept of Socrates: 'If all our misfortunes were laid in a common heap, whence everyone must take an equal portion, most people would be happy to take their own and depart'.

The wisdom of witchcraft is basically common sense, it is knowing what is possible and what is not. Some people imagine that I am a panacea for all ills, that all I have to do is wriggle my nose or wave my magic wand and I can solve every problem in their lives.

A man wrote to me that he had been unemployed for six years

and wished that I could find him a job. He lived in a basement flat which was always damp because the tenants above him habitually allowed the bath and the sink to overflow with water which dripped down his walls; he wished that I could make them cease doing this. He was lonely and wished that I could help him to find a girlfriend, but even if I did, he did not have a decent suit to wear when escorting her; neither did he feel that he could entertain her in a damp flat, nor did he have any money to take her anywhere. When he visited his parents, his father was invariably drunk and his mother never had any money because she gambled it all away on bingo. He wished that I could solve all these problems.

I read the letter to my husband and asked, 'What would you do if you were in his situation?'

He replied in a heartfelt voice, 'I'd cut my throat!'

'That,' I retorted with some asperity, 'is no answer.'

I was very tempted to reply to this man that if he used his backbone as often as he used his wishbone he would be half-way to solving at least his own difficulties. Instead, I suggested that we first tackle the job situation, when he was established and earning money he could then seek alternative accommodation, and hopefully renewed confidence in his changed life style would result in improved self-projection and he would find a girlfriend.

Another letter came from a man whose wife whilst holidaying abroad had fallen in love with another man. On her return home she informed her husband that she intended to leave him and their two teenage children, and a short time later she departed. He wrote that he was absolutely devastated by the loss of his wife, his children were inconsolable and he begged me to influence her magically to return, otherwise he would commit suicide.

It is a fallacy that people who threaten suicide never do it and I was very concerned about his state of mind. Nevertheless, I am usually very reluctant to interfere in marital affairs since the only people who know what has occurred within a marriage are the couple themselves. I meditated deeply on the matter and reasoned that since his wife was a woman of mature years and quite capable of deciding where her happiness lay, I had no justification to interfere with her free will, despite her husband's desperation, and I replied to him to this effect.

He refused to accept my decision and wrote another pleading letter, again threatening suicide if I did not accede to his request. My reply was more robust and I declined to be influenced by emotional blackmail, but to give him some comfort I examined his future trends. I saw that there would be a divorce in his life and that within a period of eighteen months he would begin an association which would result in a second marriage. He appeared slightly mollified by my predictions and said he would let me know if they came true. Two years later he wrote that he was about to remarry and, ever the opportunist, asked for a spell to bless his marriage with happiness and this time I was glad to oblige.

I am constantly surprised by the forbearance of some women within the marital relationship. A middle-aged woman correspondent told me that for several years her husband had lived in a town some miles distant with another woman. He continued to support her but on the understanding that she informed any curious neighbours that he was working away from home. His grown-up family were aware of this peculiar situation but were at a loss to know how it could be resolved.

A similar story concerned a professional man who also lived with his mistress some miles from his wife. He visited her occasionally assuring her that he still loved her and intended returning to the marital home but that his mistress completely satisfied his sexual requirements. Both women nurtured a naïve belief that their husbands would eventually return and conveniently maintained an open door so that the recalcitrant husbands could creep back should their illicit relationships prove abortive. My function would have been to speed their return although my instincts dictated otherwise.

I occasionally receive letters from people who mistake me for a house-agent and ask me to work a spell to sell a house for them. I cannot engender any enthusiasm to sell houses, although I have done it on a few occasions to oblige a friend. One needed to sell his house quickly because he was about to be gazumped in the purchase of another property. I helped to sell the first within two days, and my friend acquired the second at the price he had originally agreed. However, I refuse to make a habit of selling houses as it is very boring magic.

One of the most unusual requests I have received was from a woman who was researching her ancestry. She had traced everyone in the family except her husband's great-great-grandmother and she asked me if I could find this woman for her; I am not sure where I was supposed to look.

Another strange request was from a woman whose son was an

army officer; she had a good relationship with his wife and had two lovely grandchildren. Her problem was that her daughter-in-law had a very common voice and a loud laugh and drew attention to herself. I was asked if I could change the daughter-in-law's voice. Whilst I was amused at her request I was not really surprised, she obviously subscribed to the fairy-tale idea that a witch is capable of doing absolutely everything in a magical sense.

A woman wrote to me that she lived in a state of complete chaos, she was permanently exhausted and could not cope with either her part-time job, her children, her cooking or her housework; she asked me to work a spell on her to make her more organized.

I have lost count of the number of women who request assistance in maintaining a diet; they submit a wide variety of excuses as to why they cannot exercise self-control in their eating-habits and beg me to help them with a magical spell.

It is interesting that I seldom receive letters from the mentally ill, and only occasionally from someone with an intense obsession, which is usually too convoluted for me to offer any help. Such a case was a twenty-page letter from a woman who impressed me as being completely sane and rational, apart from an obsession that at a nearby RAF establishment was a man who was completely unknown to her but whom she was destined to marry. Various clairvoyants had given her the same message from a member of her family now deceased that her future husband was stationed at this establishment. She had even received a message from the deceased father of her future husband confirming the fact that she was intended to marry his son. Her problem was that she did not know the identity of this man, and the matter was complicated, and credence in her mind given to the prophecies, because various other events which had been foretold had actually occurred. Her request to me was that I would discover the identity of the man so that she could write to him and establish contact.

A recurring theme in my correspondence is a request to act as a psychic mediator in family quarrels; sons or daughters estranged from parents whom they accuse of irrational behaviour and vice versa; every sorrow and tragedy of human life passes through my letter-box.

I receive far more requests for help than I can logically handle. All of them touch my heart and I have a great desire to bring peace and happiness to all the people who write to me, but it is a physical impossibility, I have to eat and sleep and work, and if I practised all the magical spells that I am requested to do, I would never do anything else.

The happy results of the ones that I do work on give me immense pleasure. I received a letter from a man who was very lonely. He and his wife had been divorced for many years, he lived alone in a bed-sitter and had a married son with two lovely children who lived in a distant town. He never saw his grandchildren because he confessed that he had at one time been financially involved with an unsavoury group of people to whom he had owed money and they had threatened to kidnap one of his grandchildren. He had been obliged to warn his son and daughter-in-law and the latter had, not unnaturally, since regarded him as *persona non grata* and refused to allow him to see his grandchildren. This state of affairs had continued for several years and he asked me to help him. He provided me with a picture of the grandchildren and I made a special magical endeavour for reconciliation. He wrote to me in great excitement ten days later and said that 'quite out of the blue' he had received a telephone call from his son inviting him for the weekend.

Whilst shopping, I met by chance a man from whose finger I had removed a wart some years ago and he insisted on reminiscing about what was to me a trivial, but to him a major, event in his life. 'You put your thumb on it,' he said, 'And muttered something under your breath and after a couple of days I was amazed to find it had disappeared. I didn't really believe you could do it, and when I told you that you merely replied "It doesn't matter whether you believe or not, it's only important that I believe I can do it".'

Disbelief on the part of a person for whom I am working is no barrier to successful magic, although if they do have faith it obviously helps.

A man wrote that he had several warts on a very personal part of his anatomy and he was very disturbed because recent medical research had revealed a connection between genital warts and cervical carcinoma in women. I would have very much liked to have helped him but since it is necessary that I actually touch the warts I felt that in this instance it was inappropriate.

I receive many letters from people who believe they are cursed with misfortune and they cannot make headway in any direction, often they describe lives that seem to have been totally disastrous. It is possible to remove 'curses', and in a few cases when I am given evidence that a curse could be at the root of the problem I agree to do it. Generally speaking, however, when I exercise some psychic perception I invariably discover that they are experiencing a retrograde period which happens to most people from time to time and I am able to give encouragement by an indication of when this negative period is likely to pass.

What is alarming to some degree is the number of people who write complaining of malignant pyschic manifestations in their home environment. One woman experienced poltergeist phenomena when pots and pans flew through the air, writing appeared on walls and mirrors and she was physically attacked by a bird which would suddenly appear from nowhere and peck her face, drawing blood. Her husband told me he was a complete disbeliever, but had to acknowledge that these things were happening; he was helpless, his wife was on the verge of a nervous breakdown and they seemed to have sought help from every quarter with the possible exception of the fire brigade.

Another woman wrote that her house on the coast was haunted. The house was several hundred years old and she had discovered from its history that it had in the past been the centre of smuggling activities. At frequent periods, usually at the time of a waxing or full moon, a ghostly figure would appear and heavy footsteps were heard along a corridor leading to the cellar. A clairvoyant had told her that it was a smuggler searching for his ill-gotten gold. A superficial search of the cellar had revealed no obvious hiding-place and she required my advice as to whether I considered it worthwhile to tear the cellar apart in the hope that she would discover the gold; she was more interested in the gold than the ghost!

A client at my office told me of a very pleasant haunting of his home. He lives in a modern house and all his family have at times seen the ghostly apparition of a young girl child wearing a long white dress of old-fashioned design. They hear her singing nursery rhymes and a rocking-chair frequently rocks by itself. His aunt, a Spiritualist, is very anxious to hold a séance in the house to discover the identity of the child, but he and his family are unwilling fearing that it may result in the cessation of the haunting.

Ghostly visitations are much more common than is generally realized, and very often when I lecture on the subject of witchcraft, I am subsequently approached by members of the audiences anxious to tell me of their own experiences. One informant, who had nursed her invalid mother at home for many years, said that whenever she went in the lady's former bedroom she invariably found a dent in the pillow and the bed unmade as if the now dead mother had recently been lying in it. Various items of linen would periodically disappear from the linen cupboard, and she would later find them all neatly folded in her late mother's bedroom.

An Australian friend who was recently widowed wrote that one evening whilst she was sitting quietly at home, she heard the front door open and saw through the hall passageway her late husband. She called out 'Oh, it's you, Peter', forgetting for an instant that he was dead. She rose to greet him, and then remembering found the hall empty.

This friend told me of another experience when staying at her married daughter's home in Tasmania. The house was quite old by Australian standards and had formerly been owned by a doctor. On one occasion she woke in the middle of the night and heard a male voice say 'Are you in pain? Lie down on the couch and let me examine you'. She had for some reason associated the voice with her son-in-law and as she slept in a wing of the house separate from the family asked her son-in-law if he had been wandering around in the night but he denied it. Enquiries elicited the information that the doctor's surgery had been in that wing of the house and she was obviously sensitive to some emanation from the past.

There is a curious phenomenon which occurs particularly in old buildings. Stone, brick and wood are good conductors of psychic energy which is absorbed into them and released periodically to the surprise of people who sense or hear the emanations. Psychic investigators opine that highly charged emotions such as fear, pain, unhappiness or even great joy emit energy which is absorbed into the surroundings, and this would account for the uncanny feelings that many people experience in old houses and near ancient monuments.

The daughter of one of my friends, on moving into a modern flat complained of an eerie feeling of being watched all the time; her kitchen was always icy cold despite central heating, and household articles were forever disappearing and re-appearing in odd places, such as a teapot in the bathroom. Her child's push-chair completely disappeared from the hall and was subsequently found in the street. My friend's daughter was very alarmed by these strange occurrences and wondered if the flat was haunted and if that would account for the fact that her small daughter woke up screaming several times a night.

I was approached for my advice and with a possible view to exorcism. Now I am a witch not a professional exorcist, and whilst it is true that there is within the rituals of witchcraft a rite of exorcism I have not used it very often. I do not have the time to chase around the country conducting exorcism services and when overtures are made to me for such services I usually suggest the application of various techniques. If these fail, I put people in touch with an agency who specialize in exorcism. Since this particular haunting was in my locality, however, I agreed to investigate and made the necessary arrangements with my friend to visit her daughter's flat.

The flat was located on the third floor of a modern block, having been built a mere ten years previously. As I walked through the door into the hall I encountered a blast of cold air, despite it being a warm midsummer evening, and I sensed a presence. I walked into every room and quietly intuited the ambience of the place and decided that the kitchen was undoubtedly the source. I asked the two women to leave me alone in there. I sat incongruously in the middle of the kitchen on a stool, closed my eyes and meditated. After about ten minutes, I began to feel a blast of cold air around my legs. I ignored it and kept my eyes firmly closed. The cold air then moved over my hands and around my head, and I felt my face chilled and my hair moving in the draught, and it seemed to me that the stool upon which I sat was gently vibrating. I decided it was time to acknowledge the presence of the wraith; I opened my eyes, raised my head and enquired loudly and suddenly, 'Who are you?' Immediately the vibration of the stool and the current of cold air ceased.

It was twilight by this time, there was no light in the kitchen beyond that which permeated from the darkening sky outside, and I peered uncertainly into the shadowy corners, hoping that there would be some sort of physical manifestation towards which I could address my words. Eventually, I sensed some slight movement in one corner of the room but the spirit refused to show itself and merely indicated its presence.

I became clairvoyantly aware that the ghost was that of a very old man who had been the previous tenant of the flat. He resented the intrusion of other people into what he considered was still his home. He meant no real harm, he just wanted them to leave. He was confused and earthbound and I explained to him that he had passed beyond the bounds of this life into the next sphere of existence and no longer had a place here. I said that he should ask for help and guidance to reach him and that I would pray for him. I then spoke the ancient words of the ceremony of exorcism, and as I intoned the beautiful Latin phrases, I become aware of a light in the corner of the room which shimmered and trembled for a second, and then disappeared, taking with it the dark shadow. I continued to sit in the kitchen for a little while and uttered a simple prayer for the old man's peace and guidance. Gradually the temperature of the room returned to normal.

My friend and her daughter were agog to learn what had occurred, having been nervously waiting for me to join them. The flat was no longer haunted, and I was interested to learn later that subsequent enquiries revealed that the previous tenant had in fact been an old man who had died suddenly and his body was discovered in the kitchen.

2   A Vision, a Visitor and a Black Witch

I receive many letters from women who are involved in relationships and fear they are about to lose the man concerned. The request is usually for a binding spell to bind the man to them or, if love appears to be disintegrating, for a spell of enchantment to be worked. Witches possess a fairly high moral code in their dealings with people and we are forbidden to interfere too much in a person's free will without a very good reason indeed. Binding and enchantment spells are not permanent, they eventually lose their potency and have to be reinforced; consequently, if I agree to this type of request I have committed myself to a periodic service to the same person and I am not prepared to do this – quite apart from the fact that I consider it slightly immoral to influence magically a man to stay with a woman he no longer loves. Many of the decisions I make are arbitrary, but they have to be by the very nature of what they entail in the lives of people.

There is a tremendous effort of mind, will and concentration, combined with physical and emotional energy required in the working of magic and some of the requests I receive do not, in my opinion, justify the exertion. A typical example is a girl of twenty-five who fell in love and went to live with a man in a far from comfortable flat. In addition to his normal daytime occupation, he was training in the evenings for another job and she was left alone for long periods. He also wished to spend time with male friends which further restricted their togetherness. Unable to tolerate this sort of life she left him although they remained friends and continued to meet twice a week on a platonic level. She wrote to me that she still loved him and wished to revert to living with him, mutual friends had assured her that he still loved her, and she requested me to work a spell to bring his love for her to a point where it would be an overwhelming desire in his life.

I declined. My feeling was that the situation was just too

convoluted because implicit in this request was that he should sacrifice his ambitions to her personal and somewhat selfish needs. Even if I had been prepared to do this, she would not have been happy to live again in that particular flat and the next request would be to help them find better accommodation. I gave her some counselling instead, which probably disappointed her, but in my opinion what was required was not a magic spell but a meaningful discussion about their mutual future and intentions. People have to make efforts on their own behalf and not expect a witch to do everything for them.

So many couples, married and unmarried, appear to have a complete inability to communicate adequately with each other. Women write to me with long lists of complaints against their husbands, the things they do and the things they do not do. I am requested to remake the husband nearer to what his wife desires. I wonder sometimes why they got married in the first place if they were so incompatible.

Having said that, some women do have justifiable complaints. One woman wrote to me that the roof of her house leaked and her husband, rather than get it repaired had fixed up a Heath Robinson contraption in their bedroom to catch the water when it rained. One stormy night, the bucket hanging over their bed overflowed, drenching them both, and still he refused to get the roof repaired. I did not know whether I should laugh or weep for her.

Some of my encounters are very sad. I was approached by a boy of about fifteen who was very interested in magic and witchcraft and had read extensively on the subject. I normally discourage such young people from their curiosity, but he invariably appeared on my doorstep on a cold winter evening without an overcoat and ravenously hungry and all my maternal instincts were aroused as I concentrated on feeding and warming him. I confess that I felt rather sorry for him, although I quite soon became aware that he had a vivid imagination and was an inveterate liar as his professed experiences with the supernatural were bizarre, to say the least, for someone of such tender years. He told me that he was always in trouble at school and had been suspended on many occasions for misbehaviour and trying to involve other youngsters in what he termed 'occult practices'. He had also been in trouble with the police in his village and had been advised to 'make himself scarce' and his mother found him unmanageable.

That much was true. I telephoned his mother who was

divorced from his father, she confirmed his troubles at school and with the police and said that he was a wicked incorrigible boy and she despaired of his future. He stole from her, made trouble within the family and with neighbours and she was convinced he was possessed by an evil spirit. I suggested that she might take him to a child guidance clinic but that had been tried without effect.

He was nevertheless a pleasant, plausible boy, though it eventually became clear in our conversations that his interests lay in Satanism and black magic. I told him that he was on a dangerous path and advised him against such study which could only lead to eventual self-destruction, but he refused to be dissuaded. I had hoped that I might have some influence for good on him, but eventually he ceased visiting me and wrote saying that he was not interested in natural magic or white witchcraft and was searching for a group of Satanists to further his knowledge. He dropped out of my life and a few years later I saw in one of the seedier occult magazines an overt advertisement for recruits for a Satanist group; he openly used his own name and advised 'no time-wasters'.

An inevitable question will be 'Why did you not use some magical power to turn this boy from his Satanic inclinations?' I came to the conclusion during long conversations with him that he was a very disturbed young man with a grudge against the world; he would have benefited from psychiatric treatment, and I was reluctant in his particular case to subject him to any type of magical influence. Once more we come to the question of free-will, people have to be allowed to make their own decisions and to learn from their mistakes; that is what life is all about, to learn from experience. That wicked cynic Ambrose Bierce defined experience as 'The wisdom that enables us to recognise as an undesirable old acquaintance the folly that we have already embraced', and in a pale and painful semblance of poetry reveals the wisdom of one Joel Frad Bink thus:

> To one who, journeying through night and fog,
> Is mired neck deep in an unwholesome bog,
> Experience, like the rising of the dawn,
> Reveals the path that he should not have gone.

Two former friends of mine were a married couple engaged in psychic work and healing. Karen and Peter were well known amongst their neighbours as compassionate helpful people always available when the need arose. My husband and I socialized with them regularly in company with other friends and one day it occurred to me that I had not been in touch with them for a while. I spoke to Karen on the telephone and she told me that she had given up healing and psychic work and had joined an evangelical Christian church. The motivation for this had been a mystical vision of Christ who had said to her, 'Did I die for you in vain?' and she had been instructed to surrender all psychic activity and her friends in the psychic field.

I knew that Karen had been reared in the Roman Catholic faith and that there had always been an inner conflict in the deeper aspects of her mind, so this revelation did not come as a complete surprise. Apart from a slight element of spiritual pride, she was a very sincere person and I respected her decision. What did cause me some astonishment was that Peter had joined this church as well. I had always regarded him as an excellent healer, if a little vain and boastful concerning his talents in that direction.

Some months later Karen appeared on my doorstep crying, and obviously deeply upset. She told me that Peter had left the evangelical church they had both joined. He now attended another which was even more fundamentalist and he had changed subtly in personality over a very short period of time. He spent all his time at home listening to hymns on his record-player, waving his arms around and shouting 'Hallelujah'. The firm for whom he worked demonstrated at exhibitions and when customers expressed an interest in the product and wanted to discuss it with him he would try to convert them. The situation had reached a stage where his employers had telephoned her and said, 'Do something about your husband'. He had become violent and aggressive towards her, and she was really quite afraid of him. She refused to sleep with him and locked her bedroom door every night. This procedure had incensed him, and he hammered on the bedroom door quoting biblical injunctions concerning the marital duties of a wife towards her husband.

As she related these events to me, a sudden stillness pervaded the room, and over her head, I perceived a vision. She was lying on a bed covered in blood, and Peter was standing over her brandishing a knife with a wild maniacal expression on his face. Karen stopped in mid-sentence and said to me, 'What's the matter Lois, are you ill? You've gone as white as a sheet!' I looked at her with a dazed expression, stuttered something and tried to compose myself. I struggled inwardly, desperately wanting to describe my vision to her, but fearing to do so lest in her highly charged emotional state she should succumb to hysterics.

I took a deep breath and said, 'Karen, I have listened carefully to all you have told me and my feeling is that you are in great danger.' I emphasized the danger and suggested that she should leave her house and stay with friends for a few days. She pointed out that she had a dog and three cats and could not just walk out without making some advance arrangements. I was in a torment when she left. I wanted to telephone her and describe the vision. I argued with myself that if I did it might be counter-productive. It would terrify her and I might be the unwitting cause of the final breakdown of her marriage. Another part of me said, 'And if you don't tell her, you might be the unwitting accomplice to her death!'

I told myself that I could not justify telling her of a vision which might be born only of my own anxiety and imagination, that I could not be responsible for everybody's life. I had done my duty, I had told her that she was in danger, and if she had not totally rejected her own psychic perception she would recognize this fact.

Two days later I received a letter from Karen. She said that she had left Peter and intended divorcing him. She was staying with friends for a few days. What had compelled her to leave was that during the evening of the day she had called to see me, she had experienced a vision. She had seen herself, lying on a bed covered in blood and Peter was standing over her with a knife in his hand.

The obvious conclusion to be drawn from this experience is that I was shown a vision to warn Karen. Since I did not convey it in totality, it was conveyed to her personally. She chose to act on it and removed herself from the potential danger, but from where did the vision originate? Psychic literature abounds with examples of warnings of a similar description, and we can make the assumption that perhaps they originate from the world beyond death, where an entity, aware of a disturbed emotional situation in the life of a person highly developed spiritually and psychically, intervenes.

The alternative theory is that Karen, already aware of her husband's frustration and potential violence towards her carried a fear of it in her subconscious mind and this materialized into an image which I was able to perceive during an agitated unburdening of her personal problems. There is of course another possible explanation, that the vision was merely a product of my imagination, a manifestation of exaggerated concern as I listened to her description of Peter's metamorphosized personality. My reluctance to describe the vision resulted in it assuming strength and under stress I transmitted the substance of it to her telepathically.

One of the minor frustrations of practicing magic and working spells for people is that I do not always receive feedback and I am not necessarily informed whether the spell has been successful. On the assumption that had it not I would certainly hear, it appears likely that most of my efforts produce favourable results.

While, I was washing my hair one day, the doorbell rang. My caller was a woman who asked hesitantly if she could please speak to me. Uninvited visitors invariably receive a frosty reception, particularly if my head is swathed in a towel. I must have appeared rather unnerving because she burst into tears. Although it is inconvenient for me to be approached without prior warning or permission, on reflection I imagine it must require quite a lot of courage to knock on a witch's door if she is not expecting you. I certainly would not knock on my door, being aware that I have a short fuse!

The woman's story was that she had discovered a copy of my book *Witch Amongst Us* in an hotel in France and she had decided that I was the answer to all her prayers. She explained that she and her husband were very distressed by the behaviour of their only son, who was, I decided as the tale unfolded, somewhat of a spoiled brat. This son had received every advantage that money could buy throughout his life even to the extent of being presented with a shop to earn his livelihood. The woman's husband was Danish and their son had visited Denmark to meet his relatives and during the holiday he had embarked on an affair with a young girl who, as as result became pregnant. When the child was born, the boy refused to acknowledge that he was the father.

There is apparently a law in Denmark to the effect that if the father of an illegitimate child acknowledges his paternity the legal situation of the child is more easily established. My caller showed me photographs of the girl and her baby. The girl was quite beautiful and the baby absolutely adorable and I could well understand this doting grandmother's emotion. Her eyes were moist with tears as she said, 'All we want him to do, Mrs Bourne, is to acknowledge that he is the father of the child.' She confessed to me that her wretched son was at that time living with a most unsuitable girl who wrote them rude letters and was 'not very particular about the house', her housekeeping apparently leaving much to be desired, 'Mothers,' I thought, 'are the same the world over.'

The woman and her husband were very nice people interested only in the well-being of their grandchild and its beautiful mother, and this was one case where I felt, rightly or wrongly, that I was quite justified in interfering with someone's free-will; the boy had admitted privately to his parents that he was the father of the child, he merely had to be persuaded to admit it legally.

Occasionally I will receive a letter from a woman who has been involved in an abortive love affair and has been deserted by her lover. The request is not to establish a reconciliation but to work some black magic against the recalcitrant lover with the object of causing him injury or death. Betrayed women, and men too, at times exhibit the most primitive of emotions, but it is certainly true that the female of the species is more dangerous than the male in her desire for revenge. I explain to such correspondents that I do not practise black magic and that I am unable to recommend anyone who does.

Readers of my previous book *Witch Amongst Us* will doubtless recall that memorable and outstanding character Sonya who has, in correspondence and otherwise, provoked so much interest and comment. I have referred to Sonya as 'my sinister sister witch of the dark inclinations'; she openly admits to being a black witch and in her village in the Fens she is regarded with respect and awe. Her powers are well known and documented in the tight-knit community where she lives in a beautiful old cottage called 'Broomsticks' shared with an unspecified number of cats with extra toes on their feet! Her views are generally extreme and she despises the majority of humanity, whom she refers to disparagingly as 'mere mortals' who despoil this beautiful planet Earth and ravage her in their selfishness and greed and are fit only for the cosmic compost heap.

She feels no compunction about practising black magic against people who cross or annoy her, and this she does with the aid of her familiar spirit, one Willie by name. 'My friends prosper and my enemies don't', she says darkly but points out that instead of concentrating on her dark side it would be useful to indicate that witches are not specifically black or white but mainly neutral; no one in his right mind would make an enemy of a witch.

I actually occasionally do a tremendous amount of good, not that I love humanity in the least but I feel that the people who come into my orbit are there for a purpose; they are there for my purpose, and I am there for theirs. My friends are very important to me, I almost feed off them, I draw psychic energy from my relationship with them consequently I am very fussy about the people I choose as friends and I feel responsible for their well being. I strongly believe in reincarnation and karma and know that all the people who are really significant to me I will meet again and again in different lives until whatever purpose there is in our relationship is resolved. I act as I wish, and say what I feel because I do not care for the opinion of the world, my purpose is to fulfil my own potential in my chosen path and other people are victims.

She quoted with undisguised malevolence two lines of a verse by Emerson:

> They reckon ill who leave me out;
> When me they fly, I am the wings;

The poem continues:

> I am the doubter and the doubt
> And I the hymn the Brahmin sings.

I had asked Sonya when she first became aware of her ability and she told me that when she was ten years old a schoolteacher had incurred her wrath by unjustly accusing her of some misdemeanour. She had focused her eyes on the teacher who had promptly fallen down the schoolhouse steps, although at that time she was not fully aware that her invisible hand had pushed him. Only on reflection did she recall the power surging through her body.

During her mid-teens, she developed a passion for reading Freud, Jung and Adler, also anything and everything connected with the supernatural. Later she did some serious research into witchcraft which led her to what she considered to be its origins amongst the ancient Celts. She started to experiment and discovered with mixed feelings that she could actually make things happen; by the time she reached the age of thirty the power had possessed her.

When Sonya was about twenty-five she attended a wedding and, whilst heavily involved with a bottle of vintage champagne, was conversing with a sceptical police inspector concerning some peculiar activities in a local churchyard. It was his opinion that 'bunch of doped-up hippies' were responsible and had no connection with black magic, as had been suggested, since the mere idea of magic and witchcraft was rubbish and no intelligent person could give it any credence. He proceeded to give her a very unflattering analysis of people who were sufficiently deluded as to imagine themselves endowed with supernatural powers and he categorically stated that witches, black or white, did not exist.

Fixing him with somewhat bleary green cat's eyes she announced to him, 'Well I am a witch and I can prove it, what is it that you most desire and cannot have?'.

Eyeing her humorously he replied, 'Promotion actually, my immediate superior will not get his promotion for six years and so neither can I move up the ladder until he goes'. She asked him if his superior was likely to move elsewhere or resign, and the response was, 'Absolutely not, only if he drops dead which is unlikely as he is only in his forties and is as fit as a flea.'

A short time later she heard that the inspector had been promoted due to the unexpected death of his superior from a heart attack. She was disturbed by this since it was not what she had intended, but reported that this particular policeman avoided her studiously after that.

During a two-year period as an army wife in Germany and whilst propping up a bar in the mess, she became involved in conversation with a Welshman who remarked with a sneer, 'I am told you have the reputation of being a witch, of course I don't believe in all that superstitious rubbish'. One of Sonya's friends standing nearby warned him to be careful as her reputation within the regiment was founded on several eye-witness accounts and should be taken seriously, but the Welshman scoffed. 'Prove it,' he said. The Welshman was due to return to Wales on leave that weekend and Sonya told him that he would find it difficult to leave Germany, and when he finally reached England she would make him wish that he had not had the affrontery to doubt her powers. Knowing her as well as I do, I can imagine her sinister countenance and ominousness of her voice as she answered his challenge.

It was winter and he was fogbound at the airport for thirty-six hours. When he finally reached home he joined a mountain rescue team within a few days to search for some missing climbers. They were found safe and well but the Welshman fell into a snowdrift and spent three weeks in hospital with double pneumonia. When he returned to the regiment, she enquired after his health and asked him if he was prepared to acknowledge her powers. He laughed and said that his misfortunes had been due to coincidence and nothing more.

She decided that he required a further lesson and within a week the Welshman broke a glass, a large sliver went through his hand and the wound became septic; with his arm in a sling he slipped on the ice and broke two ribs; expediency finally convinced him that others were right and he was wrong – Sonya was indeed a witch.

3 Magic, Amulets and Black Magic

There are certain recurring themes in the questions people ask me about witchcraft and one is 'How do spells actually work?' I have explained elsewhere the opinion that magic works by resonance and that energy follows thought and sound. It has been postulated that each thought, idea or action sends a vibration into the astral plane, the first plane to which we ascend after death. There are thoughts and ideas on this plane and an exact counterpart in another dimension of every object and living creature on earth. There are no limits of time or space on the astral plane and a vibration sent from New York could produce an immediate reaction in London. When witches utilize thought and sound in casting a spell the vibration touches the astral counterpart of the person for whom the magic is intended and the recipient responds. Spells influence people to act in a certain way, usually unconsciously.

A group of trained, dedicated and determined witches using concentrated efforts of mind, will and technique can cause things to happen or change in accordance with their combined will, which becomes an entity of electrical discharge projected with force in a particular direction for a special purpose.

It was T.C. Lethbridge, a Cambridge don and now sadly deceased, the author of books on dowsing and *Witches, Investigating an Ancient Religion* who proposed the resonance theory and said that resonance was similar to electricity or magnetism but that it required an impulse from a human body which had to be tuned in like a radio. He was of the opinion that there existed in the human body an unstudied force similar to electricity and magnetism which acted like a self-starter on a car. Witches utilize this force, and American Indians appeared to have a knowledge of it when they chanted and stamped around a bonfire and made wild calls. Perhaps it was common to all primitive people when the world was young and as we became more sophisticated it was forgotten or the ability to promote and sustain it was allowed to atrophy like the sixth sense.

Witches have various methods of working magic. There are eight official ways, some are used more than others and we all have a favourite method of working. Chants, calls and dancing are used to raise and release the power, and at times a rhyme is composed containing the purpose of the spell, this serves to focus the mind as the rhyme is chanted continuously until the power is sufficient to be directed.

When we are asked to work magic on behalf of individuals, we always request a lock of hair or nail parings, a photograph and a sample of handwriting because these things contain the personal vibration of the person for whom we are working and serve further to ensure that the power reaches them and does not go astray.

Lethbridge discovered through dowsing that everything which lives has its own rate of vibration and there is even one for death. It may be that I am personally involved with a friend and when working magic can visualize her very clearly on a mental level and draw on my memory and recognition of her intimately, but the members of my coven will require the link items if they are not familiar with my friend. The personal articles also reveal a great deal of information to us, perhaps not revealed on a conscious level, and this information assists us in formulating the most expeditious way to work a spell.

Healing rituals are usually carried out by deep meditation, and we hold in our minds a visualization of a sick person in full and perfect health. Poppets or wax images have always been associated with the negative side of witchcraft and black magic since time immemorial, usually with pins or thorns stuck in them. Occasionally we use a poppet or a fith fath as a focus for healing if it is considered helpful. Plasticine is more often utilized than wax as it is more malleable and the personal items are incorporated into the image. It is then named and concentration is brought to bear on the particular part of the anatomy where there is pain or discomfort.

There is a great deal of nonsense talked and written about black magic, more than is ever actually practised. There is a theory that if negative or destructive thoughts are sent out as in a death spell, and the victim is deserving of such a spell (and who is qualified to make such a judgement!) he will cause his own destruction. The victim may be involved in a fatal accident, though Freud was of the opinion that there is no such thing as an accident and that a large proportion of road fatalities can be considered the result of suicidal tendencies. Should an evil spell be worked on someone maliciously (and it could be for no other reason) and without just cause, the thought vibrations will be reflected back from his astral counterpart to someone in tune with the perpetrator's thoughts, and who is more in tune than the perpetrator, so the evil wished on the victim will be reflected back to the sender. However, I should imagine that the very first thing any self-respecting black witch learns to do is to seal her aura so that there would be no reflection and penetration.

People who write to me and send me their personal articles are confident of the fact that I practise only white magic because these same articles can be used for black magic rituals as well. From the days of ancient Egypt and Mesopotamia and even in modern times in Haiti, Australia and Africa, healthy people have become ill and died because a curse or a spell was put on them. In primitive societies, the sorcerer declares the curse and the victim, and the community at large must subscribe to the belief. The effect can be imagined in cultures where the community looks upon the victim as already dead from the moment the curse becomes known, the victim may cease to eat or drink which hastens the curse and the end.

One method of killing is 'bone pointing' practised by the Aborigines of Australia. There is usually no physical contact with the victim. The pointing weapon can be made of stone, wood, or bone and a man who discovers that he is being boned by an enemy becomes demented, his face distorts and his eyes become staring and glassy. He froths at the mouth and trembles and begins to writhe and moan. Unless he is helped with a counter-spell by a medicine man he is destined to die within a short time.

To our western educated and sophisticated minds, it seems incredible that the pointing of a bone could produce such fear and effects, but a possible physiological explanation could be that the consequences of extreme fear are like those of a great rage, the adrenal glands produce more adrenalin reducing the supply to other parts of the body to ensure an adequate supply to the muscles for fight or flight. Adrenalin produces this result by constricting the small blood vessels in the parts of the body which can survive a reduced blood supply for a short time.

When blood supply is reduced, however, so is the oxygen supply which is carried in the blood by the red corpuscles, and when the fine capillary blood vessels are deprived of oxygen they become more permeable to the blood plasma which seeps into the tissue surrounding the blood vessel. The consequence of this in extended fear or anger is a reduction in the volume of circulating blood. This reduces the blood pressure and a potentially dangerous cycle is established. The reduced blood pressure adversely affects the parts of the body responsible for maintaining the blood circulation, and this reduction in circulation further reduces the blood pressure. These sequential events will be fatal if not checked.

That a curse can cause such physiological disorders is mystery enough to most people, but even more extraordinary are cases of death where a medical examination does not reveal either reduced blood pressure or an abnormal accumulation of red blood cells. It appears that in societies where curses are regarded as common occurrences, the power of suggestion and thought can indeed kill, and they can be regarded as psychosomatic since there is evidence that when a pointing bone has been extended against someone and then the victim is subsequently told for various reasons that it was a mistake or a joke, a miraculous recovery takes place.

The power of a curse is not only prevalent in primitive societies, there is evidence that it can work in other parts of the world. In 1946, on Friday the 13th, a midwife delivered three babies in the same area of Georgia in America, and for some evil and malevolent reason known only to herself the woman put a curse on the three babies. She said that one would die before the age of sixteen another before she reached twenty-one, and the third before she was twenty-three. The first two were accurate, one girl at the age of fifteen was killed in a road accident, the second was shot in a fight in a nightclub the night before her twenty-first birthday.

Two years later the third young woman asked if she could be admitted to a hospital, she was in a hysterical state and said she was going to die before her twenty-third birthday which was three days hence. She was examined and found to be in perfect health but under stress and she was admitted for observation. The next morning she was found dead in bed, the victim of her own belief in the power of the curse of the midwife.

The first two deaths could be regarded as accidental or coincidental but it is interesting to speculate whether the third would have occurred had the girl not been made aware of the curse which affected her psychosomatically.

I quite often receive letters from women, and men too, who are quite convinced that they are labouring under a curse.

Whilst it is true that in most cases an examination of the trends in their lives reveals the information that misfortunes were associated with regressive periods in their cycles, there have been a few cases where I suspected that a curse had been laid and took steps to remove it.

One such was a woman who wrote to me that it appeared to her that her life had been a total disaster. She had been born the only child of an oppressive mother and a weak father and had endured a sickly childhood, encountering and suffering one ailment after another resulting in long absences from school so that she never obtained any scholastic achievements.

She married at a young age a man who was quite unsuited to her temperament, mainly to escape from her home, and felt in retrospect that she had lacked the maturity to know the meaning of love. She had miscarried two babies and the third was born brain-damaged and died within days. Her marriage ended in divorce after five years, following which she had a nervous breakdown. A second marriage was also a failure and during the course of it she encountered problems with her reproductive system and a hysterectomy was performed. At the age of forty-seven, she was now into her third marriage which was faltering and she wrote to me seeking help to remove a curse which she had discovered had been laid upon her whilst she was still in the womb.

A conversation with her mother, now in her late seventies, bemoaning the circumstances of her life had disclosed the information that when seven months pregnant her mother had been approached at the door by a gypsy woman selling lace and trinkets. She had dismissed the gypsy rudely upon which the woman had raised her hand and uttered a curse that the child in her womb would be followed by misfortune all the days of her life.

My correspondent's mother had not previously related the story because she did not hold any belief in curses, or blessings for that matter. In this particular instance, there had never existed in my correspondent's mind the knowledge that her life was under a curse and she had not therefore worked subconsciously towards fulfilling it.

It is interesting that in my experience more gypsies than witches figure in stories of actual or suspected curses. One of my friends, Italian in origin, told me that as a young child she was somewhat precocious. At about the age of seven or eight she had been at the market with her mother when she had noticed a gypsy looking at her and had rudely stuck out her tongue at the woman. The gypsy scowled at her, muttered something under her breath and proceed to make a sign at my friend with her left hand. My friend's life has certainly been a procession of misfortune, partly due to wartime conditions when she was orphaned at the age of eleven, followed by wanderings in various countries, insecurity, disappointment, disasters and ill health. I know that the ability to curse is very real in some people and I suggest one should adopt a healthy respect for both gypsies and witches.

In Turkey and Greece and parts of the East, there is a genuine fear of curses and the so-called 'evil eye', and in the former two countries elaborate precautions are taken to counteract it, including the ubiquitous manufacture and wearing of blue beads of various designs which incorporate an eye. No self-respecting taxi-driver in Turkey would be without one hanging in his cab, and there is a necessary formality to be observed when expressing delight or admiration at a child's prettiness, the word *'Masaallah'* (which means 'God hath wrought wondrous things') being uttered at the end of a compliment. Tradition has it that evil spirits may be jealous of the child and this word gives protection from their maliciousness.

In the East an amulet called the Hand of Fatima is worn against the evil eye. Fatima was an Arabian Moon Goddess in a Muslim incarnation as Mohammed's fictitious daughter who was also described strangely as 'the mother of her father'. Fatima means the Creatress, she was known also as the Source of the Sun, Tree of Paradise, the Moon and Fate and was said to have existed since the beginning of the material world. In fact, she was none other than the Great Goddess and, like the Madonna of the Roman Catholic Church, her western counterpart, she was demoted to mortality but maintained most of her titles and powers.

Most reports of uttered curses which have been observed refer to a raising of the left hand as opposed to the right hand which is raised in blessing. Muslims believe that prophets and diviners receive their inspiration from familiar spirits but that prophets who are characterized by their white garments receive the words of their invisible instructors in the right ear, whereas diviners who dress in black hear the words in their left ear.

The power of the left hand always inspires terror and revulsion and is regarded as being connected to darkness, the underworld and the occult. Further emphasis is that the left is female and beings considered to possess magical powers are represented as left handed. Amongst the Maoris, the right hand is male, active and life-giving, whilst the left is female, passive and symbolic of death. Amongst the ancient Arabs and in Africa, the left is regarded as female and the right male, the right is good and the left evil, men are buried on their right side and women on their left. In some tribes, it is forbidden for women to use the left hand when cooking and in others they are not allowed to touch the faces of their husbands with their left hand.

In India, representations of Siva as Ardhanaris-vara are shown as a woman on the left side with the thigh, waist and breast in evidence and on the right the shoulder, chest and hip of a man, and in Greek tradition the Pythagorean Table of Opposites related by Aristotle shows the paired connections as right–left, male–female, and light–dark. In the classical world, the left was unlucky, and further, Anaxagoras was of the opinion that a man's left testicle produced female children and the right male babies.

The Koran of Islam states that God's elect are on his right side and the damned on his left and Tabori stated 'Allah has nothing left handed in him, his two hands are right hands'. White witches work deosyl within a circle following the path of the sun, whilst black magic is practised widdershins or anti-clockwise and everyone is aware that 'the left-hand path' is a euphemism for Satanists and black magicians. Interestingly enough, however, the Indian Tantrists call the worship of Shiva and Shakti the left-hand path, and the Mevlevi or more commonly called Whirling Dervishes of Turkey circle anti-clockwise.

There has been over the last ten years, a strong resurgence of interest in all aspects of the occult and supernatural, due probably to the fact that organized religions no longer fulfil the spiritual yearnings of many people and their longings to be more actively involved and less passively silent in their spiritual evolution. As a result, many spurious witches and covens have appeared, and the activities of some are most unsavoury if the content of my post-bag is to be believed.

A woman wrote asking if she could make an appointment to see me as she wished to discuss a private matter, one which she did not want to relate over the telephone or commit to paper. Upon meeting her, it transpired that though she and her husband were separated, she still loved him and longed for a reconciliation, and to this end she thought that magic or witchcraft might help to draw them together again. She had written to a man who advertised his services as a witch in an occult magazine and a meeting was arranged. At the meeting, she was told that a reconciliation with her husband could be arranged with the aid of a spell, but it would cost a great deal of money and, in addition, it would be necessary for her to have sexual intercourse with him in the magic circle. Not knowing any better, she had paid the money and agreed to the sex, but so far without any tangible result; her husband had not returned to her.

I listened to her story with a growing sense of outrage and incredulity at her utter naïvety, and when I remonstrated with her at her foolishness she said to me, quite understandably, 'Well, how was I to know that he wasn't genuine. I was quite desperate.' Such cynical exploitation of other people's misery makes me very angry and the letters I receive indicate that this is not an isolated case. I am at a loss to know how to preserve people from such experiences beyond warning them to be extremely cautious in their dealings with the occult world.

This particular woman's experience was not limited to being relieved of a large sum of money and being taken advantage of sexually. Her description of the events of that evening led me to suspect that a bizarre black magic ritual had been carried out. Questions asked of her produced the information that the ceremony had been conducted in a small room at his home, lined with some black, heavy, thick material, a cabbalistic circle was traced in black on the polished floor, and black candles and a heavy nauseating incense were used. On the altar was a head which she described as 'resembling that of a black goat' and in front of it was an inverted cross; the man also wore a smaller one around his neck. Only the two of them were involved in the ritual which was preceded by certain markings being made on her naked body with what she suspected was blood and the language used, for what I assumed was an invocation, 'was not English'.

A letter I received from another woman described how she and her husband had joined a coven in the north of England which was ruled by an elderly lady who exhibited all the signs of egocentricity and the coven appeared to be directed along the lines of a Communist cell.

Most covens of my acquaintance are loose-knit organizations. Members meet for the monthly estbats or festivals, and often the working of magic together and the fact of being part of a small, closed group produces a familial feeling, or of close friendship and they may socialize together between coven activities.

This elderly lady, however, required absolute submission to all her extraordinary demands which included a vegetarian diet, no smoking or imbibing of alcohol. Sexual intercourse, even between married couples was permitted only once a month. Baths, not showers, were to be taken at least once a day, and no books or articles on psychic matters or witchcraft were to be read. A monthly tithe, consisting of ten per cent of the couple's combined salaries was to be paid to her. Social intercourse between members of the group was frowned upon and she required a detailed weekly report of their day-to-day activities to be sent through the post.

If all this were not preposterous enough, they were forbidden to watch television, listen to radio or read newspapers. Women were not allowed to have their hair cut or wear make-up, and men were obliged to grow a moustache and a beard which must not be trimmed. The coven members had become restless and resentful of these rules and regulations; two had already left and been 'ritually damned'. The woman wrote to enquire if this state of affairs was usual in a coven and her letter made me laugh. I replied that the whole set-up sounded more like an extreme sect of the Plymouth Brethren than a pagan pursuit and I wondered how they tolerated it. She did not write further and I have since wondered if they all absconded.

4 Money, Magic and Light Relief

Many of the letters I receive are from people in severe financial straits who beg me to help them acquire some money by means of a spell assuring them of a win on football pools, premium bonds etc. I have to tell them that I am very reluctant to work magic for financial gain because of the risks involved. Witches utilize a primitive energy which attempts to fulfil itself on a basic level and in the least convoluted way. A simple request that Mrs Jones should receive £5,000 is full of potential danger and could result in her having an accident, losing a leg and receiving that exact amount in compensation. One needs to be direct, but also very circumspect, and it is self-defeating to complicate the spell by making the proviso '... and with no danger to Mrs Jones'. Mr Jones may have the accident and by the time I have precluded any danger to all their family my enthusiasm has evaporated. The Gods prefer simple and straightforward requests and as I do not wish to harm anyone, I do not work for money.

Obtaining money is not always the problem, some people have difficulty in hanging on to it. One man who wrote to me was well aware that he was completely ineffectual, and though he had recently held a good position with a reasonable salary, money went through his fingers like water. His wife had become tired of the struggle and had left him taking their young daughter with her. He felt that he had not achieved anything at all in his life. He had lost his job and his family, his home and his security, he had no friends, no interests and nothing to look forward to and felt he was at the crossroads in his life. It is difficult to help such people beyond trying to encourage them to become less inward-looking and to give them hope and encouragement for the future.

One method I sometimes use to obviate the dangers of working money magic is to seek for improved general conditions in people's lives, and hopefully this will include financial enhancement without specifically requesting it.

I received a frantic telephone call one day from a woman whose ninety-year-old father was making impossible demands on her. He treated her like a servant and, although she was married with a young family, insisted that she visit his house every day to cook and clean for him. If she did not accede to his every whim, he threatened that he would change his Will and leave his considerable fortune to a nephew who never did anything for him. She lived in fear of this and was exhausting herself in trying to please him.

The final humiliation was when he demanded monogrammed handkerchiefs and a shirt for his birthday. What she wanted me to do basically was to change his personality, or failing that, to dispose of him by witchcraft whilst the Will was still in her favour. I declined on both counts. It is difficult to change someone who has spent ninety years developing an obnoxious personality and I was not prepared to work black magic, despite the promise of a substantial financial reward. I suggested she take a stand against the old reprobate and, using her imagination, tell him to stuff his Will and his money, but she was not willing to do this since the money was too important to her.

I am sometimes asked if I have ever encountered unpleasantness as a result of practising witchcraft. The answer is that, on the contrary, people's usual attitude is one of respect and great curiosity. We live in a more tolerant and enlightened era than that of the Middle Ages when, it has been estimated, over nine million people, mainly women, were hanged or burned as witches for practising their natural abilities in midwifery, healing, dowsing, mediumship, etc. The persecution was the result of political moves by the ecclesiastical authorities in which scapegoats were manufactured, and the responsibility for the troubles of society were displaced. Interestingly enough, witches were never persecuted in Spain, the Inquisition were only concerned with heretics and they regarded witchcraft as a mental aberration!

Many years ago, I knew a male witch of an aristocratic family who regarded him as a black sheep. He was a great character, a man of high intelligence, who generated enormous power and psychic ability. He lived in a wooden hut in the middle of a wood in the south of England. It must not be imagined that he existed in poverty or squalor, the hut was warm and comfortable with most of the attributes of civilized life. He was a skilled artisan and made by hand much of his furniture. I particularly recall a table carved from a single piece of wood and highly polished.

He was very sociable and I have attended many ceremonies in the middle of the wild wood. My memories of soft summer evenings with the full moon shining through the trees and the sounds of a sighing wind and the crackle of bonfires at our Sabbat celebrations are very rich and evocative.

He was well known in the local village as a witch and people were wary of him, but he gave dinner parties and invited local people who interested him. The local vicar attended one of these. During the course of the evening the conversation turned to religion, and the vicar unfortunately made some slighting remark about the religious beliefs of witches and of their Goddess. Robert, who possessed a very quick temper, worked himself into a rage and attacked the vicar verbally, and was restrained from attacking him physically only by the intervention of the other guests. 'You have insulted the Goddess,' Robert screamed. 'Get out of my house.' By all accounts the vicar was glad to do so and was observed haring over ploughed fields as if the hounds of hell were pursuing him.

The following Sunday the vicar preached a sermon from his pulpit against witchcraft in general, and Robert in particular. A little while later, when Robert was away from his home visiting friends, his home caught fire and was destroyed, whether by accident on design no one really knew.

So much of my life as a witch is occupied by listening to and trying to deal with misery and heartbreak in other people's lives, but it does occasionally have its lighter moments. Witches are often great leg-pullers and I am no exception. Some years ago my husband and I spent a holiday in a small cottage in Cumbria with two friends, Colin and Jean. There was a public house in the village, and Colin who was fond of his beer repaired to this hostelry each evening. After two pints his tongue was loosened, and he told the assembled company that there was a witch staying in the cottage. As they plied him with pints, his imagination ran riot, and eager to impress them, he regaled them with hair-raising stories of my supposed powers and abilities, one of which was a Rasputin-type attribute of being able to put people into a hypnotic trance just by fixing them with my gaze, and forcing them to do my will. The landlady, who was a very sensible woman, scoffed at this, but the locals were not so sure, and they nodded sagely and assured him that they "ad 'eard o' the power o' witches'.

When Colin reported this story to us, we decided that we would give them something to think about on our last evening at the cottage and Colin was issued with minute instructions. He was to make his usual trip to the pub, drink one pint, and order another but only to drink a third of it. At 9.30 p.m. I would effect an entrance and fix him with my eyes; he was to rise stiffly from his seat and, without saying a word or looking to right or left, walk to the door leaving his beer on the table. I reasoned that no one would leave almost a pint of beer unless he was in a trance.

As I reached this part of the instructions, Colin evinced signs of revolt. 'What about my beer?' he demanded indignantly.

'Oh, nuts to your beer,' I replied. 'I'll pay you for it, it will be worth the money just to see their faces.'

On our last evening, Colin trotted off to the pub as usual. 'Don't forget you must only drink one full pint,' I reminded him. I feared that if he drank more he would forget his instructions and instead of getting up from his chair, stare at me stupidly.

I dressed dramatically in black and Jean made up my eyes, heavily accenting their darkness. At 9.30 p.m. my husband drove Jean and me to the pub. She stayed in the car to open the door to facilitate a quick get-away. As I approached the door, I could hear the murmur of conversation from inside, and composing my features into what I hoped was a fierce and frightening countenance, I melodramatically flung open the door and stepped just inside.

The effect was instantaneous. A deathly silence fell in the bar, eyes popped, jaws slackened and pints paused midway to their owners' mouths. The landlady paled, inhaled noisily and ceased polishing a glass as I fixed my eyes on Colin.

The idiot had his back towards me, and I could hear him giggling at some joke. I thought he was about to ruin the scene and imagined the wigging I would give him if he spoiled my heady moment. He suddenly became aware of the charged electrified atmosphere, he coughed, stiffened and turned slowly towards me with a glazed look in his eyes. He rose from his seat and, ignoring his beer, walked towards me like an automaton, and to his credit he kept a straight face and was very impressive.

As he reached me, I turned swiftly on my heels and he followed me out of the door. The car was waiting just outside, and we fell into it laughing hysterically, and we laughed all the way back to the cottage.

We left early the next morning, and no one ever saw us again. It is more than likely that the events of that evening will go down in history in the folklore of the village, and perhaps a hundred years hence, when great tomes are penned on twentieth-century witchcraft, one will report '... and it is recorded that ... etc., etc., etc.!'

5 A Family Affair

Whilst savouring my toast and marmalade in bed one morning, my husband walked into the bedroom and announced, 'You had a visitor at three o'clock this morning!'

I paused mid-bite into my toast and said blankly, 'Who?'

'I heard the door-bell ring, looked at the clock and wondered who on earth it was,' he continued. 'It was a young man, he stood swaying on the doorstep as drunk as a lord and said he wanted to have a discussion with my wife about Victorian paganism or pagan Victorianism, I forget which, and I told him not at three o'clock in the morning you can't, and you're flirting with death if you wake her up. I was standing there in my pyjamas with bare feet and hanging onto the dog who was straining to get at him and give him a good "goozing". He looked at his watch and said "oh, is it that time".'

'Did you punch his head?' I asked casually as I munched my toast.

'No, but I asked him not to breathe on the paintwork in case he blistered it; he was very pleasant, he ambled off up the road swaying from side to side and measuring the pavement, I expect when he woke up later he forgot all about his visit.'

'What a cheek,' I said as I drank my coffee, 'If he had awakened me I would have withered him with a few well chosen words,' or as a friend to whom I repeated this story remarked, 'the mistress of universal wisdom would have given him some!!'

'Goozing', incidentally, is how we describe what our dog Güzel does to any stranger she can reach, wriggling her rear end and generally making a great fuss of them.

I thought that my husband had behaved with remarkable restraint, all things considered, and I commended him. Sometimes it's rough being the husband of a witch. This young man was known to me although we had never met. He wrote to me a year or so ago asking me to help him cure a gambling obsession, which I think I did successfully. Then a few weeks ago, I received a poignant letter from him expressing his disgust with the world; a copy was sent to a local newspaper. He said that by the time I received the letter he would be frozen to death. The time was midwinter and I was very alarmed. Not knowing where to search for him, I telephoned the local police who put me on to a social worker and she promised to go around to the house. When she arrived, she found the police already there, alerted by the newspaper and an embarrassed and remorseful young man confessed he had written the letter to me in a mood of depression. All in a witch's day.

A question I am often asked is whether witches are anti-Christian and since I can only ever speak for myself the answer is 'no'; I think that witches are tolerant of all other religions believing as do the Hindus that 'all religions are rivers leading to the same ocean' and that 'there are as many ways to God as there are breaths in a man's body'.

On a purely personal level, my eldest son is married to a Roman Catholic and both my grandchildren are being raised in that religion which makes me very happy, since they are being taught to venerate the feminine aspect of divinity. I make a point of never discussing witchcraft or my own religious beliefs with my family, they do not share them, there is no reason why they should. In particular, I avoid the subject with my daughter-in-law because as a good Catholic, I feel it makes her nervous; witches have received bad publicity within the Christian Church. I have also studiously avoided the subject with my grandchildren who are now aged eight and five. About a year ago, however, whilst their mother was out shopping, Adam said to me shyly, 'Grandma, is it true that you are a witch?' He had obviously heard it from someone. We had a conspiratorial conversation and I asked him if he would like to see my magic wand. Both the children's eyes sparkled and when the wand was produced there were many 'Ohs!' and 'Ahs!' from the two of them. Children are so very literal and there were demands to know if I could turn the dog into a toad.

Rosalind who has an obsession for *The Wizard of Oz* and labours under the delusion that all witches are like the 'Wicked Witch of the West' opined lispingly and with great feeling, 'But you can't possibly be a witch, you're my gwandma!'. Hopefully she will at some time come to terms with this conflict.

My younger son's wife whilst on a course with the Civil Service in Cambridgeshire stayed with relatives and discovered from them that she was a descendant of Jane Wenham who narrowly escaped being hanged as a witch. The trial of Jane Wenham, the 'Wise Woman of Walkerne' on 4 March 1711–12 before Mr Justice Powell of Hertford Assizes raised great interest not only throughout her own district but in London too and she soon became 'the discourse of the town'. She had been a suspected witch for some years and when Matthew Gilson, whom she had apparently threatened began to behave in a very odd and crazy manner, a Farmer Chapman 'hailed the angry beldame as a witch'. Jane Wenham, foolishly in my opinion, applied to Sir Henry Chauncy, a local justice for a warrant against the farmer on a basis of defamation of character. He was fined one shilling and Mr Gardiner a well-known clergyman gave her a lecture about living in peace with her neighbours which she greatly resented.

A woman called Anne Thorne who was a servant at the parsonage began to have fits and told a story of walking down a remote lane, where she saw 'a little old woman muffled in a riding hood' who gave her a large crooked pin. Shortly afterwards the maid met Jane Wenham who shouted at her and abused her in the street and presently she began to have further paroxysms. The reputed witch was then taken into custody, Sir Henry Chauncy being assisted by the rector of Walkerne, Mr Francis Bragge, and Mr Strutt the vicar of Audley. A few days later in the presence of a justice and three local ministers, Jane Wenham made a halting confession. The assizes were thronged, 'So vast a number of people have not been together at the Assizes in the memory of Man.' In spite of the preliminary investigations the one charge brought was that Jane Wenham entertained a familiar in the shape of a cat. There was a curious story of cakes of small feathers set in an elaborate pattern and clotted together with some viscous matter, the Devil's unguent made of dead men's fat, which were found in Anne Thorne's pillow.

From the beginning, Justice Powell set himself against a conviction, but the evidence was overwhelming and Jane Wenham was formally condemned, only to be soon reprieved and pardoned. After her release she was taken under the protection of one Colonel Plummer of Gilston, and on his death she was allowed a small pension by the Earl and Countess of Cowper. She lived until 1730. The case provoked a pamphlet controversy and there was nothing more avidly discussed at the time. Mr Bragge's *A Full and Impartial Account of the Discovery of Sorcery and Witchcraft Practiced by Jane Wenham of Walkerne in*

Hertfordshire, upon the Bodies of Ann Thorn, Anne Street, etc. etc. till she received Sentence of Death for the same, March 4 1711–12* ran into no less than five editions within the year 1712 which must have pleased Mr Bragge. It was answered by such pieces as *A Full Confutation of Witchcraft, proving that Witchcraft is Priestcraft, London 1712* and *The Impossibility of Witchcraft, Plainly Proving, From Scripture and Reason That There Never Was a Witch, London 1712*. It seems highly likely that Jane Wenham was a medium possessed of hypnotic powers, and she had attempted to meddle in dark secrets. Doubtless the fright she received persuaded her to avoid such involvements in the future.

What interested me in this report of my daughter-in-law's ancestress was the reference to feathers. In *Witch Amongst Us* I wrote about two people in Brazil against whom black magic was perpetrated and black feathers in the shape of a ball and a cross were found in their pillows.

During the years when my sister was hospitalized, my younger son drove me monthly to visit her a distance of two hundred miles. The journey was tiring and I preferred motorway travel which is more direct but he dislikes motorways. On one occasion I was irritable on the journey and nagged him. On his return home he told his wife and said 'If you wake up next to a frog in the morning, you'll know why!'

I am fortunate to have a well-adjusted family who placidly accept that I am not the run of the mill wife, mother and grandmother, although I learn from them, and from friends that other people find me formidable and are afraid of me.

This does not please me as, unlike my friend Sonya, the witch of the dark inclinations, I do not relish the thought that some people find me intimidating. I know that I am impatient at times, preferring a broad picture rather than endless detail, and as a friend told me once when she was bent on issuing a few home truths, 'not only do you not suffer fools gladly, you do not suffer them at all!' I suspect that I belong in the category of Colin Wilson's description of some psychics in his book *The Psychic Detectives*. Of those with whom he was acquainted, some are highly dominant individuals with strong personalities, '... so here we have a common factor, naturally dominant individuals, what zoologists call 'alphas', it is a combination that often produces criminals as well as artists'.

In the course of my everyday life I am approached by numerous people with a variety of heartbreaking situations with which they are unable to cope. Some just seek advice whilst others require active assistance in the way of magic, if I am prepared to give it. If I were less strong, I would not be able to handle all the sorrow and pain laid at my door, nor could I be a support to the sad and lost. Neither would I be able to practise witchcraft, for as my grimoire, a witch's book of instruction declares, 'The Craft is not for the weak, nor is it for the vain'.

There is a general assumption that witches never encounter any sorrows of their own, but witches do not lead charmed lives, they are subject to the same pain and misfortunes as other mortals and suffer in the same way.

I am not always responsible for manifestations attributed to me as for example, on the evening I gave a talk on witchcraft to a mainly male audience. It was a dark, stormy night with a gale blowing, rain lashing the windows whilst thunder rattled them and lightning flashed; in the middle of a demonstration of extra-sensory perception doors flew open and the lights flickered and went out for a few seconds. There were nervous laughs and a few smothered screams from the women present and half the audience were petrified: the combination of a witch, ESP and the terrible storm convinced them that I had raised it.

Many years ago, when my dog Nana was alive and my younger son was in his teens, he was dating a young girl who held a junior position at my hairdresser's. As young girls do, she was chattering away to him one day about the customers and remarked, 'There's this tall dark haired woman who comes in the salon and I have to wash her hair and she really scares me. She brings a black and white dog with her and when she's sitting there, even if she doesn't say anything, you really know she's there, do you know what I mean? One of the other girls told me she is a witch' she added.

My son looked at her and said quietly, 'That's my mother.' He told me that there was a deathly silence, she paled and her jaw dropped. I roared with laughter, imagining the scene. The romance ended shortly afterwards, she obviously did not want a witch for a mother-in-law and I cannot say I blame her if I had that effect on her!

In my book *Witch Amongst Us*, I wrote of the experience of two psychic friends of mine, Kathy and Phillip who visited a crystal gazer in Leigh, Lancashire, and in the crystal ball she produced pictures of the real parents of Kathy, although she had not been told that Kathy was adopted as a baby. She said to her, 'Would you like to see your real mother, I don't mean your adopted mother, I mean your real one' and the woman waved her hand over the crystal and a sepia-coloured picture appeared of a lady Kathy did not recognize but who bore a remarkable resemblance to herself. The picture persisted whilst she carried the crystal out into the hall to show her husband. On her return, the woman produced a picture in the crystal of Kathy's real father who again bore a resemblance to her and this again persisted until she had shown it to Phillip sitting in the hall. I remarked that I would have been inclined to treat this story with a pinch of salt had I not complete faith in Kathy's veracity.

One of my correspondents gave me an interesting confirmation of the gifts of this crystal-gazer. She wrote to me from Haulgh, Bolton, Lancs, and said, 'When reading about the crystal gazer in Leigh, I wondered if it was the same lady I saw over 18 years ago. In the crystal ball I saw the face of my future husband, he was even wearing the red cravat he had on the night we met. She predicted when I would become engaged, it all sounded highly unlikely at the time but sure enough all came to pass, just as she said it would.'

Another interesting letter came from a lady who referred to a passage in *Witch Amongst Us* in which I described attending an introductory conference at the Hilton Hotel in London where the Maharishi Maheesh Yogi was lecturing on his system of meditation. This was when he first became prominent in the Western World and pre-dated the time when the Beatles popularized the movement. At the end of the meeting there was a rush of people towards him and, as I was at the front, I found myself standing before him. He smiled at me and handed me a bunch of sweetpeas. As he passed them to me, his hand brushed briefly against mine and I felt a sensation like a mild electric shock shoot up my arm. I kept the flowers in water in my home and at the end of three months they were still as fresh as the day he gave them to me. My correspondent, who was deeply involved in the teachings of the Maharishi wrote, '... I was told some time ago by a teacher that Maharishi touches or gives flowers to someone as a sign of special favour or recognition. Others have also described the phenomena of the everlasting flowers. So I do not think you would have been treated as you were without it implying a degree of recognition and approval'.

My book appears to have helped many people in diverse ways and at times almost seems to be regarded as a talisman. Some of the letters I find most moving and humbling, such as the one from a woman who took my book into hospital where she underwent a major operation. She wrote that she felt it gave her courage to face the ordeal and in some strange way she was conscious of my presence which she found very comforting. Others write that they carry the book around with them and find many of their problems becoming resolved in mysterious ways!

Others write that they have dreams about me after they have written to me. One wrote

> ... A couple of nights after I wrote to you I had a very strange and beautiful dream, it had a different flavour from the dreams I have had in the past and I truly felt it came from a special place and was an answer to my letter to you. It was a dream of a red and green room and an iron girl sitting in front of a fire, there was a woman in the dream who I felt to be you or your representative. In the course of the dream the iron girl came to life and was struggling to speak, I woke up wondering what she had to say. The problems I was specifically worried about when I wrote my first letter have eased, melted, changed, whether you had anything to do with it I don't know but I thank you.

Another correspondent, a woman, wrote, 'On reading your book I was impressed by your matter of fact acceptance of your gifts. What also came across was your sense of wonder of life, and the deep spiritual peace you have. I long to know how I could attain some measure of this, and develop the "spiritual" side of my life, to find what we are all seeking, peace.'

A most unusual letter came from a woman who wrote, 'I had bought your book but had not got down to reading it, it was on my bedside table and I went to bed one night feeling very depressed and lonely, my husband had died a few weeks earlier and I was feeling particularly lost that night as it was our wedding anniversary. I started to weep copiously and my little dog sat on the bed and looked at me sorrowfully and suddenly bounced over to the bedside table, knocked the book on the floor and stood there barking at it. I picked it up and began to read it and found it so interesting and comforting and now I always keep it with me.' I was very touched by her letter and have no explanation for her dog's behaviour except that animals are known to be very psychic creatures.

Some years ago, again when my dog Nana was alive, my husband and I heard of an occult shop which had recently opened in a nearby town. We decided to visit it and found it in a shabby back street. As we opened the door and were about to enter, we saw a cabbalistic circle painted on the floor, complete with magical symbols. We walked across it but Nana stood at the door growling softly at it with her hackles raised, and when I called her, she would not walk across it but very carefully walked around it. She was obviously aware of some residual psychic presence still in the circle. I asked the owner if it was ever used for magical purpose and he replied in the affirmative.

It is customary and preferable to have a room kept exclusively for magical work, especially if a circle is permanently in situ as this acts as an accumulator of psychic energy and when people walk over the circle indiscriminately this power is destroyed. Perhaps the owners of the shop were not aware of this, or possibly a lack of space necessitated the use of that area, but in either case I thought it a most peculiar place to draw a magic circle.

6 Encounters in Other Lands

One of my friends, who is also a close neighbour, told me that whilst at a dinner party at an old house in Lisbon, Portugal, he had a very strange experience. He was conversing with his fellow guests when, in what could only have been a split second but seemed to assume an eternity in time, the scene changed, and instead of the people with whom he was dining, he found himself in the presence of complete strangers who appeared to be British officers in uniform of the Napoleonic period. His retrospective vision ended when his contemporary fellow-diners solicitously asked him if he was feeling all right as he had visibly paled.

John, another friend whose acquaintance I made whilst I was in Russia, described an experience he had shared with a girlfriend in Egypt in 1973. They decided to climb the Cheops pyramid and spend the night at the top. After the arduous ascent they were very tired and settled down in their sleeping bags and rested for some hours but woke simultaneously at around 3 a.m.

The desert was dark with a black velvety sky and no moon and they could see the lights of Cairo in the distance as the silence of the desert enveloped them. They became aware that a strange luminous mist was drifting towards them from what they only later discovered was the direction of the City of the Dead. John told me that the mist was so lucent and radiant that it was almost like the dawn breaking but he knew it was too early for dawn. They were each completely overwhelmed by a feeling of oppression and desolation as if the whole of life were meaningless, and the idea of suicide by jumping from the top of the pyramid was a very seductive one. They became quite frightened and determined to climb down the pyramid, and when they had done so, they made their way through the Arab camps and found a rough café where they had something to eat.

They were served there by a young man who spoke English

and was actually the son of the owner. He was very curious as to why they were abroad at such an early hour and questioned them closely and attentively.

They admitted to him that they had been at the top of the Cheops pyramid, although they knew it was forbidden, and he told them that they had been very foolish to sleep in the area of the City of the Dead, and that they had exposed themselves to great danger, although he did not elaborate on the nature of the danger. John murmured that they 'could take care of themselves', and the Arab replied, 'No one can look after themselves in that place.'

The Arab was so sedulous and curious, that they began to wonder if he was interested in the money they were carrying, but realized the unworthiness of the thought when he told them that it was essential that they leave Egypt as soon as possible because their situation was perilous. He wrote some Arabic characters on a piece of paper, tore it off the pad and handed it to John with the words, 'You must not take this piece of paper out of Egypt, you must tear it up into small fragments and drop them into the sea, salt water is essential.'

They feared that they would be obliged to fly out of Egypt as the Arab–Israeli conflict was imminent, but the airports were commandeered by the military and to their relief they left by ship and during the voyage destroyed the paper as instructed.

John and his companion separated at Alexandria and she returned to Paris where they met again eighteen months later. It was only then, when they deliberated on their experience that each became aware for the first time that they had shared the awful feeling of oppressive desolation, and the idea of suicide. This had not previously been discussed or referred to between them.

They speculated on whether their experience on the pyramid of Cheops had left some tangible psychic residue around them which the Arab, his senses sharpened by the mystery and silence of the desert, and his life close to the ancient tombs, had perceived, and if the paper with the Arabic symbols had been a talisman to absorb the baleful influence and secure their safety until they had left Egypt. Was this why it had to be shredded and thrown into salt water? (In occult and magical lore, salt water has a purifying effect.)

John and his companion maintained only a loose connection during subsequent years, but a curious phenomenon developed between them which had not earlier been in evidence. It manifested in a psychic sense, a type of clairvoyant–telepathic rapport, where each become aware subliminally of important events in the life of the other, such as marriage, births of children, etc. When John's erstwhile companion married and went to Egypt for her honeymoon she flatly refused to visit the pyramids, which her new husband found most odd, but she declined to offer an explanation.

Amongst my post was a letter from a 24-year-old woman who wrote,

> ... since I can remember, I have been plagued by visions of events and things. I experience clairaudience and psychometry quite frequently. For example on a recent visit to Edinburgh, my mother and I were in the small chapel of rest where the volumes of soldiers who have died in battle are kept. I had gone to see if I could find the names of the comrades of my father who was in the Royal Scots Fusiliers in the last war. My mother and I had wandered into a tiny ante-room with the names of deceased soldiers carved into the walls, when we suddenly heard the sound of humming; I heard it first and then my mother heard it but neither of us said anything until it became so loud that we could not ignore it, the tune was 'I'm a rambler, I'm a gambler', the favourite tune of my father and his wartime companions. When my mother and I were discussing the humming, two other women in the chapel looked at us as if we were crazy as they had not heard anything. I made enquiries as to whether any soldiers in the castle had been singing and the answer had been in the negative.
>
> We left the chapel ante-room quickly and after looking through the names in the volumes of the wartime dead I was becoming disheartened at not finding my father's friends and had decided to give up when I walked into what I thought was a wall in front of me but when I looked closer, there was no wall, I was in the middle of the room with people passing on each side of me but I could not move either forward or backwards.
>
> I was beginning to panic when I heard a soft voice in my ear say 'turn left' and when I did, there on the shelf at my hand was the book I had been searching for. The book contained the names and burial places of the R.S.F. soldiers from 1940 to 1946. I would have walked straight past it had I not heard the voice. I was also given a message for my father from his friends

and only my father knew the significance of what I was told.

Whenever I am in Turkey, my psychic senses seem to be magnified and during one of my frequent trips to Istanbul I was walking in the area of Eminönü with Semra, a Turkish woman friend, where the museum of Aya Sofia is to be found. The first St Sophia (or Aya Sofia) was a Byzantine basilica of Christianity in 360. It was destroyed in the hippodrome riots of 532 and was rebuilt over the following thirty years by Justinian. It is recorded that on seeing the finished cathedral the emperor cried out, 'O Solomon, thou art vanquished!'

In 1453, Mehmet the Conqueror made it into a mosque and it came to be known as Ayasofya. Four minarets were added and the architect Sinan surrounded it with shrines. Since it had been originally built as a Christian basilica there is no inner courtyard for ritual ablutions as in mosques.

In the same way that Mehmet had wished to emphasize Islam by converting St Sophia into a mosque, Kemal Atatürk, the first President of Turkey secularized it by making it a museum. The huge gilt discs engraved with writings from the Koran which hung on the walls were removed and only after the death of Atatürk were they replaced. Aya Sofia is still a museum, and frankly rather stark in appearance, but it is an amazing feat of architecture. The big middle dome rests on two half domes and the church was dedicated to the Virgin and not to the saint who bore the name of 'Sophia' which is the Greek word for 'wisdom'.

I have visited Aya Sofia on several occasions, my main interest being that it houses several pillars which originated in the Temple of Artemis in Ephesus, but on this occasions I was not thinking of anything in particular as I walked with Semra through the enormous bronze doors where I stopped dead in amazement for I found myself looking at the interior of a Christian cathedral. The vision could not have lasted for more than a few seconds, but in that time I viewed the sumptuousness of its past glory with its gold and silver throne, the altar table, altar screens and wall panels all studded with precious jewels which scintillated in the light. My senses seemed to be pervaded by the odour of heavy incense and there appeared to be three priests dressed in beautiful coloured robes and ornate head-dresses standing by the altar, and then the vision faded and I was back in the present and hearing the echo of feet in the vast enclosure as it milled with visitors. I said nothing to Semra at the time but confided my vision to her later, and as we walked round Aya Sofia I seemed to see it for the first time with unveiled eyes.

When we walked out of the museum I decided to have my boots cleaned by one of the many *boyaci* or shoe-shine boys who are ubiquitous in Istanbul with their highly decorated and shining brass boxes containing brushes and polishes of various colours to accommodate the footwear of their clientele. Some of the *boyaci* are mature men and the one who cleaned my boots did not seem able to get a gloss on them. When I remarked on this, he told me it was because they were damp from recent rain, it was November after all, and I agreed.

The charge for this service is very modest, about two hundred Turkish lira but I had no small notes and so handed him a one thousand lira note. He then said to me, 'I have a wife and seven children and I do not have a thousand lira note in my pocket.'

I smiled at his sauciness and replied, 'Well, we all have to work for our money ...' and at this point my Turkish failed me and I said to Semra, 'tell him that I say that if he has seven children he must be careless!'

Semra blushed to the roots of her hair, as well-brought-up and protected young Turkish women do not indulge in such repartee with strange men, but she willing translated my words as I had asked. The *boyaci* looked at me and said laconically, 'My wife is very young and if I put my trousers on the bed she becomes pregnant!' Semra and I burst into laughter and decided that he had won that round and we departed.

As we walked along the road, laughing together at the cheekiness of the *boyaci*, three young Turks walked towards us and Semra greeted one as an old friend. 'He works for my father,' she explained, 'and', she added, 'he is a gypsy.' I looked at the young man curiously. Most Turkish men are dark and swarthy and sport a moustache, and I wondered if he was a Kurd with Mongolian blood, noting his high cheekbones and dusky skin colour.

When Semra had said, 'He is a gypsy', I immediately mentally associated the term with palm and tea cup reading, and without thinking I thrust out my hand, palm upwards and said, 'Read my palm for me please.'

The Kurd, if such he was, looked at me in a startled fashion and said, 'I can't read your palm.'

Whoever heard of a gypsy who could not read palms, I thought to myself, and said impulsively, 'Well give me your hand and I'll read yours.'

I really do not know what came over me, but the gypsy

extended his palm and I commenced to delineate what I saw and felt. My Turkish was not always equal to the task and I would say to Semra, 'Tell him that ...', and she would quickly translate, and the visions and the sensing came so fast that eventually it became more suitable to speak in English without thinking too deeply as the effort of mental translation on my part destroyed the psychic impulse.

I must have been accurate about his past for the Kurd became excited and demanded to know what the future held, and his friends grew impatient at the length of his reading and thrust their palms under my nose and said pleadingly, 'Bayan, Bayan' ('lady, lady'), wanting me to read for them.

The situation rapidly, if I may use a pun, got out of hand, for it is the nature of Turks to be attracted to a source of noise and excitement and I was soon surrounded by a veritable crowd of Turks holding out their hands and shouting, 'Madame, madame' whilst Semra struggled to cope with the flood and flow of the translation.

I began to wonder what I had started when a policeman strolled over to discover the reason for the disorder but, evidently deciding that the law was not being broken, he retired with an understanding smile. His temporary interest had produced a lull in the clamorous voices and I became aware of the presence, on the outer rim of the crowd, of an elderly Turkish man who was watching me quietly.

He must have been around seventy-five years of age, his back was bowed with years of labour, his hair thick and iron grey, and his face a deep mahogany colour from exposure to the hot Turkish sun and deeply lined with age and weariness. His eyes, deep set and of the darkest brown, were strangely youthful as they watched me and as Semra and I walked over to him, he broke into a slightly tremulous smile as he shuffled towards us. I said quietly, 'Merhaba baba' ('hello, father') and he silently held out a rough, gnarled and work worn hand for my inspection.

I knew as soon as I touched his fingers that I was in the presence of sanctity, of a patience and belief which had endured without complaint all the blows and misfortunes that a harsh fate could inflict, that he was almost at the end of his long and painful journey through a troubled onerous life and he sought not my reflections on his past, his present or predictions for his future, but assurance that Allah remembered him and that his strivings for submission to the Will of Allah, which is the meaning of Islam had not been in vain.

I addressed him gently, in an exaggerated Oriental vein, customary, and beloved of elderly Turkish men, 'Baba', I said, 'Allah who has watched over you and received your praise since the days of your youth looks upon you with his favour; you have lived according to the laws of the Koran, you have never failed to give alms to the poor and needy for the love of Allah. Your name is written in the Book of Life, and the Prophet Mohammed (peace and blessings be upon him) will receive you at the Gates of Paradise, and you will drink of the waters of Tasnim and dwell in a palace with a garden watered by a flowing spring, and planted with shady trees. Is Allah not the Compassionate, the Merciful, and did not the Prophet Mohammed (peace and blessings be upon him) promise you these things, fear not ...'

There was more which Semra lovingly translated, and as I spoke, a peaceful rapturous gaze came to the old man's face, and his eyes filled with tears of gratitude. When I had finished, he took my hand, kissed the back of it and raised the hand to his forehead, a traditional token of respect in Turkey, and murmuring, 'tesekkur, cok tesekkur ederim' (thank you, thank you very much), he turned slowly from me, and limped down the road.

As I watched his departure thoughtfully, I was warmed by a glow of content, that I had been able to give comfort to an old man, and the thought transcended, that if my whole life had been self-centred and deficient in acts of altruism, that one conversation might have been my redemption. I was glad that fate had brought me to Aya Sofia at that time, although the dervishes teach that nothing happens by chance; perhaps I had been there for the elderly Turk as he had been there for me.

As I mused on these reflections, I was continuing to watch him slowly limping down the road in the weak November sunshine, when to my alarm and stupefaction, he seemed to melt into the late afternoon light and disappear. The road leading from Aya Sofia was long and straight, there were few other people about and no corners around which he could turn. I thought I had imagined it until Semra said in a puzzled voice, 'Where did he go?' Where indeed? When I turned from my bewilderment, I was again besieged by upturned palms, but the mood had passed, and I excused myself and walked into Aya Sofia again and ruminated on whether I had 'entertained angels unaware'.

These psychic encounters, including my own, occurred to quite ordinary people, spontaneously, and they would seem to carry no obvious sense of significance in terms of their content, except perhaps to give us an indication that there is more to the Universe and our conception of it than appears on the surface.

One of my correspondents, who subsequently visited me for counsel on another matter, related an incident which had occurred some years previously. Her husband being abroad on business, she had arranged to attend a concert with a married couple. During an orchestral piece which she amazingly recalled as having been Brahms' First Symphony, she began to experience what she thought was an hallucination. She had a vision of a man dressed completely in black and with a black scarf on the lower part of his face, who entered the garden of her house through a back gate, and after creeping quietly through the garden proceeded to demolish a lock on the back door. He made his way through her kitchen and hall and upstairs to her bedroom where she kept a substantial amount of jewellery in a dressing-table drawer. He rifled through the drawers until he came to the one he was seeking, removed the drawer, placed it on the bed and proceeded to carefully sort through it deciding which items were the most valuable. She had left her bedroom curtains drawn back as it was daylight when she had left the house, and she saw him turn out his torch and close the curtains and then return to sorting out her jewellery. The vision faded and she was panic-stricken but unable to say anything to her friends until the music had finished. When she told them what she had experienced they attempted to pacify her by saying that she had simply been imagining it all. She would not be calmed, however, and declared that she knew exactly which pieces of jewellery had been taken and that she had seen him drop a diamond ring which had rolled under the bed. She begged them to take her home and so they did.

On reaching the house they found the back door had been forced open and the bedroom curtains were drawn. The dressing-table drawer was lying on the bed; only the choicest items of jewellery had been stolen, less valuable pieces were tossed aside, and under the bed she found a diamond ring. Further, a black scarf which did not belong to her was found near the bedroom door, obviously dropped during the man's hurried departure.

Such visions often occur when the mind is relaxed, as when listening to music, and whilst her experience was a distressing one, some paranormal occurrences are often trivial and inconsequential.

The experiences of my neighbour, the Scottish lady and John were unusual but of no great import in their lives, whilst that of my woman visitor did nothing to prevent the catastrophe occurring, it merely indicated what was happening at the time of the vision.

My encounters in Turkey were more mystical than paranormal and they have not influenced my life to any extent, beyond confirming what I already knew, that such events are not always interwoven with purely personal aspects of our lives, or the workings of our own unconscious minds, but can be extended to someone, who, however temporarily, arouses our compassion or interest. Whilst they do not recommend themselves to the scientist or the materialist, there is no doubt that they do occur and are as real as the practice of witchcraft and the efficaciousness of spells.

One of my friends for whom I have great affection, often appeals to me for aid in certain difficult periods of his life and I always oblige him with what he terms a 'bit of witchcraft' since it is very easy to work spells for friends because there is an emotional aspect involved. My workings on his behalf have always been successful. Now it may well be that without my intervention, his crises would resolve themselves anyway, I am the first to admit this, but it seems at times that it would be stretching coincidence too far to consider that they would be resolved as quickly as they are by my bit of witchcraft.

I was very busy with the demands of my own life when Richard said he was having problems at work. He could not resolve them and wished they would just melt away and could I do a bit of witchcraft. I suggested that on this occasion he should do it himself, I would give him instructions and if I knew the exact time he intended to carry out the spell I would concentrate and project power to him temporarily, and this was arranged.

A few weeks later he reported to me in an astonished voice, 'That spell you helped me to do Lois, do you know it actually worked! The problem just melted away!'

I replied in exasperation, 'Of course it worked, hasn't every spell I've ever done for you worked, do you think I've been wasting my time for the last thirty years?' He had the grace to look abashed.

7 Crystal Vision

I receive many letters from people who wish to learn how to read the crystal; having purchased one and experimented for a little while, they become disheartened if they do not immediately obtain crystal vision. I firmly believe it is possible to develop this ability with patience and determination.

The term 'crystal-gazing' is familiar to most people, 'scrying' is a less familiar word but means the same thing. The picture brought to mind is of a dark-skinned gypsy with her aura of mystery in a fairground tent, her brightly coloured headscarf decorated with tiny coins and the crystal ball before her, 'Cross my palm with silver, and I'll tell you what the crystal shows for you!'

Crystal-gazing has a history almost as old as that of the human race, and various methods of scrying have been traced to the fourth century AD. During the classical and Middle Ages crystals were used by the Greeks and the Romans as a form of divination. In Egypt the gazer or seer, placed a spot of ink in the palm of the hand and it was thought necessary to go through certain magical incantations before visions could be produced and these could only be seen by an adolescent child. According to some sources, the Pharaohs had a similar technique from which they were able to discover the state of distant provinces and so provide against famine.

Amongst various tribes in the West Indies, the liver of an animal was used as a point of concentration, this, like the scrying of the Egyptians, was accompanied by a very long formula and required a period of almost two years before visions could be obtained. Crystal-gazing also had its equivalent amongst the original Indian tribes of North America and is apparently practised today by the remnants of the Indians in the Far West.

During the twelfth century, cups and basins filled with water obtained from sacred streams were in vogue. Mirrors and other bright objects such as swords were also used. In the fourteenth century nearly all scrying was accomplished with the aid of quartz crystals and with beryls, highly polished. Crystal-gazing is very popular in India and Arabia and stories of wonderful divination feats are told by travellers to these lands. The Muslims of India employ a 'magic mirror' which is similar to a crystal only being different in shape. The art is extensively practised by the Yogis and Sunnecasses.

Literature prepared and written by the learned Dr Dee, scryer to Queen Elizabeth I, is still in existence. The crystal used by Dr Dee is preserved in the British Museum. Other records state that Aristotle made a crystal which was employed by Alexander the Great.

Men of different races have discovered that pictures or visions may be seen in a speculum of some clear depth which has led to the almost universal use of the crystal as we know it today. However, let it be understood that there is no special virtue or magical properties or qualities in the crystal itself, it is merely an instrument for astral vision, just as the telescope, microscope and other optical instruments are employed in the phenomena of physical vision. It is true that the atomic and molecular characteristics of glass, crystal, etc. tend to produce the best results but water and ink have been similarly used with success.

The term 'scrying' comes from the word 'descry', meaning 'to perceive things at a distance', and Andrew Lang, an Oxford scholar who lived towards the end of the nineteenth century was of the opinion that the effort involved in crystal-gazing objectifies images consciously or unconsciously held in the mind of the gazer. The great Arab historian Ibn Khaldun who studied the subject five hundred years earlier, wrote that scryers concentrate all their perceptions in a single sense, that of sight, 'fixing their gaze on an object they regard it with attention until they perceive the thing that they wish to announce'.

Many years ago I paid a visit to a little Irish lady who was very gifted in scrying. She produced an ordinary white pudding basin filled with water and handed me a blue bag. (For those unfamiliar with the use of a blue bag in this technological age, let me explain that it was in times past used to whiten linen. Dipped in cold water it leaked a blue substance and when white linen was dipped in the water, the whiteness was enhanced.)

I was instructed to swirl the blue bag around the water in the basin and concentrate my thoughts for half a minute. She then proceeded to scry into the basin of blue water. Everything she told me about my past life and present circumstances was completely accurate and prophecies she made regarding my future came to fruition within six months.

Various teachers use different forms of the crystal or substitutes for it, and an interesting variation for the impecunious is a cup painted black on the inside into which water is poured.

The potential scryer should then first decide what method is attractive. Some people insist on experimenting with a crystal ball; the price of rock crystal can be prohibitive but equally good results can be obtained with the use of a glass crystal and these can be purchased at a relatively economic price. Plastic crystal balls should be avoided, they are an abomination.

My personal observation is that a new crystal should before use, be 'charged'. This is achieved by allowing the light of a waxing moon to shine on the crystal for seven consecutive nights. It has been my experience that people who have followed this advice have been rewarded with more speedy results. Scrying is concerned with an inner and subjective aspect of experience which can be related to the moon. According to the beliefs of the most primitive peoples, the moon is a kind of beneficent presence whose light is considered not only favourable but indispensable for growth. The earliest representation of the Moon deity or the Moon Goddess was a cone or pillar of stone. In Melanesia, for instance, stone is worshipped as an aspect of the Moon, often found in the form of a hand carved circular stone. In Chaldea, the Great Goddess, Magna Dea who was goddess of the Moon was worshipped in the form of a sacred black stone which is believed to be the very stone still venerated at Mecca. Stone, glass and crystal are minerals, and by association under the rulership of the Moon, an aspect of the Great Goddess. By charging a new crystal we are acknowledging this divinity and association.

In the practice of scrying, it is immaterial whether the crystal is placed on a pedestal or held in the hands. If it is to be held, a black cloth or dark coloured velvet should be placed between the hands and the crystal to prevent actual contact with the hands, and prevent sweating of the glass which usually occurs when warm hands are brought into contact with any cold glass surface.

The crystal should be warmed by holding it near a fire or tightly in the hands. The scryer should retire to a quiet room free from all disturbances and first practise alone. The window curtains should be drawn to exclude nearly all light so that the room is in comparative darkness but sufficient light should be allowed to enable the crystal to be clearly seen; light from a window or a lamp should fall over the shoulder onto the crystal which should be the same distance from the eyes as a book would be when reading.

It is necessary to relax and sit passively in a comfortable chair to exclude physical sensations as far as possible, and your eyes should be closed for a period of about five minutes to seek a quiet, calm state of mind. Having arrived at this, attention should be concentrated on the centre of the crystal, look into it, not at it, and do not stare until it becomes uncomfortable. Focus the gaze on the crystal and think of whatever you desire to see, and always with the expectation of seeing pictures. During this process, do not blink the eyes more than can be possibly helped, but at the same time do not strain them by trying to keep them open any length of time without blinking. Do not allow the eyes to wander from the ball nor the attention relax from the subject in mind.

The first attempt should be limited to about ten minutes and it is possible that there will be little success in the first few attempts, but the prospective scryer should not be discouraged. The sitting should be made daily and, if possible, at practically the same time each day. Ten-minute periods are recommended at first, as the muscles of the eyelids will strengthen with practice until an unwinking gaze can be maintained for twenty minutes or half an hour.

When the ability is possessed or sufficiently developed, just before a vision appears, the ball will cloud over with a milky white mist, this is called 'clouding' and is the first sign of oncoming visions. Some people get no further than 'clouding', whilst others claim the crystal seems to change colour, starting with a dark red and going through the colours of the rainbow, the circles and rings always starting at the centre of the crystal and progressing outwards as in a disturbance of a pond when a pebble is thrown into it.

According to some traditions, the colour of the cloudiness has meanings. White predictably is a good portent and black is evil. Green or blue cloudiness indicates coming joy; red, yellow or orange clouds herald disaster. If the clouds ascend, the answer is 'yes' to any question asked of the crystal, descending clouds mean the answer is 'no'. The vision of a globe within a crystal indicates travel, a skull death or wisdom, a star success or a warning, an eye good luck or impending evil, and a bird means a message or potential rebirth.

When the ability to see 'clouding' has been attained, the faculty may be developed by a simple experiment. The breathing should be slow and deep whilst looking into the crystal for ten minutes, and then there should be a rest for five; during this time, write on a slip of paper what you wish to see, turn the paper over and think no more about it, continue passive and wait for what may appear in the ball. Notes should be taken of all that is seen, for as a dream, crystal vision is quickly forgotten.

Crystal-gazing is one method of developing latent powers of clairvoyance which many people possess. Some visions are merely meaningless daydreams produced by the imagination and directed into the crystal. Others are visions produced by the memory of forgotten events, the establishment of a connection between the subconscious and the conscious mind, created as a result of concentration upon a crystal. Many visions are of future events, and these are often so numerous and diversified, mysterious and unaccountable that the scryer may not recognize one of this type until the event has transpired, when of course the vision is recalled. There are no set rules for the meaning or interpretation of the various visions, like dreams they can only be related to a person's life and inmost private feelings and attitudes, but often an understanding of the picture accompanies it. On occasions, messages have appeared in writing in the crystal conveying information, and I have experienced the forms and faces of deceased relatives appearing in the crystal.

Some crystal images are quite small, others completely fill the ball, the small images are usually of lesser events. Images appearing on the left normally indicate past events, in the centre the immediate present, and on the right those concerned with the future.

In the course of time, as a result of constant handling and use, the crystal ball will become inbued with the personal aura and vibrations of the owner, it will in fact become a magical tool and as such, it should never be allowed to be handled indiscriminately by other persons. When not in use the crystal should be kept covered, preferably by a piece of black velvet so that no light falls on it. It can periodically be washed in warm soapy water to remove residual perspiration stains from the hands, and dried with a soft cloth, and before use it should be somewhat reverently gently polished with the velvet cloth.

When the scryer becomes proficient in the art of crystal-gazing, it will then become possible to scry on behalf of another person, and in this event the method to be adopted is as follows. The crystal should be removed from beneath its covering cloth and lightly wiped over with the velvet, the ball being held in the left hand. The eyes of the scryer should be closed, and with the right hand seven circular passes should be made over the crystal whilst mentally acknowledging that the gazing is to be on behalf of another person – this is merely a psychological technique to establish the fact.

The crystal should then be handed to the other party and instructions given that the ball must be held lightly between the hands, and whilst the eyes are closed mental directions given to the crystal for the answering of certain questions, if these are required. If this is not the purpose of the sitting and a more general scrying is desired, then the circumstances of the life of the person, their hopes and fears should be held in mind whilst they sit passively for five or ten minutes. The crystal should then be retrieved, held in the hands of the scryer, if necessary wiped over with the velvet cloth, and the reading commenced.

Another method of divination often used by witches is the use of a 'magic mirror'. The lazy occultist can purchase one of these ready-made in some occult supply shops, but there is a great deal of satisfaction to be obtained by fashioning one personally, with the added inducement that during the course of its construction one's personal vibrations are introduced into it.

A concave mirror is the most satisfactory and these can sometimes be obtained from an old clock. The glass should be cleaned and polished thoroughly and three separate coats of black paint applied, allowing each one to dry properly before the application of the next coat; the painting should be done on the convex side. It is not necessary to frame the mirror unless one particularly wishes to do so, and when not in use it can be wrapped in a black cloth, preferably velvet and stored inside a box of suitable size. The mirror method is more suitable for personal divination and the instructions given regarding the access of light should be applied as for the crystal. The mirror can either be held in the hands or propped up against some firm surface when in use. Alternatively, the purchase of a large size stand sold for the display of ornamental plates greatly facilitates its convenient use.

Curious recommendations have been made by past exponents of the art of scrying. It has been suggested for instance that good results may be obtained by drinking an infusion of mugwort (*artemisia vulgaris*) or of chicory (*cichorium intybus*) because of their tonic qualities. These herbs are under the zodiacal sign of Libra. In addition, a waxing moon is considered to be the best time for scrying since, as already stated, there is an affinity between the moon and crystal. In addition, it has been suggested that the visions seen in the crystal differ according to the mental and psychic temperament of the scryer. There are two distinctions made, one whose mental attitude is positive and another who is passive. In the former the visions are more likely to be symbols of a past or future event rather than a picture of the event itself, the passive subject however is apt to see a definite picture of the persons or event revealed.

Some modern crystal or glass balls have a small, circular flat surface on the sphere which assists in lessening the reflections which sometimes interfere with projections of mental pictures. The faculty of visualization plays a most important part in the art of crystal-gazing and a good exercise for the beginner is to attempt to externalize onto the crystal a simple picture from the memory, a cat, a dog, or a tree for instance. When these are produced satisfactorily an invisible mental barrier has been breached. Points of light are reflected from polished surfaces and these serve to attract the attention of the scryer and to fix the eye and gradually the optic nerve becomes tired until it ceases to transmit the impression outside and responds to the reflex action from the brain. In this way the impression received from within is projected and appears to come from outside. Results will therefore vary with individuals depending upon the sensitivity of the optic nerve. It is sometimes asserted that prior to the appearance of visions the whole crystal seems to disappear and a mist rises before the scryer's eyes.

The Mexicans have a legend that their god Tezcatlipuco had a magic mirror in which he could view everything that occurred in the world; to the influence of this divinity were attributed many visions and omens announced by repeated knockings, and in the Orphic poem 'Lithica' a magic sphere of stone is referred to. It was called *sideritis* or *ophitis* and was said to be black, round and heavy. Helenus the Trojan soothsayer is reported to have used this sphere to prophesy the downfall of his native city. He fasted for twenty-one days and then wrapped the sphere in soft cloth and offered sacrifices to it until by the magic of his prayers 'a living soul warmed the precious substance'.

In his life of the Emperor Didius Julianus (133–193) Spartianus wrote of the strange variety of divinations by means of mirrors which were placed on the heads of boys who were blindfolded and then proceeded to see forms or signs in the mirrors. One of the boys is supposed to have announced the approaching accession of Septimus Severus (146–211).

Divination by means of a silver cup existed amongst the primitive Hebrews which is revealed in the story of Joseph and his brothers. In Genesis 44;1–5 we read that Joseph concealed a silver cup in the sack of grain borne away by Benjamin making this an excuse for the return of his brothers. He sent messengers to overtake them demanding the return of the cup, 'Is not this it in which my lord drinketh, and whereby indeed he divineth?'

The Arabic author Haly Abou Gefar relates a story of a golden ball used by the Magi followers of Zoroaster; it was encrusted with heavenly symbols and set with a sapphire and one of the magicians attached it to a strip of bullhide and swung it around reciting at the same time various spells and incantations. It is probable that the magician fixed his gaze upon the brilliant sphere and fell into a hypnotic trance during which visions appeared to him. These he would interpret to those who had come to hear their future or obtain information of things happening at a distance.

In one of the canons of the synod held about AD 450 by St Patrick and the bishops Auxilius and Issernanus was a decree that any Christian who believed there was a *Lamia* (or witch) in the mirror was to be anathemized, and not received into the church until he renounced the belief. The vision in the crystal or mirror represented to these worthies of the church an evil spirit who gave the scryer the information he was seeking.

Andrew Lang wrote of what he termed hypnagogic visions, images which appear when the eyes are closed and before sleep is achieved. The faces which appeared to him were always unfamiliar, except that he once saw his own face in profile. The same was true of landscape and inanimate forms, the forms seemed to grow out of the bright points of light which appear when the eyes are closed and Lang suggested a similar origin for the visions which scryers obtain.

Ibn Kaldoun a Persian writer who was born in 1332, wrote a reasonable analysis of crystal-gazing,

> Some believe that the image perceived in this way takes form on the surface of the mirror, but they are mistaken. The diviner looks at this surface fixedly until it disappears, and a curtain, like a mist is interposed between him and the mirror. Upon this curtain are designed the forms he wishes to see,

and this permits him to give indications, either affirmative or negative, concerning the matter on which he is questioned. He then describes his perceptions as he has received them. The diviners while in this state, do not see what is really to be seen; it is another kind of perception which is born in them and which is realised not by sight, but by the soul.

The Persian poet Jami wrote of a magic mirror in his poem Salaman and Absal,

> Then from his secret Art the Sage Vizyr
> A magic mirror made; a mirror like
> The bosom of All-wise Intelligence
> Reflecting in its mystic compass all
> Within the sev'nfold volume of the World
> Invol'd; and looking in that Mirror's face
> The Shah beheld the face of his Desire.

The sceptre of the Scottish regalia is surmounted by a crystal globe, two-and-a-quarter inches in diameter, and the mace by a large crystal beryl. These stones were regarded as amulets in the past and their use traced back to the Druids. Sir Walter Scott tells that in his time they were still known amongst the Highlanders as 'Stones of Power'.

In the twelfth century divination by means of the crystal and the mirror was practised. John of Salisbury (1120–80) wrote that when he was a boy he received instruction from a priest who was skilled in the art, the priest would polish the fingernails of the boy with consecrated oil or ointment and then tell them to look upon the nails until some form of figure appeared.

Many of the early records of crystal-gazing show that the images revealed were produced by the expectations, hopes or fears of the gazer. In many cases the vision is only prophetic because it determines the future conduct of the person who consults the crystal. Persuaded that what has been seen must come to pass, he or she proceeds consciously or unconsciously to make it happen to fulfil the prediction. If it is a happy positive event it would stimulate the scryer to greater efforts to achieve it, but if a less happy and negative vision, it could result in despair and lethargy because 'it is prophesied'. This is a warning which needs to be heeded by any prospective scryer.

A curious story survives from the French Revolution when suspicion fell on one General Marlière. A short time before the date fixed for his appearance before the judges he met a colonel in the French Army who was a firm believer in the visions seen in a crystal ball, and not unnaturally he was eager to put the matter of his future to the test. The colonel was not very willing since he suspected what the General's fate would be but eventually he agreed, and the medium used was an innocent child. A picture appeared in the crystal of a man wearing a private's uniform struggling with another in General's uniform and the child proclaimed that the General was beheaded. However the strange dress of the executioner excited comment for the official garb of an executioner bore no resemblance to a private's uniform.

General Marlière was tried, found guilty and guillotined and on the day of the execution, Samson, the official executioner, wishing to gratify his personal vanity dressed himself in the uniform of a national guardsman. This peculiar intention could not have been foreseen by any of the people who were present at the reading of the crystal.

The Armenians practised divination by observing the images which appeared on the smooth surface of water in a well and the person who saw such images was known as a *hornaiogh* ('he who looks into a well'). An Arab woman living in Constantinople had a great reputation for her power and was frequently consulted by Armenians and other dwellers in the Turkish capital. Whoever wished to question this woman concerning the cause of an illness, the whereabouts of stolen objects or missing people, etc. usually took a child of the household with them and the scrying was done by the child. If no child was brought however, the witch herself did the scrying.

There is another story about crystal-gazing concerning an American lady who could not recall the address of a friend whose previous letter she had destroyed. She consulted her crystal and within a few minutes perceived an address in grey letters on a white background and duly wrote her reply to this address. When the reply came it was found that the address was stamped in grey on white paper, identical to the address she had first received. Gazing into the crystal had stirred up the visual impression stored in the subconscious mind and it had externalized in the crystal and it would appear that an element of self-hypnotism could be involved.

Crystal balls have been found occasionally in tombs or in funerary urns. In the tomb of Childeric (AD 436–81), the father of Clovis, a rock crystal sphere was found, and amongst those found in French sepulchres was one discovered in 1853 at Arras. It is preserved in the museum; and still has the original gold mounting which attached it to the necklace from which it had been worn suspended. Crystal balls have also been found in the Saxon tombs of England, at Chatham, in the Isle of Wight, at Barham near Canterbury, at Fairford in Gloucestershire and in Kent.

A crystal ball known as the Currahmore Crystal which belongs to the Marquis of Waterford has the reputation of possessing magical powers. It is of rock crystal and there is a legend that one of the Le Poers brought it from the Holy Land where it had been given to him by the crusader Godefroy de Bouillon (1058–1100). It is slightly larger than an orange and a silver ring encircles it around the middle. It is supposed to be able to cure cattle of their distempers, but the cattle are not touched with it, they are driven up and down a stream in which the crystal has been laid.

Whilst many witches have their own personal crystal, scrying in a coven is usually done with the aid of a black cauldron filled with water and there are traditional meanings associated with the symbols which appear in the cauldron, these also apply to those seen in a crystal and it might be helpful to a prospective seer to know what these are:

Aerial	News from far away, secret letters
Ant	Extra work involved
Axe	A road accident
Bed	Period of illness
Bee	Profit from work
Boat	Inheritance, money
Book	Success in studies
Candlestick	Long lasting luck
Car	Departure, journeys
Cat	Betrayal
Cavalier	For a woman, a new lover
Circle	Birth, pregnancy
Clover	Unexpected profit
Cross	Pain, illness
Duck	Gossip
Eagle	Power and energy
Ear	Advice, do not heed
Elephant	Success and fortune
Eye	Termination of lawsuit
Flower	One flower, joy, festivities

Flowers	Short lived happiness
Guillotine	Death
Hedge	Complicated matters need attention
Hen	Frivolous woman, gossip
Horse	Family ingratitude
Lamb	Great happiness
Leaf	Loss of hair
Leg	Carnal passion
Lion	Courage needed
Mouth	Lies
Mushroom	Blood disease
Nail	Enemy will reveal himself
Ox	Profit, victory over an enemy
Plate	Gambling win
Rat	Ruin
Razor	Care needed
Ring	A small present
Scales	A lawsuit
Snake	Important hindrances
Spider	Disappointed in love
Stick	Sudden inspiration
Swallow	Return of a dear one
Sword	Danger from a man
Teeth	People wish you harm
Umbrella	Protection from friends
Vase	Future love
Wedding rings	One, a wish to marry
	Two, broken engagement
Window	Be careful of thieves

Finally, the present Dalai Lama, the fourteenth, was located with the help of one of the alternatives to crystal-gazing. Each Dalai Lama is said to be the reincarnation of his predecessor and when the thirteenth died, the search for his reincarnation began. There was evidence that he would be found in the East. Lake Lhamoi Latso at Chokhorgyal is believed by Tibetans to show visions of the future and so the Regent made the journey of ninety miles to the lake. He spent several days there in meditation and eventually he saw a vision of a great monastery with a green and gold roof, close by was a dwelling with turquoise tiles. The vision was correct in every detail, the boy destined to become the Dalai Lama was found living with his parents and brothers and sisters in the house with the turquoise tiles.

8   *Psychometry and Clairvoyance*

Many of the letters I receive are from people who have a great longing to fulfil their own psychic and spiritual potential. Some write at length outlining their own psychic experiences and innermost feelings and ask if I can judge whether they are witches or if they have the capacity to become witches. Others with no interest in active practice of witchcraft require advice on how they can develop psychic ability.

I have explained elsewhere (in *Witch Amongst Us*) that it is not possible to become a witch as it is to become a Christian or a Freemason for instance, witches are born not made, and many of the people who are born witches wish that they were not; I am not one of them. It does not automatically follow that because a person is born a witch, strong psychic abilities will be in evidence also, these are an added bonus. A witch is someone who is able to work magic, an individual with an indefinable physical force which they can utilize and manipulate to change and influence events and circumstances in their own lives or the lives of other people for good or ill.

My friend Sonya is a witch, albeit on the dark side, but she denies that she possesses any psychic ability as such and observes that she has always been too busy working magic to seek development of clairvoyance, crystal-gazing or psychometry. She is, however, a brilliant astrologer and has said that on occasions when interpreting a chart she will receive mentally a broader expansion of something only hinted at in the chart, and it is my firm belief that she is in fact utilizing that sixth sense which is common to all humanity but is developed more strongly in some than in others.

Our ancient ancestors needed this sense to survive the harshness of their environment. It told them where there were good hunting-grounds and where enemies lay in wait, but gradually as mankind evolved the sixth sense atrophied because it was no longer needed. Vestiges of this extra-sensory perception survive in most people and can be developed with patience and application, one of the easiest of which is psychometry or object reading. By doing no more than hold an object – a ring, brooch or a photograph – a psychometrist may be able to give the most amazing detailed information concerning the person and the circumstances with which the object is connected.

The principle of psychometry is that there is a psychic connection between things once associated, and the psychometrist establishes a mental and emotional rapport with a distant scene, a period of time, a person or an object by the utilization of some form of physical material connected with the scene, time or person. There is a theory that there exists an electro-magnetic vibration between articles worn for periods of time by people, rings, necklaces, spectacles, watches, etc., and this can be extended to include hair, clothing, handwriting, a photograph or nail-parings. Strong emotional elements are absorbed into the aura of these items and can be detected psychically as will characteristics of a person, location, habits, health, etc.

It is also possible to sense the past history of an object or its surroundings by means of the object itself. A bullet from a battlefield may give the history of the battle, a portion of ancient pottery the habits and living conditions of the people who used and made it, as well as the appearance of the land in which they lived.

Strictly speaking, psychometry is mainly concerned with the past and present, but from personal experience I have found it to be also a doorway leading to the future. Its continued practice leads to the development of clairvoyance, clairaudience and prescience, and it becomes possible to make prophecies and forecasts of future events in a person's life. A lowered state of consciousness which causes the person to be less inhibited is favourable to psychometry and with some subjects an element of trance or auto-hypnosis has been observed.

It is advisable for the beginner to practise with an article of someone unknown as conscious knowledge of the circumstances of the life of a friend or relative will interfere with psychic perception. I always insist that any article I am given to read should have been owned since new and worn fairly consistently for about a year. If it has been owned or worn by someone else, or bequeathed in a Will for instance, the vibrations are likely to be confused. I explain this at the beginning of the reading so that if I am handed an article which belonged to a person now deceased, I shall be likely to pick up the circumstances of their past life.

It is helpful if the reader works with the eyes closed as this cuts off any outside stimuli; the article should be held in the hand for a few minutes and then against the forehead. It is possible that with practice there will be a physical manifestation indicating that the reader has 'tuned in' to the aura of the article. For me it is a sensation of warmth in the area of the solar plexus. Images then begin to appear in the mind, fleeting and fragmentary so that it is necessary to describe them and associated clairsentience (feelings) immediately before they are replaced by others. The reader should state clearly and in simple language what is seen and felt no matter how absurd or ridiculous it may seem and any requests for further elaboration should be discouraged as these tend to interfere with the psychic perception and break the tenuous emotional link with the aura of the article.

A great barrier to the subtle layers of the psyche is the intellect, and the beginner must learn how to overcome this and suspend rationalization of visions and feelings, bypassing the conscious mind and allowing the subconscious mind to prevail. The reader may find the urge to speak instinctively as a child would and this is a good indication that the psychic sense is functioning rather than the logical adult mind which seeks always to rationalize impressions or dismiss them as imagination.

I have observed a curious phenomenon in psychometry readings which experience has taught me to heed. For no apparent reason I will begin to think of, or see a picture in my mind of a person or a situation completely unrelated to the person for whom I am reading. One example will suffice. Once when reading an article for a young woman I mentally saw a question mark and said to her, 'You have a decision to make, don't you?' and she nodded. Into my mind came the picture of a woman friend who had recently had a hysterectomy due to fibroids. 'Now why should I suddenly see Marion', I thought to myself and then the realization dawned that I was being shown the basis of the decision that my client had to make. 'You have a fibroid, and have to decide whether to have an operation', I told her. She agreed I was correct.

The point I am trying to make here is that when the psychic senses are functioning and being utilized, no mental impression or physical feeling should be ignored. Whilst exchanging experiences with psychometry a friend told me that once when giving a reading to a middle-aged lady she experienced a sharp pain in her right sacral area and she said to her client, 'You have a grumbling appendix, don't neglect to see a doctor' and the client admitted she was having pain in that area.

Some perception may be seen symbolically, and with practice the beginner will start to recognize symbols and develop a personal psychic shorthand, the veracity and accuracy of which can only be substantiated by trial and error.

For instance a mental vision of a speeding train coming off the rails does not always represent a future accident; moving vehicles often represent the sexual and emotional life and could be prescience of a change in these circumstances, or that the owner of the article is leading a dangerous life and heading for disaster in these areas. The emotional sensations concurrent with the vision should serve to differentiate.

A summer scene of a softly flowing river or a lake, with the quierient in a small boat on a punt, lazily sailing, would most certainly indicate to me a potential period of peace, contentment and well being to come. A large expanse of water, an ocean or sea with a small boat drifting aimlessly, or being tossed by angry waves would incline me to regard the quierient as being unable to come to terms with the contingencies of life, manipulated by circumstances rather than seeking to control them.

Psychometrists can sometimes be compared with people who have difficulty recollecting a forgotten word or name, in trying to bring to mind the word required, others with an association will be thrust forward. Once when giving a reading to a young African girl, the word 'royalty' came to mind. I asked her in a surprised fashion, 'Are you a princess?' She told me that her deceased father had always referred to her as 'his princess' and members of her family continued to use this as a nickname.

Generally speaking, names come through with difficulty, sometimes only a few letters of a first or last name will surface or only a few elements of the totality of events occurring in the past of people will be seen or felt; at times bizarre hints of a name will be given. I was once reading for a woman I knew slightly when I clairaudiently heard someone singing an old song, 'Daisy, Daisy, give me your answer do ...' The woman's name was Hazel and I told her that I could hear this song and she said 'My father used to sing it when he was alive, he called me Daisy and my mother Gert!'

The perseverance and practice of psychometry can lead to the development of other psychic senses and clairaudience or the hearing of an objective voice may manifest in time. There is no clear dividing line between psychometry and clairvoyance and one leads into the other naturally.

It appears that psychometric impressions are not inhibited when an object is concealed. Many psychics hold objects which are concealed in opaque envelopes and they are able to describe the object correctly and the persons and events associated with it. It is recorded that Gerald Croiset, a famous psychic was given in a sealed envelope a medieval manuscript and he received images of a Pope, a knight and a monk. Fragments of an object are as good as the whole, the journalist and psychic investigator William T. Stead handed a psychometrist a few blank squares of paper which had been cut from letters written by famous people and the writers were identified.

To some extent it is believed that the psychometric power of an object depends on what it is made of, and objects derived from animal or vegetable sources have stronger psychic properties than inorganic matter such as metal; in one test cardboard proved to have better properties than aluminium objects.

The theory that objects act like the human unconscious in storing impressions of people, events and surroundings, would explain some types of ghosts which may be merely thought forms released into a house during a traumatic event in the past. The house has 'memories' of everything that has happened in it, especially scenes of emotional content.

I once gave a small stone picked up from the now derelict site of the Temple of Artemis in Ephesus, Turkey to a friend for reading. She described with great accuracy the present appearance of the site, and then tuned into the past, detailing the sumptuous building which once existed there with its magnificent pillars and portico, its wealth of gold and silver offerings from the multitude of the faithful who came to worship and give honour to the Great Goddess of the ancient world. She also described the statue of Artemis and revealed the unusual information that the statue was always veiled (which was true).

There was an occasion when after accurately recording the past life, and present trends in the life of a young woman for whom I was giving a reading, I became aware of an intense feeling of supreme happiness and contentment, and I said to her impulsively, 'I feel that all your dreams are shortly to be fulfilled, everything you have ever wanted will soon be yours!' She smiled at me wryly and expressed disbelief.

I saw her again a year later at a psychic festival, and she reminded me of the reading and continued, 'I went home and told my husband and we both had a good laugh. Two weeks later what you had prophesied actually happened. My husband was made redundant and with his redundancy money we were able to buy a house in Glastonbury where I have always wanted to live. I was able to give up my job and start a family. I am pregnant now, can you tell me what it will be, a boy or a girl?' I told her that she would have twins, one of each. When I saw her again a year later, she showed me her babies, a boy and a girl!

On another occasion I was stopped in the street by a strange woman who said, 'You probably don't remember me but you gave me a reading a year ago, and said you could see a removal van outside my house being loaded with furniture; that I was going to live in a white house on a hill in a foreign country. We moved on account of my husband's work and we now live in France, in a white house, on a hill!'

Movement in people's lives figures largely and extensively in psychometric readings, at least as far as I am concerned. In a reading for the wife of a BBC producer, I saw a removal van outside her house and had the feeling that it spelled some danger for her, but was unable to elaborate. I subsequently learnt that her husband left her; the removal van obviously represented his departure from her life.

It is possible to do psychometry without the use of an article, by holding a person's hand or by merely touching them and this happens to me spontaneously at times, helped I am sure by an emotional and compassionate response to someone in distress.

One of my friends has a beautiful daughter for whom she was once offered a hundred camels in the Grand Bazaar in Istanbul when they were both on a visit there! The daughter, whom I shall call Mary (although that is not her real name) is thirty-four, she has a responsible and exciting job in London with her own flat and she has always valued her independence. She has many friends of both sexes and a busy social life. Her mother one day in conversation with me was telling me about her son's recent wedding and said that Mary had stayed at home for the weekend after the wedding and had been depressed and weepy. She confessed to her mother that her single life was no longer as exciting as it used to be and she would very much like to get married, but amongst all her male friends and acquaintances, there was no one she regarded as being 'special'. My friend became emotional at this point recalling her daughter's tears. I put my hand on her arm sympathetically and I started to receive very strong psychic impressions.

'My dear,' I said, 'don't distress yourself because Mary is going to get married quite soon, it will all happen very quickly, I see a 'two' with it, the man she is destined to marry will be very tall and slender and he will have some foreign blood.' My friend was comforted by this and said she hoped it would be so.

Two weeks later it was Christmas, I was passing my friend's house with my dog when Mary, who was home for the festival came leaping down the steps looking absolutely radiant and said in great excitement, 'Lois, what do you think?' 'You are getting married!', I forestalled her, noting her glowing happy face, 'Yes,' she said, 'and it happened exactly as you foretold in two weeks! He is just as you described, tall, slender, and his father is Russian. I am so happy, you are invited to the wedding!'

Subsequent to the engagement a friend of Mary's who is a journalist wrote a feature for a London evening paper on 'Love at first sight' in which Mary and her fiancé were included. Her mother showed it to me and said, 'You have an honourable mention' and I read Mary's statement, 'A witch who is a friend of mummy's foretold it all!'

Experiments with psychometrists indicate that they are not affected by distance between the experimenter and the subject and that they can break through the barrier of time and are able to get impressions concerning people they will meet by chance in the future. W.H.C. Tenhaeff developed a test in 1946 known as the 'chair experiment'. Gerard Croiset was involved in these experiments which consisted of two separate parts. Croiset gave a description of the characteristics and outstanding events in the personal life of the individual he expected to occupy a certain chair in a lecture hall, and some weeks later the person who by sheer chance occupied the chair was questioned to discover to what degree Croiset's observations deviated from the personality and experiences of the individual involved. The chair experiments lasted for twenty years and took place in many cities in Europe.

One of my correspondents told me a story concerning her husband's grandmother who lived in Guatemala. She was on holiday in a bungalow in the mountains when she became ill with a very high temperature and was delirious. She got out of bed on several occasions and started trying to lift floorboards on the veranda where she insisted that Spanish treasure was buried. She was persuaded to go back to bed and her family put the delusion down to delirium. After the family left at the end of the holiday, the landlord, who had heard of the incident dug up the ground under the veranda and found a hoard of Spanish gold. It would appear that the high temperature had in some way released clairvoyant faculties.

A Scottish lady who wrote to me with the interpretation of her dreams also told me that when she was a young child staying with her grandmother, the latter put out the light and asked her what she could see on the white curtains of the sash window. The flickering shadows revealed to her gaze a young man in sailors' uniform. He was very young indeed with short hair neatly parted. He stretched out a hand and into the vision came a child. The sailor was the grandmother's son who had been killed in the First World War at the age of sixteen and a half and the young boy was my correspondent's cousin. Her grandmother said, 'See the big one is coming for the wee one' and within a week the young boy was dead as a result of pneumonia.

Many young children are naturally gifted with clairvoyance but the ability fades as they grow older and the wonderful gift is lost. It always seems to me that very young babies have the wisdom of the ages in their eyes, if only they could talk. When my grandson was about four or five years old it occurred to me that he might still remember his pre-birth life and I asked him, when his mother was not around, 'Adam, where were you before you came to be a part of our family?' My hopes of any innocent mystical revelations were dashed when he looked at me with his big brown eyes and said, 'I was in Mummy's tummy, Gwandma!'

I have written that the practice of psychometry often acts as a doorway to the art of clairvoyance which can be described as visionary perception of future events; often there is no actual clearly defined dividing line, one naturally leading into the other. When I placed my hand on my friend's arm and received psychic information concerning her daughter's forthcoming marriage, that was, strictly speaking, clairvoyance triggered by psychometric contact.

There are occasions when people who visit me for clairvoyance erect a mental barrier between us as a result of anxiety, nervousness or disbelief and I cannot make contact with their psyche. I ask them to try to relax because they are blocking me and request an article to hold, and this usually solves the problem as the article will break the barrier and release the visions, and once they are flowing, I can dispense with it.

Clairvoyance is another aspect of extra-sensory perception, but for those not born with the ability it is more difficult to develop than is psychometry. I do believe, however, that given time and perseverance it can be developed but it requires a teacher preferably within a development circle. These are very difficult to find and when discovered are often even more difficult to gain entrance to. In addition, the development of clairvoyance can take many years and most people do not possess the patience to undertake such a long apprenticeship without some substantial result unless they are very dedicated. A medium friend of mine preferred to describe psychic development as spiritual unfoldment, and in its highest aspiration this is exactly what it should be. Without a spiritual orientation the search for psychic power can be dangerous, and it should never be sought for selfish or unworthy reasons and never be used for financial gain.

I have made two interesting observations concerning psychometry and clairvoyance. When prophesying events in a person's life I appear to have access to more detail as the event itself comes nearer in time. It is almost as if the view of a distant place might be obscured by intervening mist but as I travel towards the place the mist obscures less and less. When lecturing I usually give a demonstration of psychometry and several articles are placed on a table or a tray before I arrive at my request, so that I do not see from whom they originate and am therefore unable to draw any conclusions on a psychological level. I have discovered on occasions that it is not always necessary for me to actually touch the article. When I commence the psychometry I am drawn to one particular article as if it radiates a strange frequency and says to me 'Read me, my owner needs to hear what you sense from me' and even before I touch it the visions start to flow. I begin to think that the dichotomy of the world into a mental order and a physical order existing side by side which is the heritage of Descartes no longer obtains, nor does the commonplace sense-centred view of physical objects as dead material things. Every object is an aggregate of molecules and has its psychical field of influence and memories, and perhaps this explains to some extent beliefs previously regarded as mere superstition and why images, sacred relics, places of worship and pilgrimage and areas where sacrifices have taken place are saturated by the emotions, prayers and mental attitudes of generations of people and are the foci of psychic fields. In a similar way this could account for the fact that certain jewels and objects are regarded as being unlucky because they have been associated with psychic fields of an unpleasant type.

9 Meditation

I receive a substantial number of letters from people who, whilst not actively interested in the practice of witchcraft are nevertheless concerned with various aspects of spiritual unfoldment and seek my advice in the pursuance of this. Many experience difficulties in the performance of meditation and seek guidance on successful techniques and ask if it will be beneficial to them. I believe that if it is approached sensibly and correctly it can be a very rewarding exercise, quite apart from any spiritual endeavour a short period of time each day which is devoted to the cultivation of a tranquil mind produces many psychological benefits.

The prime necessity is a quiet room where the daily ritual can be indulged in peace and quietness. A bedroom is ideal because of its associations with sleep, rest and detachment from the world, but any room will do providing it can be guaranteed that one will not be disturbed for at least twenty minutes at a time. Meditation is not an escape from reality, neither does it imply a loss of consciousness, a trained practitioner can meditate whilst walking or travelling by bus or train, but for the beginner peaceful and quiet surroundings are in the first instance an absolute necessity.

The best position is one of complete relaxation, it is possible to meditate whilst lying in bed but there is a danger that sleep will come in the middle of a meditation, and it is better not to meditate much after 9 p.m. in the evening because if a correct procedure is followed, a meditation produces a force of renewed energy and vitality which might make it difficult to sleep.

A comfortable easy chair is recommended with arm rests to support the arms and a fairly high back to act as support for the spine and the head, a relaxed position should be assumed and all the muscles should be loosened and all tension released. It is as well to do this methodically starting with the muscles of the face and neck, the mouth should be allowed to drop open and if this does not produce a particularly elegant countenance, no one is there to see it. There are certain techniques in vogue for inducing relaxation; the mind should be directed to various parts of the body where tension is likely to occur, from the face to the neck, the chest, the stomach and the abdomen to the thighs, the knees and the feet; a relaxed body makes it easier to achieve a tranquil mind.

When the body is quite relaxed a gentle rhythmic breathing should then be assumed, the meditator should for a few minutes concentrate on the sound and the feel of inhalation and exhalation of breath. The next step is the endeavour to empty the mind and to dismiss from consciousness any thought of a practical disturbing nature, to imagine that one is looking into and becoming one with an area of darkness, reminiscent of a piece of black velvet cloth, it is very difficult for a beginner to completely empty the mind and this exercise is a great help. It must be remembered that meditation like any spiritual endeavour, requires patience and practice, but followed regularly the routine can surprisingly quickly be adopted.

It is not sufficient to try to empty the mind or to allow aimless drifting of thought forms, stray thoughts and daydreams will intrude into an unoccupied mind and therefore an objective device on which to meditate is necessary, a nucleus around which thoughts can be reflected. For a practising Christian, a useful symbol might be a cross, for a witch a crescent moon, for an ordinary pagan a gently flowing stream but an agnostic may disdain any of these symbols and for such a person perhaps the choice of a significant word such as love, or peace, service, or friendship might be helpful.

If a symbol is chosen, with each inhalation of breath the relevant symbol should be imagined in the mind and released with the exhalation, and if a word is chosen, this word should be repeated mentally in the same rhythm of the breath.

Ideally meditation should last not less than twenty minutes, and not more than thirty minutes and with practice the meditator will sense a 'going down' into the meditation, and at the end of the set time a 'rising up' into normal consciousness.

What I have described is a simple method of meditation for someone who does not wish to become involved in any of the major disciplines which vary according to the relevant schools of thought. Some schools provide a meditator with a mantra for meditation, the mantra is exclusive to that person and must not be revealed at any time. The mantra is chosen by an experienced teacher on the basis of a psychic determination of character of the meditator and regarded as being the most suitable for his or her purpose.

Meditation was once regarded as being the preoccupation of mystics and saints but its value is now being recognized by medicine. My own doctor recommends it as an alternative to tranquillizers and sleeping-pills and it has become an established feature of holistic treatment and most spiritual organizations. It is common to Buddhism and Hinduism and to the mystical body of Islam which is Sufism but it has never been particularly prominent in Christianity. In the growing interest in achieving states of mind in which consciousness can be expanded, however, meditation has been rediscovered as a useful entry into the deeper aspects of the mind.

The most detailed meditative techniques are to be found in ancient Hindu literature with particular regard to Yoga, the aim of which is union with the Absolute through eight stages of development for the purpose of harnessing the energies of the mind to the transformation of the individual. Meditation is not particularly an invention of the East and it does not involve withdrawal from the world, changing one's life or renunciation of sex, meat and alcohol.

Our conscious awareness can be compared to a butterfly trained on first one thing and then another, it moves around with great rapidity attracted by compelling thoughts and sensations which intrude into our minds every second of the day. Concentration is quite difficult, the more one attempts to concentrate, the more one is often distracted and learning to control and concentrate attention is really the basis of meditational devices.

In the system presented by the Maharishi Maheesh Yogi, a pupil is given a specific mantra and is advised to pay little heed to the inevitable drifting thought forms which encroach into the meditation, but to gently disregard them and draw the concentration back to the repetition of the mantra. There is an exercise in Yoga which involves gazing at the tip of one's nose or turning the eyes upwards and gazing towards a point midway between the eyebrows. This should only be undertaken for short periods of time with the eyes closed, and they should be rested when they begin to feel tired, and 'Tratakam' as this system is called stimulates all the centres in the brain by means of the cranial and spinal nerve centres and assists in the control of the wandering waves of the mind.

Meditation

Idries Shah has suggested in *The Way of the Sufi* that language can have a direct effect on consciousness which goes beyond the idea that a chant or prayer can, by means of its rhythm set up resonant vibrations in the brain, to the idea that the sound of particular words themselves produce particular effects on the brain and mind. Dr Lyall Watson in *Supernature* asks, 'Is it possible that words have a power by virtue of their own special frequencies? Can magic words, sacred formulas and chants exert an influence that differs from other sounds chosen at random?' He explains that vowel sounds have lower frequencies than consonants. Explosive consonants like 'p' and 's' have particularly high frequencies which maybe why we call a cat 'Pussy' since cats' ears are tuned to high frequency sounds to help them catch their prey. It is also why we whistle for dogs.

It is therefore significant that many mantras contain many vowels and soft low frequency consonants such as 'l' and 'm', the best-known is probably the Hindu 'Om'.

In *Najmeddin Daya*, a thirteenth-century Sufi classic, instructions are given for a Sufi exercise known as 'Dhikr', a liturgical recitation which is 'the remembrance of God'. I described in *Witch Amongst Us* my attendance at these ceremonies with dervishes in Turkey. The *Najmeddin Daya* instructs:

> Having prepared a room which is empty, dark and clean, in which he will, for preference, burn sweet scented incense, let him sit there, cross legged, facing the quibla (direction of Mecca). Laying his hands on his thighs, let him stir up his heart to wakefulness, keeping a guard on his eyes. Then with profound veneration he should say aloud La Ilaha Illa'llah (there is no god but God). The La Ilaha should be fetched from the root of the navel, and the Illa'llah drawn into the heart, so that the powerful effects of the dhikr may make themselves felt in all the limbs and organs.

The *Najmeddin Daya* continues,

> He will utter the dhikr frequently and intently, thinking in his heart on the meaning of it and banishing every distraction. When he thinks of La Ilaha he should tell himself: I want nothing, seek nothing, love nothing, Illa Llah – but God. Thus with La Ilaha he denies and excludes all competing objects, and with Illa'llah he affirms and posits the divine majesty as his sole object loved, sought and aimed at.

Meditation has an important part in many witchcraft ceremonies, at least in the coven of which I am the Magistra or leader. At the commencement of all our ceremonies we meditate to a particular piece of evocative music which utilizes the Pan-pipes and reflects our pagan reverence for all life forms, which we regard as aspects of the beauty and creativity of the ancient Goddess who is the object of our worship. We meditate freely, that is to say we do not use a mantra or a symbol, but allow thoughts and images to drift across our consciousness at will. The object of this meditation is to concentrate and focus our minds on the circle and our purpose in the gathering, formation and actual presence in the circle which is regarded in witchcraft lore as being between two worlds, this world and the next, and the activities which take place within the circle are not the concern of either world.

In actual practice, what occurs is usually quite definitely the concern of both worlds, the seeking of guidance, strength of mind and will and the drawing of power from the one for the immediate benefit of individuals in the other.

The meditation is often extended beyond the music and during it evidence of clairvoyance and clairsentience usually manifests, together with personal mental and spiritual journeys and experiences in relation to individual members.

Meditation is also used as one of the eight methods of working magic which are available to witches, and in conjunction with techniques of hyperventilation, mental, as opposed to physical power is raised and directed. Meditation is often used in healing ceremonies since it has been discovered through trial and error, that it is easier in a relaxed state to hold in our minds, a vision of the person for whose benefit we are working. In addition to healing carried out in the circle some witches still prescribe herbal remedies for simple ailments, Sonya dispenses herbs and in the past, the wise woman or witch possessed a multitude of remedies which had been tested over years of use. A large number of the herbal remedies which were developed by witch healers still occupy a place in modern pharmacology. Witches knew of pain-killers, aids to the digestion and anti-inflammatory agents. Ergot was prescribed for the pains of labour at a time when the Church opined that the pains of childbirth were God's punishment for the original sin of Eve. Ergot derivatives are used today to hasten labour and help in the recovery from childbirth. Belladonna was used by witch healers to contain uterine contractions when a miscarriage threatened as it is an anti-spasmodic agent, and digitalis continues to be an important drug in the treatment of coronary complaints and this is said to have been discovered by a Shropshire witch. It is likely that other remedies prescribed by witches owed their effectiveness to the reputation of the witch as a healer.

In their book *A History of Women Healers*, Barbara Ehrenreich and Deirdre English record that the witch healers' methods were a great threat to the Catholic Church for the witch was an empiricist relying on her senses rather than on faith or doctrine; she believed in trial and error, cause and effect. Her attitude was not religiously passive but actively inquiring and she trusted her ability to discover ways to deal with disease, pregnancy and childbirth, whether through medications or charms, her magic was the science of her time. The Church by contrast was deeply anti-empirical and discredited the value of the material world showing a profound distrust of the senses. Its attitude was that there was little point in looking for natural laws which govern physical phenomena for the world is created anew by God in every instant.

It is likely that the witches who gathered for the Great Sabbats in addition to practising pagan religious worship took the opportunity to trade herbal lore and their experiences in the healing art. The fact that they did heal and help was anathema to the witch hunters. As one wrote, 'For this must always be remembered, that by witches we understand not only those which kill and torment, but all Diviners Charmers, Jugglers, all Wizards, commonly called wise men and wise women ... and in the same number, we reckon all good witches, which do no hurt but good, which do not spoil and destroy, but save and deliver ... It were a thousand times better for the land if all witches, but especially the blessing witch, might suffer death'.

Many of the people in the present time who approach witches for healing are looking for a miracle cure, medical science can find no way to heal them or relieve their pain. Some have sought help from alternative therapists and there is today a great movement towards alternative medicine, acupuncture, homeopathy, radionics, spiritual healing and the like. Many drugs prescribed by doctors cause side effects and the cure is sometimes worse than the complaint.

When people approach me for healing, whether for animal or human, I always insist that a veterinary surgeon or a doctor first be consulted and I need to know the details of the illness and its past treatment. I do not as a rule prescribe herbal remedies but there are a few homeopathic treatments of which I have received excellent reports and if I think these will help I might suggest them. For instance, a remedy called 'Devil's Claw' obtainable at health shops in tablet form has eased and sometimes apparently cured elderly friends who suffer from arthritis, others report no benefit. When my eldest son broke his leg I recommended comfrey (this is commonly known as knitbone) in tablets or tisane, this herb promotes healing of bone and tissue amongst other things. Arnica is beneficial for promoting the healing of bruised tissues and helps to prevent post-operational vomiting due to anaesthetics as well as internal bruising from surgery.

Sprained limbs benefit from being bathed in a concoction of knit-bone (comfrey) and poppy heads. These two properties are boiled together in an old saucepan, simmered until the water turns a muddy brown and when it has cooled sufficiently the injured limb is bathed or immersed in the water as hot as one can bear it for ten minutes or so, several times a day. It reduces swelling and inflammation and was a favourite remedy of my mother who used it on me several times when as a child I sprained an ankle.

I am convinced that we can all benefit from alternative methods of healing when medical science is unequal to the task and whether the healing is psychosomatic and due to suggestion is not important, it is the results which count. However, having said that, I maintain a strong grip on objective reality and common sense and will not allow myself to be diverted into the realms of fantasy by the speculations of some alternative therapists who promote their own imaginative theories.

Whilst discussing with a radionic therapist a personal complaint about which I had received conflicting diagnoses from medical and surgical specialists, and contemplating alternative therapy, a remark was made, 'Well, of course, it may be that it is something you have brought over from a previous life'. A glazed look came over my face. He subsequently confided, 'I had a communication from a woman in America whose mother had cancer and she asked me if I could help her. She sent me a lock of hair and when I made my diagnosis I found it was a karmic thing and I was told to leave well alone.' When alternative therapists express such esoteric incongruities, they lose all credibility in my eyes and I just felt enormously grateful that I lived in an age and a society, where, if I ailed, I could consult a doctor or a specialist who would give me the benefit of his experience on a practical and sensible level, and his healing of me would not depend on his opinion of my karmic record.

10   Shades of Jung and Stone Circles

I received a telephone call one day from a man who had read *Witch Amongst Us* and asked if he could come and talk with me. I was very busy at the time and reluctant to agree to a meeting, but sensed from the tone of his voice signs of some desperation, and against my real inclinations, I agreed.

He was a handsome man in his early fifties I judged. He arrived in a chauffeur-driven Bentley which looked rather incongruous parked outside my house next to my sports car and my neighbours' assorted humbler vehicles, and as he walked through my door in an obvious Savile Row suit, I wondered what he could possibly require from a witch since he appeared to have a great deal of what is desirable in a material sense.

We talked of trivialities for a while until he was able to broach the subject which had brought him to my presence, and he told me that twenty-five years before when he had been making his way in the world, he had been in partnership with a man who was his friend and who had contributed a large sum of money and mortgaged his home to their mutual business. As a result of a nefarious business deal, the details of which he did not disclose, he had cheated his friend and left him bankrupt and the man, who was not a strong character, had committed suicide leaving a wife and two young children without a home or means of support.

My visitor admitted that he had been uncaring and totally ruthless and had continued to build his business empire without remorse or a backward glance at those he had wronged. The business thrived and he made a great deal of money, and was busy for so many years amassing a fortune, he had only gradually become aware that his life was sterile and empty.

He had been married twice, and these marriages had ended in divorce, and his present marriage was heading the same way. He had business acquaintances but no friends, men and women he attempted to cultivate quickly turned their backs on him and he had no relationships with the teenage children of his marriages – even animals seemed to dislike him, cowering and becoming restless at his approach. In recent months he had been disturbed during his sleep by dreams of the man who had committed suicide so many years before, and he felt haunted by him. His working hours were agitated by strange sounds of a sobbing woman and crying children, although no other person in the vicinity could ever hear them.

There was no religion to which he subscribed and he could find no peace or comfort in his life which now seemed meaningless, and he had come to me for advice.

When I asked him what specifically he wanted from me he hesitated and then said, 'Absolution, I have confessed the darkest secret of my life to you and you have access to something beyond my understanding, I am sorry for what I did in the past and tortured by the memory of it, help me to find forgiveness.'

'I am not a priest,' I said, 'I cannot give you absolution, but I will help you if I can.'

Some months later whilst reading the autobiography of Carl Gustav Jung, I came across a similar story to my great surprise. Jung had selected it from thousands of human encounters and it concerned not a patient but a woman who arrived at his office one morning, refusing to give her name. She was to walk out of it and Jung's life without ever revealing it, just as the man who came to see me never revealed his name, nor did I ask for it.

In Jung's case, the woman merely admitted that she was a doctor and confessed that many years before she had killed her best friend in order to marry the friend's husband. The murder was never discovered and in due course she married the man and had a daughter by him. Consciously she had no moral compunction over what she had done, such unease as there was appears to have been felt by nature and the atmosphere of the murder communicated itself to all around her through the damage it had done to her own personality and the way it had changed the climate of her spirit.

First her husband died soon after the marriage, their daughter grew up estranged from her and ultimately vanished without trace from her life. Her friends, one after the other abandoned her and soon even the animals she loved appeared to be afraid of her. She loved riding but had to give it up because the horses she had previously managed so well became nervous, shied and ultimately she was thrown by one of her favourite mounts. She was left only with her dogs and clung to them, then her favourite dog had to be destroyed. Finally she could bear this exile from life and nature no longer and came to Jung to confess. After the confession she left and he saw and heard no more of her, but the vision of the woman and her total insupportable alienation from life and nature inflicted on her by the murder stayed in his mind.

He observed that though one could keep such things secret in oneself, one could not prevent life from knowledge of it, and the consequences of the murder one had done to oneself in the process found expression in the subsequent unease, estrangement and even disasters in the world without, and sometimes it seemed as if even animals and plants knew. Laurens Van Der Post repeated the story in his book *Jung and the Story of Our Time* and so on two occasions I was reminded of the man who had confessed to me. Van Der Post observed that it reminded him of a primitive people he knew in the interior of Africa who believed that there was no secret so small that nature sooner or later would not extract, and that if a person had been guilty of some great natural evil, even the grasses would accuse him of it in the sound they made against his feet as he went walking through them.

Van Der Post told Jung how impressed he had been during his explorations of the bush and desert, by the extent to which one's own most secret intent for being there seemed to make itself known to beast, bird and even plants around one. This feeling was like something imposed on him objectively. He had found for instance, that when he moved through the bush to all appearances dressed and equipped in the same manner as for many weeks, always carrying the same gun, the atmosphere and behaviour of all around him changed subtly on those days when he had to shoot buck or bird for food. He remarked that this was not only his experience but also that of many of the most perceptive of the great hunters, primitive as well as European that he had known. Jung had said quietly, and rather sadly, 'And even so, they go on denying the reality of the collective unconscious.'

Jung also had something to say which was of particular interest to me as a witch; for years, he had observed a circular movement of awareness, dreams, visions and new inner material round an, as yet, undefined centre like plants and moons around a sun. It was a strange rediscovery of what had once been called the 'magic circle'. Some of Jung's patients who could not describe it in words or paintings would even dance the magic circle for him. Stone age man still does so in Africa to this day where there are apparent mad outbursts in the bush in Central Africa when whole communities, grey-headed, middle-aged, youth and young children, dance from sunset to dawn in a circle round and round a deranged person, exhorting in song and chanting, the soul whose loss they believed had deranged the spirit, to return to the body.

Van Der Post had been amazed how the dance invariably succeeded in its purpose, and Jung was gratified because he had found this circular pattern such a compulsive one, constant in himself and others, that he had started to paint it and derived such comfort and meaning from it that for years he hardly drew anything else. He called the process and the movement of spirit the 'mandala', taking an old Eastern word for a circle, because he had seen drawings of this pattern by his patients that were almost exact copies of paintings used for religious instruction in Tibet, a fact that his patients had never known. Mandala is the Arabic (as used in Africa) for spectacles, signifying an enlargement and two way traffic of spirit.

The Arabic interpretation reminded me very strongly of the elements and intent of witches in the magic circle, when there is an enlargement of normal everyday consciousness, culminating in a combined spiritual effort, drawing power from the invocation of the gods into the circle, and the projection of the energy outwards into the world beyond the circle.

There is an ancient stone circle which has connections with a witch if a legend which has existed for over four centuries is to be believed. The circle, which comprises seventy-six stones lies midway between Oxford and Stratford-on-Avon and is known as the Rollright Stones and, but for the intervention of a witch in some ancient era, the stones would have marched on London and conquered England.

In addition to the seventy-six stone circle, on the opposite side of the road a little distance away is another stone, seven feet high and known as the King Stone. It is firmly embedded in the earth below the ridge of a hill which overlooks the village of Long Compton and a view of the extensive countryside.

> Seven long strides shall thou take
> If Long Compton thou canst see
> King of England, thou shalt be ...

These are the words the king was supposed to have heard from the witch who was the owner of the hill as he approached its crest on his march through England. As the king moved forward an earthen mound rose ahead of him blocking his sight, and the last words he heard before being petrified into stone were:

> As Long Compton thou canst not see
> King of England thou shalt not be
> Rise up stick, and stand still, stone
> For King of England thou shalt be none
> Thou and thy men hoar stones shall be
> And I myself an elder tree

According to local lore, it is impossible to count the exact number of the king's men stones in the circle, and further, if one is able to correctly count them, one's days are numbered for one will die within a year. However, the reason for the difficulty in counting them is that some barely protrude above the ground and others are joined at some point. One brave soul stuck a loaf of bread on a large stone to act as a marker and was thus able to successfully count the remainder of the stones. The story does not relate whether he survived for excess of a year.

The legend continues that periodically the stones revert to men, they join hands and dance their way down the hill at the witching hour of midnight to drink at a nearby stream. It is also said that on one night each year the warriors and their king meet under a hill in a cave where they drink and feast and remind each other of the day they will resume their flesh and blood roles and march once more to conquer England.

About a hundred years ago the locals would hold picnics at the site on May Day and on Midsummer's Eve when fairies were supposed to dance around the King Stone, the fairies left rings of bright green grass where their feet trod, but their revels were only seen by those with the 'sight'.

According to the *Folklore Journal* of 1895, Dr A.J. Evans reported that one Will Hughes of Long Compton had seen the fairies many times, as had his mother and her playmates. It was the custom for a childless woman to visit the King Stone at midnight and hold her bare breasts to it in the belief that she would become the mother of a bright intelligent child, loved and cared for by the fairies, whose path would be smoothed by the little people watching over it.

It was also thought that prayers offered in the middle of the circle for the sick would effect a speedy cure. 'Both these ideas evidently are remnants of the ceremonies of the long ago when the ancient Priests of the Temple held sway over the surrounding countryside, and taught their worshippers that an offering in the temple was more efficacious than anything'. This, according to a book published in Oxford at the turn of the century.

The diameter of the circle, thirty-five yards, is exactly that of the inner circle at Stonehenge, and the entrance too is from the north-east as at Stonehenge. The name of the nearby village listed in the Domesday Book as Rolendrich would be Rholdrwyg if written in the old script, which means 'Druid's wheel or circle'. The Irish equivalent, Roilig means 'Church of the Druids', and several characteristic barrow or burial mounds were apparently found nearby.

The legend of the king's men is ancient, and it is recorded that in the sixteenth century local people had long favoured the tradition that the stones were once men who had been petrified by a witch and 'they take it ill, if anybody doubts the story, nay, he is in danger for his disbelief by being stoned'.

Dr Evans, in the same *Folklore Journal*, also refers to the legend of the elder tree, 'the proof that the elder tree is a witch is that it bleeds when it is cut' and he records an ancient custom in the district of gathering round the King Stone on Midsummer's Eve when the elder is in bloom. 'Then, as the elder was cut, and as it bled, the King moved his head'.

In Denmark he says, an elder tree has been seen to move about in the twilight, and its magical properties are referred to in the Hans Andersen fairy tale in which the mystical power of elderflower tea enables drinkers to see in their dreams the Elder Mother herself, seated amidst her sweet-scented flowers and foliage.

The earliest associations of the tree with witchcraft is a record preserved in the ancient Canons of King Edgar which speaks of the 'vain practices which are carried on with Elders, elder flowers, everywhere in the country are used as a spring lotion for the complexion, the young leaves bruised in lard, are considered a capital preparation for the skin, while the blood-like berries in autumn, when made into a thick wine is unrivalled for relaxed throats, or served hot, forms a splendid pick-me-up after a long tiring journey on a wet cold winter's night, and is to be found in nearly every country home.' Little wonder therefore that legends gather around the Elder tree which has so many magical properties.

Conversely, however, another legend reports that if one has

an elder tree in the garden, one will never be bothered by witches! Yet another legend has it that a witch does indeed reside in each elder tree and before lopping branches off the tree, permission should be asked of the residing witch. There is no report of what would occur if she said 'No', I should imagine that a disembodied voice issuing from an elder tree would provoke some alarm at least.

The origin of the stones is lost in antiquity, and in a cornfield about four hundred yards to the south-east a further group of five stones exists huddled together. They are known as the Whispering Knights because they appear to be, from a distance, kneeling men with heads close together as if in secret conclave.

Last summer on a visit to the Rollright Stones, my husband and I in conversation with some other visitors to the site were told that a party who had been officially surveying the stones, and staying in a nearby hotel had one evening been sitting in the circle when a peculiar atmosphere had arisen. One of the party appeared to go into 'a kind of trance' and before him appeared a wild female figure dressed in skins and brandishing a knife and threatening him, it was reported that 'her eyes blazed'. The fear generated by him spread to the rest of the party and they fled in disarray.

Enquiries at local hotels elicited no further information and I can only assume that what occurred was the 'Old Ones' protecting their holy place.

The Rollright Stones are privately owned and now fenced off, but visitors are allowed during daylight hours. Many years ago, a coven to which I belonged had a ceremony there on Midsummer Eve, and we spent the night in the circle, and one of my most enduring memories is of the sun rising over the stones and driving home at 5 a.m. with the early morning mist on the surrounding fields. It was a magical and beautiful experience. Unfortunately, since that time there have apparently been less innocent and more unsavoury activities at the stones on particular dates in the occult calendar resulting in special protection of the site at these times.

Some years ago, I was associated with a programme that BBC Television Manchester made concerning the area around Pendle Hill in Lancashire, which has long been reputed to have been the haunt of witches in the seventeenth century.

It was a place of worship in pagan days and acknowledged as such by the Romans who climbed the hill to salute their own gods. The hill has a strange shape. It appears to stand out against the sky from the south, yet merges into the moorland around when circled on a series of country roads through Sabden, Clitheroe, Downham and Roughlee. The book, *The Trials of the Lancashire Witches* by Edgar Peel and Pat Southern is a scholarly account of the proceedings in the area when a pair of rabble-rousing local families by their squalid fights and accusations delivered each other to the hangman in 1612. Altogether, almost a score of 'witches' were executed although it was never really proved that witchcraft was involved.

The saddest victim was a widow named Alice Nutter and it has always been recorded that she lived in the grey stone manor Roughlee Hall which is still in existence and visited by the curious today. However, Mrs Gladys Whittaker, a regular member of the Nelson Historical Society who has made extensive exploratory forays into the history of Roughlee Hall, can find no evidence that she ever lived there. When Edgar Peel and Pat Southern were researching their book, the only evidence they discovered was the signature of her son, Miles Nutter on some deeds belonging to Dam Head Farm at Roughlee. All who tell the story of the Lancashire witches, whether as a novel or plain history, inevitably draw on the chronicles of one Thomas Potts, clerk to the Judges in the Circuit of the North Parts who, in November 1612 at his lodging in Chancery Lane, wrote of the late *Wonderful Discoverie of Witches in the Countie of Lancaster*. Potts did not actually record that Alice Nutter resided at Roughlee Hall, he merely specified Roughlee which was a 'booth' or living area, and Pendle Forest was not a wood, the word 'forest' simply implied an area originally set aside for hunting. It is because most of the people arrested lived there and nearly all their supposed mischief was performed within its bounds that they are equally well known as the Pendle Witches.

Pendle Hill is a lonely, brooding, sombre place, it is eerie and awesome and virtually unchanged in appearance since the seventeenth century with a certain quality of wildness. I have spent many hours exploring Pendle Hill whilst staying at the home of Edgar Peel and his wife Ana, and I never fail to be moved by the strange ambience of the area which hints of secrets yet untold and fires the imagination by what might have occurred there three hundred years ago.

Now however, according to the local newspapers, the area has become proliferous with numerous ersatz 'witches' and 'Satanists' and the local churches have become so concerned with this occult explosion that there is talk of erecting an enormous Christian cross on Pendle Hill to emphasize the prevailing Christianity of the area. It would seem, however, that the local authority would not give planning permission. The situation generated such hysteria that the local television station recorded a programme, and fundamentalist Christians thundered out their age old message that the Devil was at the bottom of it all.

We can at least depend on the Devil being blamed for anything which smacks of being unorthodox.

11 Weather, Wedding and Familiars

I receive very odd letters occasionally asking me to kindly work a special spell to ensure that the correspondent's holiday weather is warm and sunny, outlining the dates involved and the resort to be visited; not unnaturally these are invariably English resorts, English weather being notoriously unreliable, and though I never cease to be amazed by people's requests, there appears to be a general belief that witches can influence the weather. I once attended a garden party given by Sonya, there had been a heatwave for several weeks before the party, but on the actual day, in the middle of it the heavens opened, there was a cloudburst and the water poured from the garden into her cottage. I said to her teasingly, 'I thought that at the very least you would have organized the weather for your own party!'

She scowled at me and retorted, 'Don't blame me, blame my apprentice' indicating a young friend, but Sonya never really lived that day down.

One Heinrich Kramer published a learned treatise on witchcraft in 1484. He accused witches of killing humans and cattle, blasting the produce of the earth, changing humans into animals and inflicting terrible disorders on humans and rendering people sterile. He also believed that hailstorms, rain and thunderstorms were controlled by witches. He gives an account of a male witch who was expert at producing hailstorms. When asked how he performed it, he said that he used certain words to obtain the services of an evil spirit and sacrificed a black cock at crossroads, advising the spirit where the hailstorm was required. After the sacrifice a hailstorm did occur, but unfortunately not always at the place named.

According to Kramer a witch was tried in Kilkenny in 1324 for producing a hailstorm but she sacrificed nine black cocks at a crossroad. An alternative method to produce rain and hail did not involve sacrifice, the witch took a small bowl of water and dipping her finger in it solemnly stirred the water uttering secret phrases and naming the place where she required rain to fall. Both these methods can be compared with the activities of modern rainmakers amongst primitive tribes in Central Africa and their efforts are often very successful.

Since black cocks are a bit thin on the ground in my part of the world, I am relieved that I have never yet been asked to produce rain or hail, and only on very rare occasions do I make any attempt to interfere with the natural course of the weather. It is very boring magic, as boring as selling houses, and even when it is successful, although I always take the credit, in all honesty, I am never completely convinced that I am responsible. My teacher and mentor many years ago taught me how to disperse the odd cloud by the recitation of certain Latin phrases and mental concentration, she did it very easily but I felt that something stronger was required to dispel the dismal grey skies which had been pouring torrents of rain unendingly for three weeks. Mary's wedding, which I had prophesied, and to which I was invited was imminent and each time I saw her mother she moaned at me, 'Oh Lois, I do hope the weather is going to improve before Saturday and the wedding!'

It crossed my mind that I might sacrifice Güzel the dog who had been incurring my wrath by paddling mud on my clean kitchen floor five times a day, but I decided against it!

Quite apart from the fact that Mary would expect me to organize good weather for her wedding day, I had a further anxiety remembering a story my mother had told me of an incident in the 1920s when she and my sister had gone out for a cycle ride and been caught in a rainstorm. My mother was wearing a straw hat at the time and the rain had caused a remarkable restyling of the crown which had risen to a point so that it resembled a witch's hat.

Rosalind, a friend and neighbour was loaning me a straw hat for this auspicious occasion, one of the few hats I had experimented with in recent weeks which did not make me appear half-witted, and whilst, if it got rained on and subsequently restyled itself as my mother's hat had done, it would be useful for advertising my profession at the reception, I did not dare contemplate Rosalind's reaction when I returned it to her. I am aware that umbrellas have been invented but they are clumsy and anyway I always lose them; a spell therefore was imperative.

The rain was pelting down as I gathered my ingredients together the night before the wedding. I pronounced the arcane words and mixed the compounds together, scattering them to the four corners of the earth as I stood in the garden saturated, with water plastering my hair and running down the back of my neck and off the end of my nose; my glasses were steamed up and I could not see what I was doing. I squelched back indoors miserably and dried off, telling myself darkly that after all that effort, it had better work or else.

Miraculously, Saturday dawned bright, warm and with the sun shining from a cloudless blue sky. I could hardly believe it! As my husband and I left for St George's Church, Hanover Square in London, I kept looking at the sky anxiously for threatening dark clouds but none appeared. An aspect of this spell is continuous concentration and I managed to maintain it throughout the ceremony and the celebrations until 3 p.m. when at the reception, and under the languorous influence of several glasses of champagne my concentration lapsed, and as I looked out of the window slightly befuddled I noticed it was raining. It was to continue almost unceasingly for another week.

Betty, my friend and mother of the bride announced to all and sundry '... and we have Lois to thank for the lovely weather this morning' and there were congratulatory murmurs from the other guests for my prowess and a kiss from the bride as I sat there smugly with Rosalind's straw hat set at a rakish angle and contemplated yet another glass of champagne of excellent vintage, and mused on the vagaries of the English weather.

There is never a stage in the practice of witchcraft and magic where one can adopt the illusion that all there is to be learned has been learned. I am constantly making new discoveries. I am, I hope a very practical person, and accept that there are limitations to any power.

The authors of *The Trials of the Lancashire Witches*, Edgar Peel and Pat Southern, both live in the Pendle witch country of Lancashire. I was introduced to Edgar by a mutual friend when he required information on contemporary witchcraft in relation to the book and we subsequently became friends. BBC Television in Manchester expressed an interest in the book and a documentary on the Pendle witches was proposed with Edgar acting as narrator. Since I was also mentioned in this book, the BBC recorded an interview with me in my home.

There is a riding school in the village of Reade in Lancashire which is in the area of Pendle, and each Hallowe'en the members of the school dress up as witches and a contest is held to decide the most imaginative and prizes are awarded. I was invited to Reade to judge the competition and television cameras recorded the event; I found it very difficult to make a judgement since all the costumes were excellent.

The producer of the programme wished to make a feature of the 'witches' on horseback riding at night, in line, each holding a flaming torch. It promised to be very effective, but George the producer was worried about the weather which had been consistently wet, he was afraid the rain would extinguish the torches and ruin the scene and asked me quite seriously if I could organize a dry evening. Equally seriously, I promised that I would and he looked greatly relieved.

Without conscience I telephoned the local weather centre and was informed that the rain would cease at around 7 p.m. and it would stay fine until midnight – and it did. George with gay abandon did his filming and several times expressed his gratitude to me.

Disaster fell back in Manchester when that part of the film was reviewed and it was found to be quite blank. The assumption was that the film had been faulty. The producer and film crew had to return to Reade to film the sequence again and this time (because I was not present!) the rain poured down. However, when the complete documentary appeared on television, the rainy sequence with the light of the torches reflected on the wet roads and undergrowth was most effective.

The most significant age for witches and witchcraft was the pre-Renaissance Period when scholars in Europe began to examine the laws governing scientific phenomena, and the superstitious Middle Ages which had seen the climax of the witch hysteria produced many investigations of which Kramer's treatise was only one. It was his belief that invisible devils were at large in the earth constantly seeking to involve themselves in nefarious activities, and people who made contact with the devils were in some mysterious way able to inherit some of their power. Since it was an age when women were considered to be the harbingers of all evil, it was usually women who made contact with the devils and so became witches.

It is recorded that in very ancient times people consulted witches to learn about the future, one of the first chronicled instances was when Saul consulted the Witch of Endor. Kramer opined that the ability to foretell the future came from a devil raised through incantations by a witch. Kramer also believed that witches in the Middle Ages were able to make men suppose that they had been transformed into an animal by penetrating their minds, and in addition, altering the minds of other people so that when they observed the bewitched person, they saw an animal instead of a human form.

My friend Sonya who enjoys her reputation as a black witch, has a familiar elemental spirit named Willie who does her bidding and works for her mainly on a prosaic level. She created him as a thought form and he adopts the shape of a small dragon since Sonya is 'into' dragons. When shopping she will send him ahead to find her a parking-space, and occasionally she will loan him to friends for this purpose. He is not a particularly good demon and at times acts in a recalcitrant fashion and has a will of his own. Once when sailing with friends in a deserted part of the coast they ran out of petrol and Willie was despatched to find someone to tow them in, three boats appeared from nowhere almost simultaneously. Willie apparently works by influencing minds and events rather like an instant spell. Such thought forms have to be reinforced frequently by means of emotional energy which can be quite debilitating.

Probably the most famous report of a thought form creation was that of Alexandra David Neel, who mentally produced what the Tibetans call a 'tulpa' during her travels in Tibet. He appeared in the shape of a monk and eventually became stronger and more malevolent as she became weaker and only with supreme effort was she able to disperse him.

All witches are reputed to have familiars, certainly in the historical witch trials they were ubiquitous and no self-respecting witch was revealed without the possession of a familiar. There were three types, the friendly spirit of a dead person, an elemental spirit thought form such as Sonya's Willie, the small dragon, or an actual creature, a dog, cat, toad or bird. Apart from Sonya, I know of only two contemporary witches who admit to a familiar. One was the late Sybil Leek who had a jackdaw called Hotfoot Jackson which perched on her shoulder, incredibly tame and of raucous voice doing 'whoopsies' down her back; not an inspiring sight, and the other has an indeterminate familiar who resides in a coconut shell in her house.

It is interesting that Spiritualist mediums are inspired by spirits who they refer to as 'guides' and who act as doorkeepers particularly in the production of trance and materialization phenomena; the guides are attracted to particular mediums for various reasons, similarity of temperament and interests for example, and whilst assisting the medium in her psychic work the guide contributes towards his or her own spiritual evolution, and there would appear to be some resemblances in the functions of a witches' familiar and a Spiritualist's guide.

There are certain ceremonies in the practice of witchcraft in which we make contact with the spirits of deceased craft members who have passed to the next stage of existence and hopefully increased in wisdom and knowledge. The method is not totally dissimilar to that of Spiritualists who also utilize a circle in which they sit on chairs with men and women alternating. Witches share a belief with Spiritualists that there exists in the human body a particular power and that under the right conditions and with the correct mental attitude it can be controlled and used for psychic manifestation. Many witches possess mediumistic gifts but whilst all true witches have the ability to work magic, not all are mediums.

Although I have loved and been owned by many animals in my life I have never regarded any of them as a familiar and when I am asked half-seriously if I do have a familiar my answer is in the negative. I do however have two thought forms which reside in my mind and are therefore mainly subjective, neither of them have a name, they simply exist, one is a black panther and other a golden eagle. When I wish to learn the progress of some event in a local area, I mentally send the black panther to gather the information, but if the event is at some distance, then the eagle is despatched. The knowledge I seek is relayed to me on a psychic level. I have never seen the eagle objectively although I have heard the beat of his massive wings, he is a male eagle, and only on one occasion have I glimpsed the black panther. Walking through some dark woods one day I began to think of him, I heard a flurry in the undergrowth ahead of me and saw him cross my path at enormous speed, muscles flexed and with the filtered sun shining through the trees reflected on his magnificent black coat, in a flash he was gone but my dog Güzel was alerted and went bounding after him, she returned to me looking very puzzled. I should think that a psychoanalyst would be able to make some interesting observations on Sonya and myself, she with her dragon and me with my eagle and panther!

There are many traditions throughout the world which can be associated with witches and their familiars. In the East for instance, fakirs and magicians ally themselves with spirits of the elements and produce incredible phenomena. Dr Paul Brunton has related some of these stories in his books *A Search in Secret Egypt* and *A Search in Secret India*. During his travels in India he became acquainted with a Muslim fakir who demonstrated his strange abilities by opening a linen wrap and taking out several tiny dolls which were about two inches high, the heads were made of coloured wax and the legs of stiff straw shod with flat iron buttons. He placed the figures on a plain table so that each stood on its iron button. Withdrawing a yard or so from the table he issued commands in Urdu and the dolls began to walk around the table and then started to dance! They moved along the surface of the table but avoided falling over the edge. The fakir indicated to Dr Brunton by means of words and signs that he should point to different parts of the table, he did so, and on each occasion the dolls massed themselves together and danced in a body towards the precise direction indicated. He did the same thing with a coin and a ring which Dr Brunton removed from his finger, the ring responded to commands in Urdu, rising into the air and falling again and whilst the fakir played his accordion with both hands the ring proceeded to dance upon the table.

The mythical eastern stories of the genie which was fabled to have been under the control of Solomon are also related to the idea of familiar spirits, and in the western world when the earth was younger and less complicated than it is today nature spirits were freely accepted and acknowledged. The Romans and the Greeks were aware of the presence of nymphs of the mountains and the rivers, each tree had a nymph and the forest its goat-footed fauns and altars were raised to them in wild uninhabited places. Such an altar was discovered near Roxburgh Castle and is preserved in the Advocates' Library in Scotland with an inscription 'Diis campestribus' which translates as 'The Fairies'.

With the advent of Christianity nature spirits were relegated to the dark realms of the world and the mind and associated with witchcraft and the domain of Diana the goddess of the woodlands and so became anathema to true believers but the memory of them lingers in folklore and if we are wise we give courtesy to the old legends as many do, myself included when I spoke to the fairies at Fairy Bridge in the Isle of Man and wished them a good morning.

Occasionally one hears of owls being associated with witches as a familiar, the owl was sacred to the Goddess Athene and the Latin word for owl is 'strix' which also means 'witch'. It was thought in ancient times to embody the wisdom of Ishtar the early Mesopotamian Eye Goddess with the huge staring eyes. The owl was also a totem of the Celtic Blodeuwedd, the Triple Goddess of the Moon and is associated with the notion of the Trinity. Perhaps these ancient gods are the creators of life; Robert Crick the discoverer of the double helix has postulated that the genetic structure of life is so intricate that it seems designed, and according to studies instigated by Dr Allan C. Wilson of the University of California there is genetic evidence that the entire human species arose from a single female in North Africa between 140,000 and 280,000 years ago; it is therefore possible if incredible to consider, that we all started from the womb of a single woman.

Strangely for a witch, I am not particularly superstitious but I possess a peculiar and awesome attitude towards owls, my mother heard one hooting at the moment of my birth and I have always sensed in the deepest recesses of my mind that I will hear one at the moment of my death.

It is reported in historical witch trials that toads were often familiars of witches and it is certainly true that toads are highly intelligent, quite psychic and quite harmless. One of my women friends who is not a witch kept one as a pet in her garden. It lived under a large shady stone beside her garden pond – they apparently must live close to water since they inhale partly through the skin and if it dries out they suffocate. She demonstrated his tameness to me one day by standing near the pool and clapping her hands three times upon which the toad hopped out from under his stone and blinked at the sun with his enormous eyes and then gazed at her questioningly as if to say 'what do you want?'. 'He always comes out when I clap,' she told me, 'he is very fond of the odd cream cracker and eats the insects in the garden.' She laughed when I told her that in the Middle Ages she would have been suspected of being a witch and said 'Nonsense'.

I quite like toads and frogs and it is recorded that when a toad is angry or afraid it will discharge a milk like fluid from glands in the area of the neck which gave rise to the name of toads' milk which was sometimes used in witches' brews, it has also since been discovered that it contains an hallucinogenic substance; it is interesting to speculate that witches rubbed toad milk into their skin, and this in combination with other drugs gave them the illusion of flying to the Sabbath, an event often referred to in historical witch trials.

Exactly what was the function of the familiar? As in the case of my two thought form familiars, the black panther and the golden eagle, one function was doubtless the collection of information from a distance. Another would be to despatch magical influences to individuals as in the case of one Elizabeth Francis who was the pupil of a witch named Mother Eve of Hatfield Peverell in 1566 from whom she had received the gift of a familiar in the name of Sathan, a beautiful black cat. She confessed that she had fed the cat on drops of her blood and the cat helped her to seduce a man with whom she had fallen in love, one Andrew Byles. When he refused to marry her, the familiar revenged her by touching him 'whereof he died'.

She repeated the process with one Christopher Francis who did marry her, a child being born three months later. However within six months Elizabeth had become bored with the marriage and she requested the cat to kill her child which he did and still unsatisfied with her life she asked the cat to lame her husband 'and he was forthwith taken with a lameness whereof he cannot be healed'.

A further function of the animal familiar was a form of divination, the witch would cast a circle, invoke her Gods to send a spirit to control the familiar and she would set before it a number of objects which represented different meanings to her and watch to see which one it selected.

Since animals are very psychic creatures and a strong rapport would exist between the witch and her familiar, it is also likely that the familiar was able to warn her of approaching danger before she was herself aware of it. The situation however became extreme in the persecution era when any lonely old lady with a pet was regarded as fair game for the witch hunters, and thousands of innocent women lost their lives simply because they had a pet which was regarded as evidence that they were witches.

12 Invocation and Artemis

In my grimoire, a witches' book of instruction, is a section on invocation. The grimoire is divided into three sections because there are three degrees in witchcraft. Upon initiation, a witch is entitled to copy 'in her own hand of write' the first part of the grimoire and as she proceeds to further degrees, she is entitled to the second and third parts of the grimoire.

Aleister Crowley, in his book *The Sacred Magic of Abramelin the Mage*, a very strange manuscript, described invocation as 'enflame thyself in praying'. The invocation from my grimoire, which I suspect contains elements of the works of Crowley states:

> What is important is that invocations impart atmosphere. Properly recited in the tense enclosure of the circle, when the intelligence is enormously keyed up, after the elementals have been evoked, and anything could or might happen, there is a quality within those words which actually, not merely figuratively, thrill. Unless this dynamic thrill is imparted by the vibration and the vigorous enthusiasm of the invoker, the ceremony may fail in effect. It must communicate and thrill, for apart from all else, the rite is conducting through the Path of Mars, where there should be fire and energy, and excitement literally vibrating within the air. If the members respond to the invocations so that they are strongly stirred to that as music, and the excitement springs up as from the depths of their souls, then the force invoked may properly impinge upon their natures and the corresponding aspect within their beings.
>
> By this special and persistent type of magical activity, the power of the soul will eventually be so developed and stimulated that the actual external ceremonial can be dispensed with, though the spiritual pilgrimage may proceed without the props which the rites afford.

Let it be admitted that magic is an artificial system of props and aids, as is the ritual of all religions, so that the rites are principally of value to the beginner, in that they dispose to, or confirm a habit of mental concentration. The rites produce this, as few, or no other system of aids will. These aids may be discarded when the preliminary training has been fulfilled, but it is very foolish to eliminate this training before full skill has been achieved.

You should perform the rites until they become part of your nature. For in the path to the future life and the ineffable light, and in spiritual things generally, most of us die beginners. We, therefore, cannot possibly afford to dispense with what provides the knowledge and stimulation of the spiritual power to assist our onward progress.

I have stated elsewhere, and it certainly bears repeating, a definition of magic as given by one Phillip Bonewits in *Real Magic* (Sphere Books): 'Magic is a science and an art comprising a system of concepts and methods for the build-up of human emotion, altering the electro-chemical balance of the metabolism, using associated techniques and devices to concentrate and focus this emotional energy, thus modulating the energy broadcast by the human body, usually to affect other energy patterns, whether animate or inanimate, but occasionally to affect the personal energy patterns.'

My friend Sonya is a lone witch and practitioner of magic and she has her own method of working. I know how she does her cursing spells because she has told me, but I have not enquired how she carries out the occasional beneficent magic which she admits to doing periodically in weak moments, and when she is in a good mood. Since she lives in the country with the great power of nature itself around her, she may dispense with the trappings of coven magic and rely on her own inate magical ability, but doubtless she draws on the potency and energy of the full moon and the elements.

Ideally, most witches would prefer to work in the countryside and so utilize the natural elements, but since unreliable weather is the norm in England at least, and a sudden shower can douse bonfires and candles, it is more usual and certainly more convenient, to have a room set apart for magical working indoors. Witches work within a circle which can be of any diameter from nine feet upwards, and the size is decided on the basis of the number of people the circle can contain comfortably.

A coven normally consists of thirteen witches, six men, six women and a leader who, in the tradition to which I subscribe, is always a woman and known as a Magistra. The function of a coven is to provide an environment where psychic and spiritual gifts can unfold and flourish, and where the potentiality for magical working can be developed.

As the Magistra of a coven of witches, I am not stricly speaking a teacher for,

> No man can reveal to you aught but that which already lies half asleep in the dawning of your knowledge. The teacher who walks in the shadow of the temple, among his followers, gives not of his wisdom, but rather of his faith and his lovingness.
>
> If he is indeed wise, he does not bid you enter the house of his wisdom, but rather leads you to the threshold of your own mind.
>
> (*The Prophet* by Kahil Gibran)

Witches are encouraged to develop in their own way and their own time. Although witchcraft is generally regarded as being the Old Religion, there is no creed and no dogma, but there does exist perfect freedom to formulate a personal philosophy, and witches are united by their love of the Old Gods and by a desire to experience the ultimate in spiritual enlightenment and in varying degrees to serve the Gods and mankind.

Witches work within a circle in order to concentrate the power which is raised within. It may be imagined that a circle is drawn to protect witches from potentially dangerous or hostile manifestations outside it, but unless black magic is being carried out, this is hardly ever the case. A cone of power arises from magical rites and this is the symbolic origin of the witches' tall pointed hat. The circle has always been considered to be a perfect shape and a symbol of infinity and eternity without beginning or end. The concept of the magic circle is of great antiquity and is described in writings of ancient Assyria on baked clay tablets which have been translated by scholars. The magical circle was called *usurtu*.

I have said earlier in this book that the circle is regarded as being between the two worlds, this world and the next, and that what occurs in the circle is not the concern of either world.

To me, the circle represents a place apart, it is a separate state of existence where, for a brief while, I feel a quickening of the spirit and I am able to recentre myself and find expression and flowering of my own desire and volition. I rediscover anew each time I draw and consecrate the circle, the relationship between spirit and matter and retreat to that world within which is transcendental and incapable of expression in non-transcendental terms. All that is unconscious in my life rises to consciousness, as if I have been merely dreaming the dream of life and have awakened.

The well-spring of creativity is touched and I have the feeling that in the midst of my own partial knowing, a great secret is about to be revealed. My perceptions are widened and heightened and I feel that I am outside time and space and change to which we are all so irrevocably subjected; and as the universe encloses the earth, the circle encloses me and shows me the spirit of the natural world, divine in its most lasting and incorruptible physical form.

The sonorous words of the invocation, the flickering of candles and the clouds of sweet-smelling incense all have their contribution towards these almost inexpressible atavistic perceptions which are shared in diverse ways by other witches in the circle.

It is the gods of the witches who are invoked into the circle. I have said elsewhere that witchcraft is a pagan, pantheistic, mystical religion which embodies the worship of life, it is a matriarchal religion in which women take the chief place and life is personified by the Earth Mother, and Her Consort, a Horned God, these are the female and male principles of life.

A writing from Thebes, Egypt in the fourteenth century before Christ declares:

> In the beginning there was Isis; Oldest of the Old. She was the Goddess from whom all becoming arose. She was the Great Lady, Mistress of the two Lands of Egypt, Mistress of Shelter, Mistress of Heaven, Mistress of the House of Life, Mistress of the word of God. She was the Unique. In all Her great and wonderful works She was a wiser magician and more excellent than any other God.

Another writing from Boghazköy, in Turkey, dated from the fifteenth century before Christ, states:

> Thou Sun Goddess of Arinna art an honoured deity; Thy name is held high among names; Thy divinity is held high among the deities; Nay, among the deities, Thou alone O Sun Goddess art honoured; Great art Thou alone O Sun Goddess

of Arinna; Nay compared to Thee no other deity is as honoured or great ... Thou controllest kingship in heaven and on earth.

The ancient Mother Goddess has been worshipped in antiquity all over the known world, Her names are legion, expressing her various attributes and aspects. I have recorded elsewhere that in remote ages the menstrual cycle, pregnancy and the birth of new life from a woman's body profoundly impressed primitive man, especially since the sexual act and pregnancy were not understood to be connected, and men were at that time unaware that they played a part in the creation of life. It was regarded as female magic and the reincarnation of an ancestral spirit which caused fecundity and so deity was regarded as being a woman, the Great Mother of the Earth, fertility itself for mankind, animals and plants.

The scholarly work, *The Witches' Goddess* by Janet and Stewart Farrar, (published by Robert Hale) identifies and details over one thousand names of the goddess, and readers are referred to this work for further study. It is inevitable that individual witches will be drawn to one or more particular aspects of the Goddess, and in my case I have an interest in Tanit who was a fertility and Moon Goddess of Carthage (a Phoenician colony). She was the consort of Baal-Hammon and was known as the 'face of Baal'. Excavations in the Balearic Island of Ibiza off the Spanish mainland in recent years have revealed evidence of her worship there. Ibiza was in ancient times a Phoenician colony and hundreds of votive statuettes and several larger ones are exhibited in the museum on the island.

I have in my collection, several small votive statuettes of Tanit, and one larger, measuring eight inches high, dating back to 300 BC. It was discovered in a ship wrecked off the coast near Tunis thought to have been travelling from Phoenicia to Carthage.

I have an even greater personal interest in the Mother Goddess aspect of Artemis Ephesia, or Diana of the Ephesians, since during one of my visits to the site of her temple I had a very strange psychic and mystical experience.

Artemis Ephesia is a Mother Goddess from the very earliest times of history. Her temple, where she was worshipped as a fertility goddess was one of the Seven Wonders of the Ancient World; her cult was said to go back to the Amazons. The name Ephesus comes from the Hittite word '*Aphasus*', meaning 'home of the bees' (or bee hive) and the bee was sacred to Diana. The temple was organized like a hive, and the sheathed, veiled figure of the Goddess represented a queen bee. In the ancient world, insects were looked upon as aspects of the divine. Scarab beetles were sacred in Egypt, flies (honey flies?) in Canaan, the praying mantis and the tarantula of Southern Italy.

The temple of Diana faced west, and being outside the city of Ephesus was connected to it by a sacred way or road. There was never any mystery in the archaeological world as to the location of the city of Ephesus, but over two thousand years had passed since the apogee of the temple and it had passed into obliteration. When interest was aroused in excavating it, the remains could not be discovered.

An engineer called J.T. Wood who lived from 1821–90, went in search of the temple under the auspices of the British Museum. One of the reasons why it was so difficult to find, was that most of the stonework had been stolen by the Christians to build churches and there was nothing above ground. Quite by chance J.T. Wood found a milestone indicating the direction of the temple and following the distance shown he discovered a swamp which, when drained, revealed what remained of the temple. The historian Pliny, who had visited the temple had written in praise of the beautifully carved columns presented by Croesus and when he found a few pieces of these columns in 1869 Wood realized he had at last found the actual site; these pieces are now housed in the British Museum and other columns are to be found in Aya Sofia in Istanbul.

It is interesting that the temple faced west as most temples and places of worship face the east. Although the temple was originally built in 700 BC it is thought that an altar occupied this site even earlier than that time and excavations produced gold, silver, ivory and bronze, statuettes, old coins and other pieces of jewellery of an archaic period which are now to be found in the Istanbul Archaeological Museum.

The temple was destroyed several times, and its rebuilding was still unfinished at the time of its capture by Croesus in the middle of the sixth century. The king celebrated the event by completing the building of the sanctuary and sending pillars and heifers of gold. The drum of a column in the British Museum bears an inscription testifying to the interest that Croesus felt for the cult of Diana.

It is recorded that two architects from Crete, Kessrifron and Metagenes built the temple, and according to Pliny the Younger, it measured not less than 190 metres long and 55 metres wide, and had 127 columns of which 36 were carved. It was destroyed by fire and restored towards 450 BC and it was burned down again in 356 BC on the night of the birth of Alexander the Great ('the Goddess being in Macedonia on obstetrical duties') by a madman called Herostrates who wished to immortalize his name. He got his wish, for in spite of a town decree forbidding the use of his name it became a byword for meaningless destruction.

When Alexander the Great visited Ephesus, he offered help in the reconstruction, but the Ephesians told him, 'A god would not give an offering to another god', and so he was deprived of tax from the Ephesians who reconstructed the temple from their own funds, although it is recorded elsewhere that the Macedonian King did eventually contribute to its embellishment.

The magnificence of the temple attracted thousands of pilgrims to offer sacrifices and gifts to the Goddess, whose statue was carved from a black meteorite. The statue of Diana possesses three rows of breasts which are thought to represent a lactating mother with the ability to feed all her children. However, the breasts are without nipples. I have taken special note of this on my visits to Seljuk Museum where several statues are housed, because of her association with the bee, the breasts were alternatively considered to represent the ova of the bee.

Recent excavations in the area of the temple have produced the remains of bulls, and it has been suggested that the breasts represent the testicles of bulls sacrificed to her. There is dissension about this theory since the bull is a masculine symbol and we know that bulls were sacrificed at the altar of the nearby Temple of Domitian, a much later example of Roman Emperor worship. No doubt pieces of bone can still be found, but it is unlikely they have any connection with the Artemision.

It is known that the Goddess was associated with a boy lover, a flower god called Hyacinthos, and in his essay 'Flowery Tuscany' written in 1926–27, D.H. Lawrence suggested that the breasts represent a grape hyacinth, reminiscent of Hyacinthos. This theory holds little credibility with scholars but appears to be as useful a theory as any other.

The temple was finally plundered by Nero, and then destroyed by the Goths in AD 263 when it was rebuilt on a smaller scale. Later it was stripped of its marble for the building of Aya Sofia in what was then Constantinople, and for St John's basilica in Ephesus itself. One of the statues of Artemis was buried by a last worshipper in the 'bouleuterion' (senate or town hall) to save it from destruction by Christian fanatics, and another colossal figure from the first century AD has recently been unearthed in excavations.

The temple and the statue, were, said the priests, the gift of the gods, and the Artemision had the right of sanctuary. By Artemision was meant both the temple and the month of the year dedicated to the cult of the Goddess.

Ancient sources reveal that only the priests and priestesses were allowed to enter the sanctuary where the statue of the Goddess was kept; the people, especially married ones for some reason, did not have this privilege. The worshippers could only observe from the façade of the temple but the sacred courtyard was open to everyone.

The cult of Artemis in Ephesus is based on the Mother Goddess of Anatolia, a fertility goddess. The concept came from the Neolithic age under several names and beliefs, and originated it is believed in Ephesus, from Kuppaba of the Hittites and Cybele of the Phrygians and spread to other countries around the Mediterranean during the Roman period.

Artemis was the main Goddess of the City of Ephesus, evidenced by the castellated head-dress on some of the statues which indicate a city Goddess. Her figure is not simple and human as is the virginal Greek Artemis (or Diana the Huntress) who was the sister of Apollo and the goddess of the hunt and of chastity. So chaste indeed that overseen bathing in a stream of Actaeon, she changed the young hunter into a stag to be torn to pieces by his own hounds. From Greek and Roman mythology, Diana the Huntress was known as the daughter of Zeus or Jupiter and on their farflung travels the tolerant Greeks were prone to identifying their Twelve Olympians with local gods and goddesses in the most incongruous amalgamations. In Anatolia they came across the worship of Cybele, daughter-in-law of Heaven and Earth, and wife of Time, Kronos. She was also known as Ops, the wife of Saturn, god of Nature; as Rhea, mother of Zeus; as Vesta, the Roman Goddess of the Hearth, and as the 'Earth Mother', symbol of fertility. There are many reasons for this strange-seeming shift to chastity. One of course is that on her travels Cybele, like all gods, was made over in the image of her worshippers. Another is that her very relationship to time and to nature made her, following the earth's rhythm, both fruitful and barren according to season. In Ephesus, the Goddess of Chastity becomes Mother Nature, Artemis Polimastros with three rows of breasts, oriental in style with many decorations and ornaments incorporated into her statue, animals are carved into her skirt and her head-piece including deer and bees.

After the death of Alexander the Great, his empire was split amongst his lieutenants, Ephesus falling to the lot of Lysimachus. By that time the port was half choked by sand from the Kaystros River.

In the second century BC, Rome took over Asia Minor. Ephesus belonging to the kingdom of Pergamum became the capital of the Roman provinces of Asia, and the town of 300,000 inhabitants prospered and grew.

A crossroads of trade, it quickly became a centre of culture attracting the preachers of Christianity who founded there the first of the Seven Churches of the Apocalypse. In the Acts of the Apostles, St Luke, a physician from Antioch (today Antakya), writes at length of the cult of Artemis, known under the Romans by her Latin name, Diana. It was the silversmiths of the city who drove out St Paul from Ephesus, for fear that his preaching would lessen the sale of the silver shrines for Diana and Acts 19:27: 'So that not only this our craft is in danger to be set at nought, but also that the temple of the Great Goddess Diana should be despised and Her magnificence should be destroyed, whom all Asia and the world worshippeth'.

When Paul addressed the entire town in the ampitheatre, urging them to accept his doctrines, 'they were full of wrath and cried out saying, "Great is Diana of the Ephesians" '.

In the fourth century, the balance of power of the known world swung the other way, Constantine made Rome the seat of the Church and Byzantium the seat of the Empire. The pagan temples were plundered and in AD 431 the Roman Catholic Church held a council at Ephesus to decide the tenets of the church. It was the second Theodosius who held the Third Ecumenical Council, when the Patriarch of Constantinople Nestorius who claimed that Jesus was God in man but not God, and who denied the virgin birth was charged with heresy and cast out of the Church. It was at this time also that Artemis Ephesia was incorporated into Christianity at the insistence of the populace, fearing that she would be lost to them at the advent of the new religion, and they cried, 'Great is Diana of the Ephesians, give us back Diana'. She was given the title of Theotokus, or the God Bearer and in course of time evolved into the Blessed Virgin Mary.

In 1971, R.E. Witt wrote *Isis in the Graeco-Roman World*. In this book he points out that the worship of the Goddess as Isis and Artemis, names that had become widely used by the time of Christ, was the target of the apostle Paul. He also quotes perhaps the most revealing line in the story of the destruction of the Goddess religion, in that Clement of Alexandria reproduces a saying from the Gospel According to the Egyptians. Christ's words are in such a context that they are almost certainly directed against the current worship of Goddesses: 'I have come to destroy the works of the female'.

This then is the historical record of Artemis Ephesia, and inspired by it, I had always nurtured a great longing to visit the site of the temple at Ephesus and have been fortunate enough to do so on several occasions, usually at the time of year when the site reverted to its marshy norm. In October 1986, however, after a long hot summer, it was quite dry and one was able to wander amongst the fallen pillars and stones. My husband and I had made the journey to Ephesus from the coast where we were holidaying, together with Ergün, a Turkish friend who had travelled from Istanbul to see me.

Despite being early autumn it was a hot sunny day. Ergün and my husband had wandered off to another part of the site, and I was sitting on a fallen stone absorbed in trying to rewind the film in my camera preparatory to inserting another film. I had been quite keyed-up at the prospect of seeing the site of the Artemision once more, and having wandered around the city of Ephesus for some hours, it was already late afternoon, and we were the only visitors in evidence. I was a little footsore from several hours walking, and it was very pleasant to sit for a while in the sunshine with the sound of the crickets, ubiquitous in that area, around me.

As I sat there fiddling with my camera, I became aware of an all-pervading silence in the air which was slightly unnerving, and I shivered despite the warmth of the sun. I sensed a strange pressure on my head which it is difficult at this distance to define, the crickets had ceased their chirping and there was a slight buzzing in my ears. I rubbed them in an attempt to ease the buzzing and the feeling of pressure, and as I did so, I looked up and around me, and to my astonishment the scene had changed.

Instead of stones and fallen masonry around me there was water, to all intents and purposes it was water which reflected the blue of the sky, and it was wet, and yet it was divorced from me, inasmuch as I was not sitting in it! As I tried hard mentally to make some sort of sense out of this strange phenomenon, I became aware of a building some little distance from me, the pillars and roof of which were reflected as white in the water, but the building itself was a pale and very peculiar metallic shade of green, and it was not stable, it shimmered in the air and shook slightly, rather like a jelly, almost as if I was actually looking at a reflection in water which was disturbed by undercurrents. The late afternoon sun was reflected on the pillars and what appeared to be an enormous bronze studded door. As my reeling brain computed that what I was seeing was another glimpse of a past age, and that this was the Temple of Artemis, it began to disintegrate before my eyes, not suddenly or quickly, but in slow motion, it simply faded and as it did so, the 'jelly wobble' increased until my eyes could no longer maintain their vision of the vibration, and it was gone, and with it the surrounding water. I sat there for some time trying to make sense of what I had experienced, as the pressure lifted from my head, the buzzing in my ears ceased, and the crickets resumed their chirping. I wished that I had possessed the wits to take a photograph in my now film-restored camera, and wondered if in any case the camera would have recorded it, and whether it was really a subjective vision which only appeared objective, though I argued that if it had been only subjective I would have seen the building as white, not pale green. I was unable to judge how long the vision had lasted. It could only have been a matter of seconds but it seemed timeless, and I was very reluctant to leave the site of the Artemision that day and kept hoping the vision would return, but alas, it did not.

Naturally I have attempted to analyse the events of that day many times and can only conclude that having spent many hours deeply involved in the history of the area, walking and talking about the city of Ephesus, and with my abiding interest in Diana of the Ephesians, my mind was receptive to a paranormal experience; however only I had the vision of the temple and the surrounding area as it must have been in that ancient time, and I have wondered whether my husband and Ergün would have shared the experience with me had they not been in another area of the site.

Instinctively I feel they would not, the vision was for me, and perhaps it arose out of an overwhelming desire to know more of that period of history, when the world was young and the Goddess reigned in the hearts of men and women, and her place was unchallenged until the advent of the rival religion.

13 The Goddess in the Ancient World

In the study of the ancient world and in conversation and correspondence with a friend who is a classical scholar, odd snippets of information surface to be mentally filed away after they have, as Homer puts it, 'pointed the way to the gates of the sun and to the land of dreams'.

One such snippet was that it was in 2500 BC that the Hittites established Cappadocia, and their decline started around 1200 BC. My friend wrote,

> ... one must understand that the Hittite decline caused the Siege of Troy. The Greeks were after the Dardanelles giving access to the Black Sea, it was a trade war. The story about Helen and her harlotry is just an amusing justification invented at a later date. The Greeks were successful (they prayed to Argive Hera) but they were weakened by their victory and the Dorians (with Apollo and the Huntress) marched in.
>
> It is customary for the gods of conquerors to take over the temples and altars of their predecessors but this does not mean that they are the same deity. I am aware that some people think the revengeful old God of the Jews, Jehovah, Allah and the Christian God of love and forgiveness are the same. I find such ideas quite unacceptable and without substance. I would agree that Mother Goddesses have much in common, but they are not the same; furthermore, they are completely different from the specialised deities of Wisdom, War, Fate, Love, Death, etc. Of recent years there have been too many people who try to juggle facts to suit their theories (Graves for example), this, although amusing is not the scientific way to study the ancient world.

Further research on Helen reveals a triple goddess connection, in which she was an incarnation of the virgin Moon

Goddess, the enchantress and the crone, the embodiment of Hecate, herself a triple goddess. Helen was also called Helle or Selene and was worshipped as an orgiastic deity at the Spartan festival *Helenphoria*, featuring sexual symbols carried in a special fetish basket, the *helene*.

Trojan Helen married Menelaus, 'the Moon King' who was promised immortality because he made a sacred marriage. However, Helen deserted him for her new Trojan lover Paris, and Menelaus lost both his immortality and the Trojan fiefs that Helen's matrimony brought. He sailed with his armies to get her back and this was the start of the legendary Trojan War which pitted patriarchal Greeks against matriarchal Trojans.

Further, as Elen, Elaine or Hel-Aine, the same Moon-virgin became the queen of pagan Britain, a 'Lily Maid' who made the first alliances with emperors of Rome. The oldest British histories said the first British King was a Trojan named Brutus, a relative of Helen. After Troy fell, he sailed west to the island of Albion and founded a city, New Troy, later renamed Lugdunum (London) after his descendant the god Lug.

There is a goddess connection in the Old Testament stories of Moses. Research on the basis of the Ten Commandments reveals that on the Babylonian monument known as the stele of Hammurabi, the king is represented as receiving from the God Shamash, the Sun God, the ancient collection of laws, commonly known as the Code of Hammurabi. The sanctity of the code was affirmed because the god gave it to Hammurabi in exactly the same way as Jehovah gave it to Moses.

Moses, being brought up as a Prince of Egypt would be conversant with the laws of Babylon and the laws of Egypt, and when he was traversing the wilderness with a tribe of runaway slaves, and at a loss as to how he could control them, he formulated laws according to what he knew already, and the storytellers promulgated the theory of divine inspiration.

The miracles of Moses were equally derivative, drawn chiefly from Egyptian myths, the drying-up of a body of water to cross dry-shod was a miracle of Isis who parted the waters of the River Phaedrus on her journey to Byblos. Moses's extraction from a rock of a spring of water, was performed by Atalanta of Calydon who did it by striking the rock with her spear and calling on her Goddess. Mother Rhea performed the same miracle and she was also the giver of law tablets on a holy mountain.

It is recorded that another lawgiving mountain deity was Mother Rhea of Mount Dicte, or Ninhursag. She was probably a model for the masculine lawgivers. Moses took over another matriarchal myth in the tale of the plagues of Egypt. This came from the third dynasty reign of Tcheser (or Joser, whom the Hebrews called Joseph). The Nile flood failed for seven years, and Egyptians starved to death by thousands. The pharaoh sent a desperate message to Mater (Mother) ruler of Nubia, to ask how the Goddess might be propitiated. Mater's reply described 'the couch of the Nile', a double cavern called Qerti or Khert, the underworld, likened to 'two breasts from which all good things poured forth'. Mater said the trouble was caused by a jealous male god, who wished to be called 'father of gods' and to hold the Key of the Nile.

When the story was written down many centuries afterwards in the late Ptolemaic period, priests of Ra pretended their god had ended the drought, by spreading a 'red beer' over Egypt's fields to distract the attention of Mother Hathor who was killing the people. This 'beer' was said to be 'as human blood'. What transformed it into blood was a holy substance from the Nile's source, called 'dedi'. This was sometimes said to be a salty red earth, like ochre, likened to menstrual blood. Or again, the red colour was pomegranate juice, another symbol of menstrual blood. The pomegranate represented the vulva in Biblical times and was worshipped as an emblem of the Goddess on her holy mount Rimmon (Pomegranate).

What really turned the Nile into blood was not Moses's magic wand, but the red silt of flood time, supposed to be the Goddess's life-giving uterine blood bathing the land in the substance of life.

Moses's followers pretended that Yahweh (Jehovah) had caused the slaughter of Egyptian firstborn sons (Exodus 12:29) while the Israelites were permitted to redeem their sons with the blood of lambs (Exodus, 13:15). However, Yahweh had long copied the Egyptian custom of firstborn sacrifice. He said, 'Sanctify unto me all the firstborn, whatsoever openeth the womb among the children of Israel, both of man and of beast, it is mine' (Exodus 13:2). Like early Egyptian gods Yahweh forgave sins only when his altars were soaked in blood: 'without shedding of blood there is no remission' (Hebrews 9:22).

The Goddess has returned, and her re-emergence is a revolution, though not in the Roman Catholic Church where she has long been acknowledged and incorporated, albeit in a sanitized, de-sexed and purified image, and where in truth she rules over her divine Son. I always feel very comfortable in a

Roman Catholic Church, and when I have attended family events concerning my grandchildren, such as a christening or a first communion, as I walk into the peace of the sanctuary, before me at the end of a long aisle is the altar, and upon it, the crucifix, but above it, on the wall in ruling splendour is an overwhelming and beautiful mosaic of the Goddess in her disguise as the Virgin Mary. I smile and genuflect to her, and reflect that she is venerated by millions of people who neither know nor care that she is in reality and originality, the Great Earth Mother.

The Goddess is the Earth; she is the mother who nurtures us and brings forth life, she is fertility and generation, all things proceed from her and return to her; she is the life of trees and plants, of grain and herbs, all that lives is a part of her. She is the air and the sky and the elements, she is the celestial Queen of Heaven, the Star Goddess and the Muse who arouses the creative spirit of humanity. She can never be grasped, penetrated or understood. Who can express the inexpressible or know the unknowable? She is nemoral, the essence of life and the mystery of the waters, she is manifested and orchestrated in the bounty of Nature. She is the Three and the One. As the Moon Goddess in the waxing, she is the Maiden, in the full moon, the Mother, and as the moon wanes she is the Crone; the perfect Trinity.

The Goddess is the *anima*, the feminine aspect in man. The history of civilization is a story of domination by man and a patriarchal god where the basic cultural pattern has been the work of man. History is darkened by ignorance of the truth, that men can only create through the feminine element of their own natures, and the rebirth of the lost feminine principle and its reliance on love is the real transmuter in poverty of spirit.

At the still centre in the storm of all our tumultuous being is a world which is ourselves, Origen in *Leviticum Homilae* wrote 'You yourself are even another little world and have within you the sun and the moon and also the stars', our lives are a journey of the human spirit between departure and return, and the Goddess governs this journey and the little world within ourselves. Unrecognized, unacknowledged yet she unveils herself within an unfathomable mystery, and in the context of the spiritual life there is a need for mystery and a need for silence. Through meditation, grace, effort or divine inspiration, great truths are often revealed, and although these may be confirmed inwardly, to talk about them can be unwise and is not to be recommended. Silence and reticence are an important part of all spiritual disciplines, and within religious traditions those whose work and contemplation are the most valued are those who say as little as possible. In silence, things may be seen, known and experienced which are quite beyond words to explain.

'Soul receives from soul that knowledge
therefore not by book nor from tongue,
If knowledge of mysteries come after emptiness of mind
that is illumination of heart

Mevlana Jelalu'ddin Rumi who wrote those words understood that spiritual experience and being admitted into the truth of great realities is something which is individual to the person who has it and attempting to communicate that experience to someone who is not ready for it is unwise. One may perhaps discuss it in later times when other experiences have overlaid it, but in the immediate aftermath of the experience it is better to savour it inwardly.

There is a tendency in the present day to require to make all of religion vernacular and comprehensible to all people. It is true that if one is too secret and obscure then religion is removed from the people but witchcraft is not a religion for all people and only a certain amount of openness is necessary and the Goddess in her incomparability is a mystery which cannot be fathomed.

I have seen on Muslim tombstones these words 'Huwa al-Baqi' – 'He is the One who remains'. At the end of all discussion, all study, all writing and all great scholarship and after hundreds of years of spiritual effort in order to understand, after all the realizations of great mystics, saints and gurus, 'Huwa al-Baqi', the Muslim God Allah remains and his mystery remains untouched. It is the same with all Gods, and Goddesses, they do not need our study, devotion, worship and aspiration, they are unique and self-sufficient in the mystery of their aloneness and unrelatability, it is we who seek them out.

There is a story in the Mathnawi of Mevlana Jalaluddin Rumi where the aspirant who comes to adore God knocks on the door and the voice within asks 'Who is it?'

He answers, 'It is I'.

The response is 'I know not an I'.

Ultimately the man at the door answers 'It is Thou' and is let in. To know the gods demands complete effacement and humility and the admission that we are before mysteries that are not for the profane and only those who are elected by grace to know them.

In a discussion with Sonya, I asked her if she involved herself in elaborate rituals and she replied simply, 'My garden is my temple, all I need is there.' She considers formal, stylized rituals superfluous, unnecessary and artificial in that they ape conventional religion and detract from the essential simplicity and naturalness of pagan, pantheistic orientation emphasized in a prayer she volunteered:

> O Goddess without end and without beginning, Thou art the Best that can be conceived by those who seek to know Thee. As a ray of light is contained in whatever shines, so does a ray of Thy beauty sparkle in every form of Nature. Whatever we can love, whatever is lovely, presents to us a part of Thy essence, a manifestation of Thyself. All earthly beauty is but the shadow cast by heavenly beauty. Make us as like to Thee as is possible to our gross nature, that we may so far participate in Thy happiness as life allows.

My temple is the countryside where I walk, it is the desert and the wilderness and the mountain fastness, wherever there is silence and stillness in which I can discover the eternal essence deep in the mind of the Goddess whom Sonya refers to as 'my Lady'.

The God of the Witches is less real to me, he who is the Lord of Death and Resurrection is a shadowy figure, her consort, who seldom appears to me in dreams or visions. Among his various identities is Pan, the God of Nature, and sometimes in meditation on a grassy knoll in a favourite place, I fancy I hear the sound of his pipes, carried by the wind from a distant spinney, and my mind wanders back through the years to childhood and mossy banks of flowing streams, of warm sunshine, and careless days and from Stockhausen's Hymnen:

> Into my heart an air that kills
> From yon far country blows,
> What are those blue remembered hills?
> What spires, what farms are those?

That is the land of lost content
I see it shining plain
The happy highways where I went
And cannot come again.

A.E. Housman

The Goddess has in the past been banished from two of the world's major religions. In seventh-century Arabia it was the prophet Mohammed who was instrumental in bringing to an end the national worship of the Sun Goddess, Al Lat, and the Goddess known as Al Uzza. Al Lat was originally much the same deity as Asherah in Arabic religion. Mohammed inculcated the worship of Allah as the supreme god. Allah, means God, as Al Lat means Goddess, and he incorporated many of the legends and attitudes of the Old and New Testaments into the Koran, the Holy Book of Islam. It was Mohammed who said, 'When Eve was created, Satan rejoiced'.

In this present day, Hebrew males are instructed to offer the daily prayer: 'Blessed Art Thou O Lord our God, King of the Universe who has not made me a woman'. The word 'Sabbath' which has strong associations in witchcraft has no connection with Jewish practices, and it is thought possibly to be a derivative of 's'ébattre' meaning 'to frolic', an apt description of the joyous gaiety of the gathering of witches. Another meaning of the word, however, is Goddess, a particular Goddess, the Shekinah, who to this day in every Jewish temple or synagogue is welcomed in the Friday evening prayers with the words, 'Come O Bride', although the old greeting has lost its mystical significance and is now a mere poetic expression of uncertain meaning.

Despite the fact that Yahweh (Jehovah), the tribal god of the Jews was in origin a volcano god who had two wives, the sad story of the exile of the womanly spirit of God, the Shekinah, the Lady, Queen or Matronit in the history of the Jews occurred, and this is to be found in Raphael Patai's book, *The Hebrew Goddess*. Just as in Tantric Hinduism, with its emphasis on sexual experience and visionary states, Shiva the God has his consort, the Shakti, so Jehovah had his lover, Sabbath or Shekinah, reflecting that in Orthodox Jewish law when sexual congress takes place between a man and his wife, the Shekinah or the female spirit of god, descends into the house and dwells there. That is why the Sabbath is holy for in the Orthodox Jewish tradition, sexual congress occurs on Friday night and Saturday is a day, not merely of rest but of reverie and reflection, of love,

The Goddess in the Ancient World

poetry and inner discovery, but the Sabbath of the Jews has, according to Patai, become an empty observance whose true meaning has been forgotten.

Catal Hüyük is a broad mound 42 km. south-east of Konya in Turkey, between the towns of Kuckkoy and Karkin, and around 1959 pieces of pottery discovered at the top of the mound drew the attention of archaeologists and excavations were instigated. What was found there was a culture dated 9000–7000 BC, the remains of a Neolithic settlement of a completely unknown civilization. This civilization had not yet discovered writing, but they were not only the most advanced civilization of that time in Anatolia but in the whole world. This ten-thousand-year-old civilization had left houses, temples, palaces, food, ornaments, bowls, weapons and statuettes of the supreme deity, the Mother Goddess. The white-plastered walls made of sun-dried bricks were decorated with frescoes depicting people and animals. Their houses, which were generally joined one to another, were entered by steps going down into the houses from the roofs. They had ovens, and because they had not yet discovered metal, they had made weapons out of obsidian. Stone and clay figures of pregnant women were found, making it clear that the core of their belief was in the Mother Goddess. Their painted pots and bowls were decorated with geometric designs of great beauty and delicacy, and inside one house which was excavated the grave of the owner was discovered. Beside the skeleton was a shining hand mirror made of polished black obsidian and on the other side a small clay pot containing dark red paint which was assumed to be the woman's rouge and lipstick.

A similar excavation at nearby Hacilar discovered a Neolithic community dated at 5800 BC and again statuettes portray a Mother Goddess and the male occurring only in a subsidiary role as child or paramour. The statuettes of the Goddess which I have visited in the Ankara Museum of Anatolian Civilizations are incredibly beautiful in their own way and tremendously evocative of an age when the Earth was young and the Goddess was given deserving homage.

Far from being a primitive civilization, excavations have revealed sophisticated gold jewellery, and death presents laid in the graves of kings and princes. Amongst them are a gold ewer, a gold cup, gold necklaces and brooches, a gold sword hilt and bronze sun discs and stags, works of art made before the Hittites in the Early Bronze Age. At this period various metals had been discovered by the people of Anatolia, copper, lead, tin, gold, silver and various alloys such as bronze and electron were used to make ornaments, etc. The pottery pitchers, footed fruit bowls, teapots fitted with strainers, vases and bowls were decorated with geometric designs.

Quite often the statuettes of Mother Goddesses discovered at ancient sites are very basic and merely rough models of a pregnant woman with huge belly, pendulous breasts and enormous thighs, but the stylized statues such as those found at the Temple of Artemis in Ephesus are the work of artists, and executed with love and finesse. One in particular which was found at Ephesus in 1955 and has been dated at the second century BC is the object of some mystery since it is very different from other Artemis statues in the various museums of the world. Art historians and experts world-wide came rushing to Ephesus to see the statue which soon came to be known as 'The Beautiful Artemis'.

This statue depicts the Goddess standing clothed and with a crown on her head. She appears to be leaning against a cushion decorated with the figures of sacred animals. Her expression is a sweet seriousness with drawn eyebrows, oriental almond-shaped eyes and full lips. She is wearing a necklace and there are the usual three rows of egg-shaped symbols and on her skirts are the figures of other sacred animals. She holds two staffs in her hands and on each side of her is a deer. She is thought to have been inspired by the Mother Goddess Cybele who was worshipped in Anatolia for thousands of years and it is considered by experts that the worship of Artemis was a continuation of the traditional Mother Goddess cult of Anatolia. On the skirts of the Goddess are the bee symbols of the City of Ephesus, as well as being sacred to the Goddess the bee was also the symbol of the city.

The worship of the female, the Mother Goddess is as old as time, and Witchcraft, the Old Religion, carries on her worship with its alternative spirituality. It is unlikely ever to become a world religion and it is defiant of patriarchal Christianity. In a sixteenth-century Church report is written: 'Woman is more carnal than man; there was a defect in the formation of the first woman, since she was formed with a bent rib. She is imperfect and thus always deceives. Witchcraft comes from carnal lust. Women are to be chaste and subservient to men'.

According to *The Times* religious affairs' correspondent:

> A warning that the admission of women to the priesthood in the Church of England would be a subtle shift towards the old

pagan religions was given by the Bishop of Exeter, Dr Mortimer, to the convocation of Canterbury.

In the old nature religions, he declared, priestesses were common – 'and we all know the kind of religions they were and are'. The church has too often adapted to changing conditions in the past, and had to be doubly careful 'in a sex obsessed culture'.

As far as I am personally concerned, I have no religious prejudice, I consider that all religions are rivers leading to the same ocean, and I feel no conflict in the study of and participation in the rites of other religions. I am as willing to attend a service in a Christian Church as in a mosque and I can talk to a Muslim within the framework of Islam, and if necessary recite the traditional Muslim prayers to the dead: 'Inna li Allah, wa, inna, ilayhi raji'un. La illaha ila Allah, wa Muhammad rasul Allah'. ('To God we belong and to Him we must return. There is no God but Allah, and Muhammad is His Prophet'.)

The Goddess and the memory of her is everywhere, from the night sky in her aspect as Moon Goddess when Sappho in the seventh century BC was inspired to write: 'The stars around the lovely Moon flicker and shine less bright, when She, full orbed upon the Earth sprinkles her silver light', to a bugle sounding what in the British Army is Reveille, but in the French army is called La Diane, and indicates that Diana the Huntress has returned to Earth from her night-time incarnation as the Moon.

Further evidence of fertility rites and Goddess worship in England is to be found at a flint mine called Grimes Graves, near Brandon in Norfolk. Some of the shafts have been excavated and one can be visited. A large quantity of red deer antlers which were used as picks to move the chalk show that the miners either hunted themselves or else traded with hunters of deer.

On a crust of flint found at Grimes Graves is a roughly scratched drawing of a deer which suggests the style of Mesolithic art (the period between the Palaeolithic and Neolithic Ages). The most interesting find, however, was a shrine at the foot of a pit where the flint had been exhausted, of a little pregnant statuette of the primitive style I have described earlier. There was also a phallus and testicles carved from chalk, and a mound of flint blocks and antler picks. Perhaps the offering was to placate the earth and make the next mine more fruitful but the Goddess belongs to a family going back far beyond the Neolithic, into Palaeolithic times.

Although the Goddess throughout the ancient world had many names, Isis is her true name, and she possessed two aspects. She was the creator, mother and nurse of all, but she was also the Destroyer. The name Isis means ancient, and she was sometimes called Maat which means Knowledge or Wisdom, and so Isis is Maat, the ancient wisdom. This means the wisdom of things as they are, and as they ever have been. The inborn, inherent amplitude to follow the nature of things in their present form, and in their inevitable development in relation to each other; the wisdom of instinct.

As Isis is Destroyer as well as life-giver, her statues frequently represent her as black and as Virgin and Child, suckling the infant Horus. Ancient statues of Isis were sometimes mistaken for the Virgin Mary and the Infant Jesus, but she was in fact believed to be the Mother of God and worshipped as virgin as were many other Moon Goddesses, and Robert Briffault in *The Mothers* (New York and London, 1927) referred to the relationship of the Virgin Mary to the moon. Orthodox Catholic Fathers called her the Moon of the Church, Our Moon, the Spiritual Moon and the Perfect and Eternal Moon. She is also said to control the Moon and all the stars and planets, and she is known as Stella Maris (Star of the Sea) and Ruler of the Ocean. In France, the Moon is called Notre Dame and in Portugal, the Mother of God.

It is recorded that in Mexico women would hold up their children to the Mother Moon asking that they should be given eternal life like her own. Sir John Barrow in his *Travels in China* (London, 1806) related that the most common female deity in China was Shing-Moo or Holy Mother and the early Jesuits found a striking resemblance to the Virgin Mary. Her statue was held in a recess behind an altar, which is the position of the Christian Lady Chapel. She was veiled and carried a child, on her knees or in her arms and had a halo around her head, and her story was similar to Mary's for she conceived and bore her child whilst a virgin.

The Great Mother is always represented as virgin despite the fact that she has lovers and is the mother of a son who dies only to be reborn year after year. J.G. Frazer has pointed out that the Greek word 'parthenos' which we translate as 'virgin' meant no more than an unmarried woman, and referring to the line in Isaiah 'and a virgin shall be with child' says that the Hebrew word here rendered as 'virgin' simply means a young woman and that 'a correct translation would have obviated the necessity for a miracle'. Philo of Alexandria wrote profoundly, 'For the congress of men for the procreation of children makes virgins women, but when God begins to associate with the soul, he brings to pass that she who was formerly woman becomes virgin again'.

In the ancient world the women of that time found in the Mother Goddess the reflection of their own feminine natures, as in the present day the Virgin Mary serves the same purpose within the confines of the Roman Catholic faith. Although in the continent of India the Goddess in various guises is still the object of reverence and worship, the West has rejected her, her shrines are neglected and her statues line the walls of museums, but the ancient feminine principle is reasserting its power as a religious tenet and also as a psychological force arising from the unconscious.

When the pale dawn of reason crept across the pagan sky, mankind grew out of believing in the Goddess, but mankind has yet to grow out of the need of her.

14 Hallowe'en

The festival of Hallowe'en is the most important date in the witch calendar and it is one of the four Great Sabbats associated with witchcraft that everyone has heard about. It is held on 31 October and is the Celtic Eve of Samhain meaning 'summer's end' when it was regarded that the winter half of the year started on 1 November. On this night and during the first week of November great ritual bonfires were held and it is recorded that on these fires were burned the troubles of the preceding year. During winter, fire gives the light and heat required to preserve life and becomes a substitute for the sun. The fire ceremonies had two main purposes; in some cases they were regarded as sympathetic magic in order to encourage the sun to return after the winter solstice, and in others they were a form of purification and the sacred flame was a means to burn up evil and to protect the good from the supernatural powers of the wicked.

In North America the Hopi Indians light a new fire which must be lit from the embers of the old one and this burns on the central hearth of the tribe throughout the year. The ceremony can only be acted out by the fully initiated men who are incarcerated in underground *kivas* for eight days before taking part in the festival on the ninth day and the ceremony is very solemn and long. This ritual is similar to our knowledge of the Samhain fire festivals of the Iron Age Celts. The chief druids in Ireland met twelve miles from the sacred hill of Tara to light the fire which was used for the sacrifices of Samhain. On November Eve every fire in Ireland had to be extinguished and relit from the newly created sacred fire.

The Celts regarded the tradition of the November fire as essential to the life of the community and it continued after the advent of Christianity. Until the eighth century 1 November was reckoned as New Year's Day and this continued until the eighteenth century. The Church on the Isle of Man where this tradition held, objected to the pagan practice of beacon fires being lit on hilltops and attempted to put an end to the custom but without effect because the people believed that the flames held a special power to increase the fertility of cattle forced through them and the virility of men who jumped over them. This fertility also extended to plant life and in the nineteenth century the country folk paraded in fields with torches lit from the Hallowe'en bonfire in the firm belief that the flames they carried would aid the fertility of cattle and crops as the sun does.

In Lancashire 31 October was called Teanday which is derived from the Celtic word *'tan'* or *'teindh'* meaning fire or light. Families gathered in the fields and collected bundles of straw on pitchforks and prayed for the souls of their beloved dead, and fires lit on Findern Common in Derbyshire on 1 November were to light the souls out of Purgatory.

In Scotland the Samhain fires continued until the end of the eighteenth century. A bonfire was burned in every village, young boys would vie with each other to get as close to the flames as possible to allow the smoke to roll over them and their companions would take turns to jump over the bodies.

The word 'bonfire' derives from 'bone fire' and the bones burned were those of cattle slaughtered at the beginning of the winter. It was on 'bonfires' that sacrifices to the gods were made, and because Guy Fawkes Night falls during the first week of November, it has been suggested that he and his conspirators were members of a witch coven. The Celts were a pastoral people and time was calculated by nights rather than by days, and by winters rather than summers, and Samhain was the start of cold dark weeks and so marked their New Year. Some of the sacrifices made were of a practical nature, some animals could not be fed over the winter and so were slaughtered at Samhain whilst they were still in good condition from summer grazing.

It is believed that some of the sacrifices were human ones, an old leader of the tribe whose powers were failing would give his life so that a younger and stronger man could rule and provide for the people. It was a great honour to be chosen to die for the tribe but as years passed, an animal or even an effigy would be substituted.

These sacrifices whether practical or ceremonial subscribed towards Samhain becoming a festival of the dead. The Celts believed that a time of change such as that from months of light to months of darkness was a magical time when barriers between the natural and the supernatural were less distanced as were those between the living and the dead. They felt that the dead were very near to them at this time and they feared to encounter the ghost of a person they had known in life, to disguise themselves, they blackened their faces and wore masks. Nevertheless they wished the dead to feel welcome should they return, so the doors were left unbolted, food was left out for them and a warm fire awaiting on Hallowe'en.

It was suspected that fairies as well as the dead were abroad at this season and they also needed to be placated; the fairies were supposed to be restless at Hallowe'en and moved around from one place to another and if they were encountered whilst moving house it was considered unlucky. Gifts of hazel nuts were left for them and on the Isle of Man the remains of supper on Hallowe'en were left with a jug of water for the fairies. At ceremonial gatherings the food eaten was to be shared with ghosts and at Knutsford in Cheshire soul cakes are baked and eaten and the room lit by candles to guide the spirits of the dead back to their earthly abode.

Just as within Christianity, Christmas was regarded as the season of good will, so in the ancient world at Samhain it was the custom to try to heal quarrels between people and to be at peace with each other so that no negative vibrations were available to be used by evil spirits. With the advent of Christianity, the Church attempted to Christianize the festival by making 1 November All Saints Day or All Hallows and Samhain became All Hallows Eve but the pagan celebrations continued and the Church eventually banned the festival. In 1928 it was restored on the assumption that the pagan associations were forgotten and many of the Celtic gods were converted to Christian saints.

It was traditional at this time to seek omens for the future, and one form of divination which was practised until well into the eighteenth century was that on the eve of Samhain every member of the family group threw into the embers of a fire a marked stone, and on the following day the stones were retrieved from the fire and any which were missing indicated that misfortune would follow the family in the coming year. Hazel nuts were used in the same way and one which burned brightly meant good luck but one which crackled and became blackened signified death and general disaster.

Ducking for apples has always been associated with Hallowe'en and the apple has since time immemorial been regarded as a talisman between men and the gods. According to the druids, immortal souls were obliged to pass through water in order to reach Avalon, the land of apples and immortality; that belief has now degenerated into ducking for apples in buckets of water. Apples are also used for divination at Hallowe'en, the peel was cut in one long strip and whichever letter the form resembled indicated the future mate of the enquirer; simply eating apples at Hallowe'en was also supposed to bring good fortune.

There is a tradition of turnip masks at Hallowe'en and this is a relic of the masked dancers of Samhain when men wore masks or blackened their faces either to impersonate the dead or hide from them. Pranks were played similar to 'Trick or Treat' which occurs in America at Hallowe'en, chimneys were blocked with turf and the masks served to protect the tricksters from the vengeance of the living. People in Scotland who carried out these winter rituals were called guizers, and the ones who begged from house to house wore straw dresses and were called sheklers.

The Hallowe'en ceremonies of witches are serious ones and unconnected with the activities of popular folklore. Samhain is to them a festival of the dead when they remember the old ones who have gone before. Since witches generally believe in the theory of reincarnation they regard death as a door to a future life and believe that those who have already passed retain an interest in the living and are prepared to help them. The Hallowe'en ceremony is a very beautiful one in which the spirits of the dead are invited to join with us in our celebrations and those of us who are clairvoyant are aware of their presence with us in the circle, and their joy at being able to share with us the Sabbat.

I receive many letters asking me about ceremonies and rituals in witchcraft and the reason for the celebration of the four great festivals. I see the festivals as a celebration of the presence of the past. They are social bonds and work on a subtle level bringing the influence of ancestors, and the connection of the past is made explicit and expressed through ritual. Rituals all over the world are conservative in nature, and for it to be effective, a ritual must be done in the same way that it has been done previously, and the language is usually very conservative. Sanskrit is used for Hindu mantras and it is no longer spoken as a living language, until recently the Roman Catholic Church used Latin, the Russian Church uses old Slavic, old Egyptian is used in the Coptic Church of Egypt.

Rituals connects us with the performers of the original ritual, the primal act. The Feast of the Passover which is an important Jewish ritual refers to the first Passover when death swept through Egypt decimating the first-born of the Egyptians and their cattle. The Israelites had made a vicarious atonement sacrifice of a lamb instead of their first-born, and smeared their doors with the blood of the lamb, and they subsequently ate this Passover feast in celebration that they had been spared.

The Eucharist in the Christian Church has the same ritual tradition as the Passover, the death of Christ occurred at the Passover and the Last Supper was a Passover dinner, the body and blood of Jesus in the Eucharist refers back to the sacrificial lamb, Jesus is the Lamb of God, the *Agnus Dei* is said or sung before the eating of bread and the drinking of wine.

In the Book of Revelation, the pattern of the seven terminal curses to which the world will be subjected refer back to and are cross referenced to those great curses suffered by the Egyptians.

On 5 November is celebrated the Gunpowder Plot and the burning of the effigy of Guy Fawkes, but it is believed that this is connected to the great Celtic Festival of the Dead, Hallowe'en, when there was a crack in time and the living and the dead came together; 5 November is a displaced version of the Fire Festival.

There is a type of morphic resonance at work in the conservative nature of rituals, things done in the same way, using the same words and the same actions place people in morphic resonance with those who have done it before, and there will be a connection between the people doing the ritual now, and those who did it in the past, a tuning in so to speak which produces a feeling of continuity with the past.

There are within witchcraft, secret words and rituals which are never spoken of or referred to outside their immediate connection, and when I work magic or spells for people I warn them not to speak of it to anyone. 'To know, to dare, to will, and to keep silent.' This is a witchcraft maxim and it means, to possess the knowledge, to have the confidence and the courage to use it, to will it to happen (to do the spell) and not to talk about it, because discussing it dissipates the energy. Having agreed to use my ability on someone's behalf, I counsel them 'please do not tell anyone that I have done this for you, do not discuss it with anyone at any time and if it is successful never divulge how you acquired your desire. In short, forget that you wrote to me (or spoke to me).'

When we work within a circle as a coven the same rule applies, we work the spell, seal the articles we have used within an envelope and never refer to it again. If a photograph needs to be returned it is sent in a plain envelope without a covering letter.

In India, there are certain sacred phrases or mantras which when chanted possess a particular power to effect the state of consciousness and mind of people chanting them. They tune in the person to a tradition of people who have previously used the mantra; gurus initiate people into mantras, and these teachers have been initiated by other gurus; there is a lineage of transmission associated with meditative states, and if a guru has used the mantra and by it achieved a particular meditative state, then the disciple through the mantra will be able to achieve it.

If the mantra is revealed casually and outside the circumstances of its mystical use, it is believed that its force will be weakened. All religious traditions prohibit blasphemy, witches never reveal the true names of their Gods because, like the inappropriate use of a mantra, the inappropriate use of sacred words weakens their force and power. Sacred words are not just words, they are particular vibrations in the air associated with certain elevated states of mind and consciousness, and their morphic resonance has an attachment to a subconscious level.

A mantra in the Judaic, Christian and Islamic traditions is 'Amin' or 'Amen'. It is said to mean 'so be it', and is usually at the end of every psalm, prayer and *gloria*. It is the same word as the name of the great Egyptian God at the time when the Jews were in Egypt, Amen the great God of Karnack, Luxor and Tut-Ankh-Amen. Tutankamen is believed to have been named after that God. The Jews were there in Egypt building temples, is it perhaps coincidence that they are the same word? Muhyiddin Ibn Arabi, a twelfth-century mystic and saint once said, 'What is left to us from tradition is merely words, it is up to us to find out what the words mean.'

One of the main purposes of any religious or mystical pursuit is that of transformation, but it has little connection with acquiring a better life in this world, and does not involve using Buddhist chanting techniques to obtain a new Rolls-Royce car. Transformation for a Muslim Sufi, a Catholic or a Zen monk is a matter of delivering one's self into the possession of one's deity. Meister Eckhart explained it when he wrote, 'We must become as clear glass through which God can shine'; in the witch tradition, 'through which the Goddess can shine', and it involves surrendering aspects of the self which can feel like a little death.

A traditional witch has a dedication in life to the service and veneration of Our Lady the Great Mother of Many Names and

Many Forms, and of the God, Her Consort. This involves the cultivation of a style of approach to Life reflected in the Natures of the Goddess and the God who represent the ebb and flow of life and death and the ritual of the changing seasons of the earth which echo the changing seasons of our lives. The injunction of the Goddess is 'No other Law but love I know, by naught save love may I be known, for all things living are Mine own, from Me they come, to Me they go.'

Every culture and civilization has developed its own language, often religious and outwardly philosophical in the form of expression in an attempt to indicate the central core of meaning, the language is an attempt to translate into human comprehension things which cannot be fully translated into human comprehension, not a description but more as an indication.

It has been said that what distinguishes man from animals is the capacity to know that there is a reality beyond his own knowledge, he is the only creature who can be aware that there is more and can thus appreciate analogy as indication (rather than description, because description is impossible when it applies to absolute infinite reality), and he can develop forms of expression outside words to indicate that which lies beyond all language.

Symbolism is such a form of expression; symbols are universal, all religions possess them, often they express the inexpressible and there are many symbols used in witchcraft the most important of which is probably the triangle. Buckminster Fuller called it the 'fundamental building block of the universe'. It represents growth in many traditions and an understanding of it is the key to many mysteries, amongst them the riddle of the Sphinx and the pyramid as eternal life. Gurdjieff related it to the 'three holy forces' of creation and it is the basic Holy Trinity.

In its normal position with the apex uppermost it represents fire and the aspiration of all things towards the higher unity, the urge to escape from extension (signified by the base) into non-extension (the apex) or towards the Origin or the Irradiating Point. In this position, it is a symbol of the God of the Witches.

A triangle inverted (with the apex pointing downwards) represents the Great Goddess. Two complete triangles, one in the normal position and one inverted superimposed so as to form a six pointed star (called Solomon's seal), representing respectively, fire and water, constitute a symbol of the human soul. A triangle surmounted by horns was the Carthaginian symbol for the Goddess Tanit (or Tanith).

In the life of man the triad is seen as the primary force of growth, a triangle with the 'bindu' or spark of life in the centre is connected with the Triple Goddess ruling past, present and future. In Christian cosmology, life is seen as having emerged from the Unity of the Trinity representing three dimensions, breadth, depth and height.

The Roman Goddess Hecate had also the name of 'Three Ways', and at crossroads, her three-faced image received gifts of money, cake and fruit. Her ancient shrine the Trevi Fountain, continues to receive three coins in the fountain in the hope that one will be blessed with good fortune.

Among the ancient Arabs the trefoil or three-leafed clover was called '*shamrakh*', and was a symbol of the male trident of fertility. The ancient Irish God Trefuilngid was patron of the trefoil, he is known as the Triple Bearer of the Triple Key, a designation extended to Shiva, Astarte and Ishtar who were three ancient representations of the Triune Goddess.

In ancient Egypt the triangle was the symbol of Men-Nefer the ancient city goddess of Memphis, and worship of the Yantra was to establish a state of oneness with the Mother of the Universe in her forms as Mind, Matter and Life.

The Sumarian Ishtar was the Triune Goddess, Ishtar means star, and the Babylonian scriptures refer to Ishtar as the Light of the World, the Opener of the Womb, Forgiver of Sins, Lawgiver and Leader of Armies. It is from the legend of Ishtar that the story of the descent into the underworld enters so many of our traditions. In witchcraft the legend tells of how, being immortal, without beginning and without end, delighting in the beauties and the joy of life, the Goddess outlives her companions and watches them suffer and pass away. Despite her powers and abilities, she eventually arrives at a stage when life can no longer be embraced and enjoyed with the knowledge of its inevitable conclusion, and out of love and sorrow and compassion for the creatures of the Earth she descends into the underworld to search out Death himself and discover the reason for suffering. The giver of life overcomes the taker of life and rebirth emerges.

The triangle is the symbol of transformation, 'Know thyself' was the admonition of Apollo and the ancient Greek mystical philosophers, perhaps if we learn to understand the mind we will understand the universe. Meister Eckhart, the thirteenth-century Christian mystic, referring to the Holy Trinity said 'God laughed and begat the Son. Together they laughed, and begat the Holy Spirit. And from the laughter of the three, the Universe was born'.

In Islam there are said to be ninety-nine names of Allah, descriptions of his attributes, there is a hundredth, but only the camel knows the Hundredth Name of Allah and this is the reason for his supercilious countenance. Names possess power, they have their own vibration, the ancients believed that if a witch was in possession of a person's name she could work magic against him, and the Ancient Egyptians believed that their names were a reflection of their soul. The equation of name with character and destiny had its influence in descriptive names such as that of Osiris which means 'he who is at the top of the steps' (of evolution) or that of Arabia, signifying 'he who walks in silence'.

Names are important in witchcraft and upon initiation a witch takes a new forename which is normally used only within circle and magical activities. The individual chooses the name which reflects a rapport with a certain vibration and the name adopted is usually a pagan name.

In Subud, devotees receive a new name which is received on a spiritual level by their Spiritual Guide the late Pak Subuh. The new name indicates the nature of the person and the direction in which they should go. The initial letter of the name is very important, the shape of this letter has a special significance 'H' for instance is a well-balanced letter in an earthly and a spiritual sense.

The Mevlevi dervishes also receive a new name, usually an Arabic or Oriental name since all these names have a distinctive and spiritual meaning and often these names are adopted and used in every day life and the original given name discarded.

As I have written previously, the true names of the witches' God and Goddess are never revealed to outsiders, and only to witches who achieve a particular degree. One of the reasons is so that the True Names can never be used in blasphemy, and also because they contain a particularly evocative power.

Another important symbol in witchcraft is the sword which has its place in every magical ceremony. Its symbolic meaning is of a wound and the power to wound, and hence by association, liberty and strength. It is a masculine symbol and in megalithic culture the sword is the counterpart of the distaff which is the feminine symbol of the continuity of life. The sword and the distaff symbolize death and fertility and the sword is seen as a sign of physical extermination and psychic decision as well as of the spirit and the word of the God. A sword has the magic power to fight off the dark powers. The western type of sword with its straight blade is because of its shape a masculine symbol, some covens use an oriental sword which, being curved is lunar and feminine, and it is always a symbol of spiritual evolution and the transcendent all-conquering spirit.

In the ancient world, the Scythians used to make an annual sacrifice of several horses to the blade of a sword which they conceived as a god of war, and the Romans believed that iron, because of its association with Mars was capable of warding off evil spirits.

15 Major Festivals

As a result of my friendship with Edgar Peel, I was invited to the home of Robert Neill, famous for his historical novels, many with a witchcraft content, especially *Mist Over Pendle*. Robert Neill is now sadly deceased but at that time he and his sweet wife lived in a lovely house in the Lake District where I was made very welcome. He regarded me very curiously, here was a man who had spent a great part of his life writing fictional novels about witchcraft and now he was actually entertaining a real live witch.

The very idea seemed to amuse and excite him and he was positively ebullient in his close, but never intrusive, questioning about my life and activities as a witch. He was a small, nervous, quickly spoken man and sat in a chair which looked too large for him. He strongly believed in the powers of witchcraft and was fascinated by the unknown quality of the occult.

It was whilst we were conversing after tea, that I became strongly aware of the spirit presence in the room of a young man who wished to communicate with Robert Neill and his wife. He was most insistent that I should pass on his communications, and I, for some reason I could not quite define, was very reluctant to do so. Perhaps because it was a social occasion and I did not know the Neills very well, but the spirit form would not leave me and eventually I took a deep breath and conveyed what the young man was saying to me.

They both looked at me in a startled fashion and Mrs Neill paled, but neither said a word so I was unable to judge whether what I gave them was accurate though I felt that it was.

Robert Neill subsequently wrote another book, I think it was his last, called *Witchfire at Lammas*, he sent me an inscribed copy and wrote me that I had been the inspiration for the book.

I was not very surprised that he had chosen this title for the book since I remembered that he had been very interested in the celebrations of the four great festivals of witchcraft of which

Lammas or August Eve is one. Lammas is cross-quarter day and falls at 15 degrees Leo and it marks the beginning of the Harvest Season. The name is derived from the Anglo Saxon '*Hlaf-mas*', the time when the first corn is harvested. Ancient man saw the corn as an aspect of the life force, personified as the 'green man', a god figure which grows sturdy and strong through Spring and Summer and is cut down at harvest and then sleeps through Winter in the earth to return in the Spring, green again, this cycle was honoured by rituals and feasts.

It is interesting that King William Rufus was killed mysteriously in the year 1100 in the New Forest. Rufus as a memory is very dear to the hearts of witches and the name is a very popular one amongst the renaming ceremony of male witches. He has been regarded by scholars as a sacrificial victim, and a member of the Old Religion. It is recorded that he was shot in the eye by an arrow near an oak tree which has since disappeared due to vandalism over the years. A pillar was erected to mark the site in 1745, but this was also defaced and has been replaced by a memorial to him. He was apparently very popular with the peasant population but the Church despised him. There was a Druidic festival held around the beginning of August which was dedicated to Lugh the Celtic sun god. The Welsh version of this god, known as Llew, as told in the *Mabinogion* was murdered and then restored to life.

The celebration of Lammas in witchcraft is a very happy one. We give thanks for the warmth of the sun and the greenness of the earth and for the gifts of the earth presented as a harvest at this time. Lammas brings the first signs of Autumn when the sun is dying and its heat is in decline. Perhaps for our ancient ancestors this was a somewhat anxious time as they anticipated the colder months ahead and looked forward to Candlemas on February Eve when the coming of the Spring was celebrated. In the ancient world, Lammas was a major summertime festival of the Great Goddess of the grain, Ceres, Ops, Demeter or Juno Augusta who was the ruler of the harvest month of August.

Opposite the festival of Lammas was the Celtic Feast of Imbolg or Candlemas, and it is sometimes referred to as Groundhog Day, animals were said to come out of hibernation to provide predictions for the end of the winter. An old rhyme records,

> If Candlemas Day be fair and bright,
> Winter will have another flight,

> If Candlemas Day be shower and rain,
> Winter is gone and will not come again

To Roman pagans Candlemas was the day honouring Juno Februata as the virgin mother of Mars, when people carried candles burning in worship of this Goddess. It was a season considered sacred to women and to the Goddess of love. For witches Candlemas anticipates the Spring and the renewal of life which comes with the warmth of the Sun, and during the ceremony for Candlemas there is an invocation to the God thus:

> Dread Lord of Death and Resurrection, of Life and the Giver of Life, (Lord within ourselves, whose name is Mystery of Mysteries) encourage our hearts, let the Light crystallise itself in our blood fulfilling of us Resurrection, for there is no part of us that is not of the Gods ...

Candlemas was one of the old pagan festivals taken over by Christianity, and because it fell forty days after Christmas, it became the Festival of the Purification of the Virgin Mary, since, according to Judeo-Christian tradition, women must be purified after childbirth, an event which was considered to render mothers unclean. The Bibles specifies forty days of impurity after the birth of a son, and eighty days following the birth of a daughter. Females were considered to be twice as unclean as males. Women were not allowed to enter churches until they had been 'churched' which was the name for the ritual purification. To the best of my knowledge the practice of 'churching' has not actually ceased officially, but in these more enlightened times it is seldom carried out.

There is some evidence that a February festival was performed well before the Celts observed it. At Castlerigg in Cumbria, there is a Stone Age stone circle with so precise an alignment to sunrise at Candlemas, that it is difficult to believe it was a matter of chance.

May Eve, or Beltane, is the fourth great festival in witchcraft, and it is my personal favourite festival because it is a time of almost-Summer and there is a sense of excitement in the air. Nature is fully awake, the Earth is green with plants growing and flowering, birds are nesting and there is a feeling of anticipation of long Summer days and warm Summer nights ahead.

The Winter festivals are dedicated to the God of the witches, but the Summer festivals are for the Goddess and she is at her most glorious on May Eve. We give thanks for the warmth of the sun and the fecundity of the earth,

> We invoke and call upon Thee O Mighty Mother of us all, by seed and root, by stem and bud, by leaf and flower and fruit, by life and love do we invoke thee.

May Day itself was always celebrated in the countryside, there was the dance of the Morris men, and the foremost characters were Robin Hood, Will Scarlet, Maid Marion, the Fool in cap and bells, Little John and of course a hobby-horse. They are all symbols of early ceremonial magic, and the phallic symbol of the maypole around which girls danced weaving their coloured ribbons in and out, is of course pagan in origin. I recall as a small child dancing around the maypole and have a photograph of this event.

May is known as the Month of the Goddess, and the fertility connotations of the past had a link with the Roman games dedicated to the Goddess Flora held on 28 of April. It is an old tradition that the dew on May Day is good for the complexion, and in parts of Europe, it is the custom for girls to roll naked in the magical dew of May morning.

Amongst witches, the festival of the winter solstice is called Yule, an Anglo-Saxon word. According to Bardic tradition, the druids celebrated a Celtic festival when the Chief Druid cut mistletoe from the sacred oak tree; this plant is sometimes banned from Christian Churches at Christmas-time, due to its pagan associations but Pliny records that the Celts saw in mistletoe certain healing properties and they regarded it as a sacred plant. The wearing of a sprig was once thought to guard a person against witchcraft and it also was supposed to have aphrodisiac attributes which probably accounts for the popularity of kissing under mistletoe.

The Winter Solstice celebrated the return of the sun, and the idea of a festival to celebrate its rebirth was traditional in the ancient world. Inevitably Christianity adopted it and converted it into a Christian festival to represent the time of the birth of Christ. The Romans called the Winter Solstice Saturnalia and dedicated it to Saturn, an agricultural deity. The Romans like us gave presents, and the practice of hiding coins in the Christmas pudding was also inherited from them as they cast lots with items of food to determine the king of festival or lord of misrule.

The origin of the yule log was with the Saxons, and it holds an important symbolic meaning in witchcraft. During the ceremony the leader of the coven stands behind the cauldron in which a fire is burning and the members of the coven dance round her deosyl or sunwise with burning torches. It is called the Dance of the Wheel or Yule and its purpose is to 'cause the sun to be reborn'. The cauldron represents the womb of the Great Mother and the fire in the cauldron is the Sun-Child in her womb.

According to some scholars, the word 'Yule' comes from an old Norse word 'Iul' which means 'a wheel' and in the ancient world the year was regarded as turning as a wheel does. The spokes represent the old celebrations of equinoxes and solstices and the four main festivals of Candlemas, May Eve, Lammas and Hallowe'en.

At the witches' ceremony of the Winter Solstice a special incantation is used:

> Queen of the Moon, Queen of the Sun,
> Queen of the Heavens, Queen of the Stars,
> Queen of the Waters, Queen of the Earth,
> Who ordained to us the Child of Promise.
>
> It is the Great Mother who gives birth to him
> It is the Lord of Life that is born again,
> Darkness and tears are set behind
> And the star of guidance comes up early.
>
> Golden sun of hill and mountain
> Illumine the land, illumine the world
> Illumine the seas, illumine the rivers
> Grief be laid and joy be raised.
>
> Blessed be the Great Mother
> Without beginning, without ending
> To everlasting, to eternity
> Ivo Evoh! Blessed be!

On the opposite side of the wheel is the Summer Solstice when the cauldron is filled with water and wreathed with summer flowers. The leader of the coven, always a woman invokes the sun thus:

> Great One of Heaven, the Power of the Sun, we invoke thee in thy ancient names, Michael, Balin, Arthur, Lough, come

again into this our land and walk upon her high places as of old. Lift up thy Shining Spear of Light to protect us. Put to flight the powers of darkness. Give us fair woodlands and green fields, blossoming orchards and uprising corn. Bring us to stand upon the Hill of Vision and show us the Path to the lovely Realms of the Gods.'

Many primitive tribes believe that the Sun and the Moon, located on either side of the 'world axis' are the eyes of heaven and there are in existence prehistoric drawings and engravings which have been interpreted thus. In the ancient world it was considered that midsummer was a hazardous time during which evil spirits were active and witches rode to their Sabbat on toasting forks on a black three-legged horse. In parts of Yugoslavia they were supposed to attack Christians with tree stumps and so these weapons were safely disposed of beforehand. It was said that if a person sat in the church porch at midnight a procession of apparitions would pass into the church and that those who did not make a reappearance were destined to die in the following twelve months.

Young girls would gather yarrow from a man's grave and place it under their pillow on Midsummer Eve and this was said to produce the spirit or shade of a future husband. Fern seed gathered on Midsummer Eve had the ability to make men invisible. Shakespeare referred to this in *Henry IV*, 'We have the receipt of fern seed. We walk invisible.' It was also said to reveal treasure by giving off a blue glow in the earth. Belief in the magical powers of vegetation at Midsummer Eve was once common in the Middle East and throughout Europe too.

There is a common superstition that witches can make themselves invisible, but the truth of the matter lies in 'not being seen' rather than actually becoming invisible; the ability is dependent upon the individual power and the training of a witch.

The human brain is constantly projecting electrical impulses which impinge on the electrical fields of other individuals, thus making people aware of each other. The training consists of learning how to attenuate the electrical impulses and become so inconspicuous as to be able to walk slowly through a crowd of people without being noticed. I know that it is effective because I have done it.

Since the publication of *Witch Amongst Us* I have received

hundreds of letters. Most seek advice or magical help but others merely ask questions relating to the book, one such was from America.

> My first question is regarding being born a witch. Is every witch born knowing she/he is a witch? Or, could someone who is interested in witchcraft but has never noticed any great psychic ability or special powers study Wicca, develop their powers and become a witch? Must one know all their life that they have a special talent or can this be discovered later in life?

From my experience, it would appear that true-born witches exhibit early in their lives the powers of extra-sensory perception and other psychic abilities which they often find disturbing, and many report that from an early age they are drawn strongly to the natural world, to a love of and an affinity with animals and an implicit understanding of the Goddess element within them which makes them feel an alien in a religiously patriarchal-orientated environment.

I consider it possible with patience and serious endeavour to develop one's inherent psychic capacity, but the unfolding of this does not automatically make one a witch. A witch is a man or a woman who is born with a special power to work magic, to manipulate the forces around them and to control events at a distance. One can be taught how to manipulate and use this power but not how to develop it, the power is congenital and it eventually manifests in a variety of ways.

One witch of my acquaintance told me that she began to suspect she was a witch when she wished ill on someone who had upset her and her desire was fulfilled. 'I began to walk around in a state of neurotic benevolence towards everyone, because if I thought an unkind thought about someone, it would happen. Only when I discovered or was guided to you did I learn how to control this power.'

It seems entirely possible in my experience for the witch power to remain dormant until well into middle age and certain hormonal changes seem to have an influence on this. Another witch was during most of her adolescence aware of unseen forces around her which originated at pubescence. During her busy life she gave scant regard to them, but as she reached the menopause they re-surfaced and became stronger and she was overwhelmed to discover that she had the ability to only strongly envisage an occurrence in order to make it happen and it occurred on too many occasions for it to be mere coincidence.

Coincidence is said to be the alibi of the gods. Perhaps the answer in this particular case is that with the advent of the menopause and increased age, the tempo, and family responsibilities of this woman's life eased and she simply was able to give more attention to the more subtle emanations of her mind.

'My second question' wrote my correspondent from Methuen, USA, 'is regarding the coven. How does one distinguish a good coven (white) from a less than honourable (black) one? Are there any special points of 'red flags' [warnings] which one could look for when evaluating the purpose of a particular coven?'

An elementary precaution would be not to be tempted by advertisements in dubious occult magazines, these are often recruitment areas for so-called 'black' covens or Satanic activities. Generally speaking, it is usually very difficult to gain entry to a genuine coven, and converts are actively discouraged. The character and background of the people involved should be examined and their motives for offering initiation scrutinized. The occult world contains a variety of poseurs who seek to manipulate and gain power over sincere but misguided seekers, and multiply their own powers by vampirizing the natural resources of the weak-minded and unstable. There are many phoney and disreputable so-called 'witches' and 'covens' in various parts of the world, and the only way to steer clear of their dangerous and unsavoury activities is to treat any approaches with suspicion in the first instance and seek guidance from people known to be reputable.

My friend Sonya, whose views on most things are usually extreme, has some very strong opinions on counterfeit witches and covens and wrote to me thus:

> So, to be a witch is to be the most privileged of beings, by that I mean true born and not converted or pretending for kicks (usually by answering an advert!). Now there is nothing essentially wrong with the humans worshipping the Lady, but my feeling is that anyone who gets persuaded or pressurised into a so-called coven will probably join almost anything that is available – born-again Christians, Moonies, Scientology,

Mormons, Krishna, etc. Depends on their psychology. By and large, these converts to paganism are harmless and provided they do not bring the Craft into disrepute can be regarded with amused tolerance. The ones who incur my acute wrath are the decadent perverts who court the publicity of the gutter press and by associating themselves with the sisterhood deem us also to be orgiastic, Satan-worshipping, drunken, nymphomaniacs. Such people are an abomination.

I have never actually met another witch except for yourself, but then I keep myself to myself, although I have been approached by an occasional weirdo to either join or start a coven, but these persons have always been dismissed with the contempt they deserve.

She continues in typical Sonya fashion,

True born witches are extremely charismatic of course, intelligent, cultured, talented, eloquent and attractive, having the greatest of all gifts, that of Magic, the knowing, the Sight with a penchant for being easily offended and unpredictable in their actions. Secretive and Stealthy they are gifted in the art of being one step ahead of the humans, it is a rare human indeed who can outwit them.

Sonya does have this inclination to refer to all non-witches as 'mere humans'!

16 Questions on Witchcraft

A further question from my American correspondent was, 'My third question is regarding the practice of Wicca. Must one be part of a coven to practise or can one do it alone. I understand that one's scope of power is probably increased when exposed to a coven but is it absolutely necessary or required?' It has been said amongst witches that the practise of the Craft is not so much a question of learning as of remembering. This presupposes a belief in reincarnation and a conviction that one was a witch in a previous life and will continue to be a witch in subsequent lives.

Sonya expressed some views on this when she wrote to me, 'Unless you have changed your opinions over the years of our friendship, then we still disagree on one of the basic tenets of our beliefs – that of reincarnation – I have never understood how this could be so, how else could you be a true-born witch if you had never been born before? Once a witch, always a witch, over many lifetimes.'

There exist very rare individuals who maintain that their memory remains extant through various lifetimes and it is not necessary for them to relearn and rediscover their powers as a witch, I have encountered several such women, they live quiet, solitary, self-contained lives and practise the Craft alone having no desire to be part of a coven. History records numerous such women, and they were often persecuted as witches simply because they did live alone. They were the wise women of their time combining the duties of medical adviser, midwife, and confessor, knowledgeable in the virtues of herbs and potions, the dispensers of wisdom and psychotherapy. In the history of witchcraft there is more evidence of solitary witches than of the activities of covens.

I consider that it is advantageous to work as a member of a coven because this gives access to combined knowledge and experience in the working of magic, quite apart from the association with people of similar outlook. More magical power is available in a coven, and for witches endeavouring to unfold their psychic abilities the help and guidance of a more advanced teacher is of inestimable value.

> 'My fourth question', wrote my American correspondent, 'is regarding compensation for your services. I noticed throughout your book that you never accepted compensation for helping people. Is this common practice amongst white witches? Could one's gift be diminished or taken away for accepting compensation for helping others? Most known witches (or people involved in psychic sciences) in the US will not give you any notice unless something green [money] is flashed in front of their faces.'

When I was initiated and trained in my first witch coven some thirty years ago, I was taught idealistically that witches do not accept reward for the magical work they do for people; the powers were given to witches in order that we could aid humanity and that if we exercised our gifts with humility, altruism and compassion, the Gods would ensure that we received sufficient for our needs.

It is probable that in times past when the village wise woman practised her art, the barter system obtained and the witch would be glad to receive a chicken or a stack of wood for her fire. Today, I think that it depends on the attitude of the individual witch as to whether she expects compensation for her work, and whether she herself believes that her gift will be diminished or withdrawn if she accepts money.

There is an enormous amount of time, energy and effort involved in the working of magic, and some of the problems presented are convoluted, and the actual deliniation of them exhausting. Many people insist on a personal consultation and have a deep psychological need to discuss their worries and despair endlessly. A witch is often expected to be a combination of psychiatrist, psychotherapist, sex-therapist, priest-confessor, marriage guidance counsellor and solicitor, and I can see no reason why a consultancy fee should not be accepted. Most specialists require payment for their services, and a witch is a specialist in her own field.

Everyone needs shelter, food and clothing, and psychic consultants such as clairvoyants, tarot readers and healers often have no other source of income. I am surprised when people complain to me that they have been to visit a healer and were charged a fee. Some healers give their services free of charge, others ask for free will offerings, and some make a specific sum as remuneration. We live in a material world and a labourer is worthy of his hire.

Having said that, there are ruthless and greedy people in the occult world as in any sphere of life, people who are prepared to exploit misery and despair. Care, common sense and judgement need to be exercised before parting with enormous sums of money for so-called 'initiations' into covens, spells, potions, or other occult work, in short – '*caveat emptor*' ('let the buyer beware').

'My last and perhaps most important question is regarding the 'power' behind white and black witchcraft. I have noticed that there seem to be many similarities between white witchcraft and black witchcraft (i.e. symbols, alphabet, rituals, etc.)'. So, continued my American correspondent, 'Where does the power for white witchcraft come from? Is it from the same source as for black witchcraft, except that the power is used differently? In other words, do both forms of witchcraft derive their powers from Satan? If you strip away all the symbols, rituals, beliefs and so on from both white and black witchcraft, is the power or source behind each craft the same?'

The energy itself is physical and emotional and derives from mental and spiritual power, which is in itself neutral and can be used for good or ill depending on the mind and will of the operator. In white witchcraft we believe that the power emanates from the minds and bodies of the witches, and as a result of certain rituals combined with mental and concentrative techniques there is coalescence and direction. There is also additional power through invocations to the guardians of the circle in which we work and from the Gods we worship.

The power is comparable to ordinary muscular power which can be used for good or evil; someone at a risk of his own life may dive in the sea and save a drowning man, he could also, using similar muscular force, mug an old lady and steal her handbag. The methods are the same, but the motives are different, compassion inspires one, callousness the other. So it is with mental and spiritual abilities, we can use them for good or for evil. Everything that can be used for good can be used harmfully, electricity wrongly used can be lethal, used correctly it is of great benefit to mankind.

In the tradition to which I belong there is no connection with diabolism in any shape or form, the Devil or Satan is a Judaic/Christian symbol for evil which has no meaning for pagans. To the uninitiated it may seem that the symbols, alphabet, rituals are the same, but there is a difference and Satanism is something quite separate and divorced from witchcraft; unfortunately the term 'witchcraft' has been used as a blanket expression for all these types of occult activity.

Satanists are often highly intelligent but disturbed individuals who derive satisfaction and pleasure from the worship of the Devil in whom they believe, because it follows that they must have a strong belief in him in order to worship him, and they obviously enjoy the development of the dark side of their nature and the cultivation of deliberate evil and corruption, they perhaps seek a short cut to power but I do not pretend to understand their motives.

However, my friend Sonya who likes to be regarded as a black witch is not a Satanist, she merely uses her psychic forces for purposes different from those of my own or other witches of my acquaintance, and whilst one may choose to deplore such actions, she views her functions differently. It is worth mentioning that if one can catch her in an unguarded and pleasant mood, she is capable of generous and helpful motivation. She is in some ways eccentric, but she is intellectual, cultured, articulate, eloquent and well-read, and she is her own woman, caring nothing for the opinion of the world and not beyond attacking me if she feels inclined. Disparaging my hesitancy regarding the theory of reincarnation, she wrote:

> I think you must have been (in a previous life) one of those mealy-mouthed self-negating Christians, all that stuff about white witchcraft, as you know my feelings on that I scarcely need to repeat my contention that magic is neither black nor white, the power is neutral, and what pray is the purpose of being of the élite if one does not exercise the power in any way one sees fit? No one but ourselves judges our actions and if the power is not used and regenerated it atrophies and we become as the humans. Why would the Lady bestow her power on her daughters if not to be used to its fullest potential (incidentally, I do not, and never have regarded any male as being a witch, merely as consorts, but then I also think witches should be celibate to conserve their psychic energy,

another point on which we disagree.)

I don't understand Christianity or Islam when compared to the gentleness and autonomy of our religion. Who ever heard of a pagan making a holy war? The humans are so self-orientated as if mankind were the most important creation on this planet, what arrogance. The Mother makes no such distinction, in her eyes everything that lives and breathes and has its being is all part of the great nurturing at her bountiful breast. We, of the Old Religion, are the guardians of this beautiful earth, we are no less than the gods and no greater than the smallest creature.

What does it matter if humanity is obliterated as a result of its greed and immorality, so long as the planet and all its myriad life forms survives and thrives? What has mankind ever done for the nourishment of this Earth, but raped plundered, pillaged and destroyed all in the name of its greater glory, greed and lust for power, usually called progress. Look what has been done in the name of its Gods, the Crusaders, the Inquisition, the Conquistadors, even the missionaries who destroyed indigenous religions which had given happiness and prosperity to primitive races for centuries and converted them to their self negating beliefs, what a catalogue of cruelty, bloodshed and intolerance is in the history of orthodox religion.

No one can condemn us, we have nothing to be ashamed of, we have only ever tried to defend ourselves and our religion against the onslaught of the patriarchal invaders who saw only evil in our gentle Lady and her horned consort.

The humans should know that we are not wrinkled, wart-ridden hags, dressed in filthy rags, living in stinking hovels and brewing up noxious potions in cauldrons. It is more likely that we are civilised ladies with neat cottage gardens growing wild flowers and herbs, giving elegant dinner parties, listening to Bach on compact disc and usually wearing jeans and green wellies!

During question time, after I have lectured on witchcraft, I am sometimes asked rather coyly, and usually by a man, if it is true that witches work naked, and periodically when the press resurrect the subject of witchcraft, a theme perpetually fascinating, there are startling newspaper headlines, and eye-popping descriptions of devil-worshippers and their nude sexual orgies.

Throughout the pagan world, nudity was accepted as part of magical and religious rituals; the pagans desired to feel close to and at one with nature, and the freedom of nudity lent itself to this desire. In Ancient Persia, young women rose early and danced naked in the dawn, and according to Pliny, the women of the ancient British Isles performed their religious devotions naked. There is an ancient belief that a woman can be cured of barrenness by dancing naked in her vegetable garden on Midsummer Eve, a day, which incidentally is one of the Sabbats of witchcraft.

In a book called *Aradia* or *The Gospel of the Witches* by C.G. Leland, the witches, followers of Diana were instructed that they should be naked at their rituals as a sign that they were truly free, and with this injunction in mind some covens today practice their rituals in the nude, but not all.

Many wear traditional magical robes which are kept specifically for use in the magic circle, they are often handmade and beautifully embroidered, and the colour chosen by the individual witch often reflects major colours in the wearer's aura.

One of the reasons for working naked was the belief that power emanated from body pores, and the wearing of a robe would impede it, but this has been disproved. Witches who work naked do so because they feel comfortable that way, and not for any reason of sexual titillation, although I am aware that some people may find this difficult to believe. I have never heard of any sexual orgies within such covens. Most members are married couples and it seems rather pointless to gather in a circle for magical and religious rituals and then waste time and energy on an orgy.

I once asked Sonya if she worked naked and she was outraged, 'Certainly not!' she said, bestowing a withering look on me, 'It is completely unnecessary.' Sonya is very Victorian in her outlook.

Whether witches work naked or robed, it has been found that within a magic circle, energy is intensified, and one reason may be the use of lighting solely by candles as these are known to give off negative ions and are stimulating in much the same way as are showers, compared to baths.

I am often asked what function men have in what basically

appears to be a purely feminine society, and I repeat that women raise the power and men act as an earth for it. Sometimes male witches are referred to as warlocks, but this is not strictly correct as the word warlock is a Scottish term, nor is the word wizard really applicable though it means a wise man, the word witch can be directed at either a man or a woman.

Because there are three degrees in witchcraft, I am sometimes asked if there is any similarity between the rituals of Masonry and witchcraft, and some witches who are also Freemasons have asserted that there are similarities in the various initiation ceremonies, and the three degrees have a resemblance to the degrees of Freemasonry, Entered Apprentice, Fellow Craftsman and Master Mason. It is there, however, that I think the similarity ends. Freemasonry at its most ancient is a male-dominated organization and compared with witchcraft is more dogmatically orientated.

I was once asked during a radio phone in, 'if witches can work magic, why is there so much suffering and misery in the world, and could not witches work to change this?' I seem to recall my answer was that there were very few genuine witches in existence, and though we worked within the framework and our capability to aid individuals who approached us, our number is insufficient to affect world events, but that 'it is better to light one little candle than to curse the darkness'.

Witches traditionally have the ability to fly through the air on a broomstick, and whilst any intelligent person realizes that such a thing is impossible, nevertheless, I am still asked questions about the origin of this legend, somewhat wistfully at times, as if the questioner would like to think that such a thing could have been possible in the dim, distant past.

I have written elsewhere that the earliest account of broomsticks say nothing of levitation, but there are suggestions that upon initiation witches were blindfolded and smeared with a toxic flying ointment consisting of foxglove (*digitalis*) to accelerate the pulse, aconite to numb the feet and hands, and belladonna, cowbane or hemlock to confuse the senses. The novice's face was fanned and when she could no longer feel her feet on the ground, the other witches would cry loudly:

Horse and hattock
Horse and go

Horse and pellatis
Ho, ho ho.

This is sometimes carried out upon initiation in present day covens, mainly in a light-hearted fashion and it is not a part of any ritual.

It is recorded that prior to their journey by broomstick, stave, fork or on the backs of demons in animal forms, witches smeared their bodies and the object on which they were to ride, with a magical ointment. A number of writers in the sixteenth and seventeenth centuries described the recipes of flying ointments, and they all contained extracts from poisonous plants. The most common ingredients were aconite, deadly nightshade, hemlock and grease, dramatically described as the boiled marrow and fat of unbaptized babies.

Other ingredients mentioned were cinquefoil, sweet flag, poplar leaves, the blood of bats or lapwings, parsley, soot and some sort of oil if human fat was omitted. Learned opinion was never, quite decided as to whether witches actually flew, or only imagined that they did, and some held that the witches' confessions of flight were merely vivid dreams or hallucinations. In my grimoire there is a story by Nider in *Formicarius* dated 1517 which suggested that flying dreams might be caused by a magical ointment and quotes the experiences of a woman who anointed herself with an unguent whilst sitting in a kneading-trough; she slept and dreamed that she was flying and shook the trough so much that she fell out of it injuring her head.

It is known that the poisons in flying-ointments would produce strong psychological effects, especially if rubbed into broken skin, for instance scratches or insect bites. Aconite causes irregular action of the heart, hemlock and belladonna produce excitement and delirium, and a combination of these drugs would cause delusions, which, in most cases would account for confessions of magical flight.

It is possible that the story of witches riding on broomsticks arose because someone once saw witches leaping up and down on poles in a cornfield performing sympathetic magic, the intention being that the higher they jumped, the higher the corn would grow. One can imagine some peasant staggering home in his cups observing this ritual and believing that he was actually seeing witches flying.

When my eldest son was about twelve years of age, he was

subject to bronchial asthma, which he subsequently outgrew, but during one attack he was treated with a drug which shall be nameless and described to me a strange experience.

I walked into his bedroom one afternoon to check on his condition, and he awoke suddenly and said in a frightened voice, 'Oh, Mummy, I have been flying! I saw my body lying on the bed and just sailed through the window and over the housetops and landed on top of the war memorial in the town; I watched the traffic through my feet. I got scared and wished I was home and found myself on the pavement looking at my bedroom window. I just wished I was in bed again when you came in and woke me.'

I reported this experience to his doctor and the drug was changed, and I have often wondered if the original plant of which the drug was a derivative was associated with witches and their reports of flying.

Traditionally, the witches' besom or broomstick on which they were reputed to fly is made of ash stake, birch twigs and osier binding; the birch twigs are regarded as being a protection against evil spirits, which when expelled are likely to be caught in the twigs. The ash stake is a defence against drowning, apparently witches were supposed to be rendered harmless when detached from their besoms and thrown into water. The osier binding was in honour of one of the aspects of the witches' Goddess Hecate, the triple Moon Goddess.

The besom has its place in certain witchcraft rituals, and most witches own at least one besom. The broom or besom is actually the symbol of woman as a pitchfork is a male symbol. I can remember as a child visiting a northern town and seeing a broomstick propped against the door of one of my aunt's neighbours. She apparently did this when she went out and an alternative was to push the broom up the chimney with its end sticking out at the top.

It was superstitiously believed that witches left their homes via the chimney. In Yugoslavia, according to one of my friends who was born there, muskets were fired in the air as a defence against flying witches at Hallowe'en, and billhooks were scattered on the ground so that, should a witch become unseated, she would have an uncomfortable landing.

Aside from its associations with witches, ancient legends abound with the stories of broomsticks, also some not so ancient.

In the north of England, 'living over the broomstick' was a euphemism for a couple living together without benefit of clergy, and it is reported that a Dutch admiral once hoisted a broom on his masthead which was a symbol of his intention to sweep English ships from the oceans of the world.

17 *Healing and a Visitation*

A large proportion of the letters I receive consist of requests for healing and these always receive priority. Although I am not personally healing-orientated the other members of my coven are powerful projectors of a healing force and I am always prepared to contribute my own psychic energy from a sense of compassion and caring for the suffering of others. Healing rituals consist basically of a transfer of vital energy from thirteen strong and healthy individuals to a person depleted by pain and illness. As with all magical rituals we perform, we require links with the patient, a lock of hair, a picture and a sample of handwriting. A spot of blood on a piece of blotting paper would produce a vigorous direct link but most people are too squeamish to prick a finger deliberately and I therefore never ask for this.

The method used in healing is one of clear visualization of the person in perfect health, the power is raised, concentrated and directed. I am sometimes asked how the healing rituals performed by witches differ from those of divine or Spiritualist healers, and the answer is that all healing comes from the same source it is merely tapped in a different way. Witches work as a group and use concentrated energy forces directed at a patient over a distance, we seldom give contact healing individually and I am referring now to my own group. There have been only a few occasions in my entire life when I have felt inspired to give contact healing and these were immediately incredibly successful. I use these words advisedly, since whilst we are gratified always to learn of improvement in a patient's condition, we do not automatically attribute it to our own efforts as it could be due to a variety of factors. What is important is that suffering is relieved, not who is responsible for relieving it.

Many of the cases referred to me are of illnesses for which medical science has no cure and a person is told that he must live with it. I can imagine nothing worse than enduring constant pain without relief, such suffering colours the whole of existence. One such letter came from an elderly widowed lady with multiple sclerosis; she said that she could cope with this but in addition had intense pain continuously when sitting or standing and could only find relief when lying down. She told me that doctors could offer her no help and she was desperate and would commit suicide if only she could think of a way to do it. I responded immediately to her need and at the earliest opportunity we worked as a group to relieve her of her pain.

One of my husband's friends complained that since the age of seventeen he had endured constant pain in his back and my husband suggested he should visit me, although he is aware that I do not consider myself to be a particularly proficient healer. This was one of my rare inspired occasions. I gave this man contact healing and from that moment on, if he is to be believed, his backache vanished never to return.

Another of my friends was given surgery for an ovarian cyst, and when the incision was made it was discovered that the cyst was malignant which indicated a hysterectomy (surgical removal of the womb). My friend is continental, highly emotional and volatile at the best of times and to recover from an anaesthetic and be told that she would have to undergo another major operation was traumatic in the extreme. She telephoned me from the hospital in a state of great agitation. She wept and sobbed and my heart went out to her. I longed to be there to comfort her. I did the next best thing, I talked to her quietly and calmly and told her that I would help her to bear this latest catastrophe and that things would turn out well. She said to me, 'Oh Lois, I am so scared, I don't want to die! Please help me.'

That night there was a gathering of my coven. I already possessed a photograph of my friend, even if I had not we could have worked without it because the most important element in the working of magic was already present, and that element was love. We asked that my friend should be surrounded by an aura of peace and tranquillity and quiet assurance, that she should be relieved of all tension and anxiety and uplifted in spirit.

The next day she telephoned me again from the hospital. She told me that she had felt wretched and worried all day and had hardly ceased crying; she continued in her accented English, '... and then I was sitting in bed at about ten o'clock when suddenly I began to feel very calm and peaceful and as I looked around me it seemed as if a golden light was shining around my bed and I knew that everything would be all right.'

I had not told her that we would be working for her that night. Although she is aware that I am a witch she attaches little importance to the fact and never refers to it. Neither did I ever inform her that we had sought to soothe and calm her fears. We had been successful and that was all that was important. The hysterectomy was performed and today, many years later, there has not been any metastasis.

An interesting observation I have made is that whilst spells for prosaic matters appear to take an average of ten days to produce effects, healing from a distance seems to be almost instantaneous. I was approached by a woman I knew slightly and asked if I could send healing to her three-year-old son who had developed asthmatic attacks. She had recently given birth to another child by Caesarean section and had not yet fully recovered from the operation. She was very tired and found it exhausting to cope with her son's attacks as well as caring for a young baby.

We immediately carried out a healing ritual and I telephoned her three days later to enquire about the progress of her son. She told me that three days earlier he had started to improve greatly. Whilst carrying out the ritual, I had received a clairvoyant impression that the asthma was psychosomatic caused by the sudden appearance of his sibling and that it would clear up quite quickly once he had accustomed himself to the presence of another child in the house. I urged her to give him extra attention and love so that he would not be jealous of the new baby.

One of the questions I am asked is whether faith is necessary for healing to be efficacious and the healing of this child would indicate that it is not; there have been many other cases when I have been asked to give healing to people who are unaware that they are receiving it and good results have been obtained. Although in our healing rituals we contribute a part of our own energy we are only the instruments through which the healing power passes *en route* to the patient and we can only work within the framework of natural laws, we cannot reverse the dissolution of the body as a result of the ageing process although we can hopefully reduce the pain that ageing often brings.

Sadly, some of my mail now includes letters from AIDS victims, haemophiliacs who were infected with the virus as a result of blood transfusions. Whilst we are always prepared to try to help anyone in need, I always insist that people should consult their own doctors and obtain the best orthodox medical treatment in addition to anything that my group can do for them.

Some of my most harrowing correspondence comes from people with a terminal illness, who, knowing that they have only a short time to live, seek reassurance and comfort from me that death is not the end of their existence and that a greater life continues in another sphere. They probe me concerning the experiences I wrote of in *Witch Amongst Us* when as a young nurse I observed the spirits of the dead who manifested at the bedside of my dying patients, and they ask me if I still encounter such visions.

Since I am no longer an active member of the nursing profession, I am not often in the presence of the dying unless they happen to be members of my own family and at such times there is naturally a high degree of personal grief and emotion involved. Nevertheless, I still function on that psychic and spiritual frequency and am able to observe the activity on a subtler level as the spirit is released.

I reiterate to my correspondents in letters and in personal counselling my experiences of the past, and of those which have occurred more recently when I have been involved with the dying.

My father-in-law became very ill and was taken into hospital and one evening whilst visiting him I became aware of his etheric or spirit body slightly separated from the physical. It resembled a silver opaque shadow against his pillows and he looked at me with a piercing gaze as if he could read in my mind what I could see. My husband, despite his father's serious illness, was optimistic of his eventual recovery and voiced to me that perhaps he would soon be home. I said to him, 'I think you should try to accept that this will not be so.' Eight hours later, my father-in-law died.

Whilst visiting an elderly lady in hospital, I was happily gossiping with her and only idly glanced at the other side of the ward. Gathered around the bed of another elderly patient who appeared to be sleeping, I observed several spirit forms, two women and a man. Distrusting the evidence of my eyes, I looked away and then back again. They were still there, ethereal and vaporous and glowing with a light that was not of this world. I excused myself and went out of the ward into the reception area where at a desk a woman doctor was reading some notes. 'Excuse me,' I said hesitantly and very quietly, 'that patient in the second bed, I think she is dying.' The doctor looked up at me in a startled fashion and hurried into the ward and to the bed I indicated. She examined the woman and within seconds two nurses came into the ward and removed the patient into a side ward whilst the doctor looked at me curiously.

Towards the end of her long life, my only sister suffered several cerebral thromboses which robbed her of her mobility and eventually her speech, and although with the help of speech therapy she was able to speak again, it was never with the same lucidity as formerly. She had always been a very active and independent person and constantly rebelled against her invalid condition and longed to die. She particularly hated being in hospital for long periods and railed against it. One day she told me tearfully that our mother had appeared to her and said 'Now Betty, you have to try to settle down here.' She never did. I realized yet again that the so-called dead are still aware of our trials and tribulations in the flesh and attempt in every possible way to mitigate them and to support us.

Eventually my sister reached the end of her troublous and painridden life, and as I sat by her bed as she lay unconscious, easing her way to the final stages of release and listening to her laboured breathing, I had a vision. I saw her etheric body slowly exteriorizing, and behind her, slightly misty but suffused with a vibrant golden light was a narrow river and on its far bank were members of my family; my parents and my brothers I recognized first; they were younger and more vital than I remembered them, and yet in some strange way it was possible to discern that they were of different generations. There were other people there also whose countenances I remembered only vaguely from photographs, never having known them in the flesh. I recall being surprised to see a nephew who had died as a young child, a man now and obvious with his deep auburn-coloured hair.

They appeared happy, and there was an air of expectancy about them, as if they were awaiting with barely concealed impatience, the arrival of someone. I was very much aware of the naturalness of the vision, they moved and talked and smiled at each other, and prevailing always, was the sense of expectancy. I remember thinking to myself that it was like any family awaiting the arrival of someone greatly loved, from a long and tiring journey. In the background I had the impression of a green landscape and amongst it were what appeared to be buildings, radiating multi-coloured hues like the flashes of colour in a beautiful opal.

The vision endured for only about thirty seconds, but I was intensely comforted and felt that it had been vouchsafed to me to reassure me that my sister's passage was a natural one from my love to the love of those waiting for her in the next stage of her voyage, and when she slipped quietly away, in the midst of my grief was a sense of rejoicing that her sufferings were over and that she was reunited with all those she had loved in the past and been separated from for so long.

Some weeks later, whilst attending a conference, a strange woman approached me and said, 'I have to tell you this, the spirit form of a woman has been with you all evening. She says that she is your sister and wants you to know that she is very happy. She is showing you her hands, particularly her nails and says you will understand the meaning of this gesture.' I did. Each time I had visited my sister in hospital I had taken the opportunity to give her a manicure since the nurses were always busy and the last thing they ever had time to do was manicure patients' nails. 'In addition,' the woman continued, 'your sister is patting her hair, does that have a particular meaning to you?' It did. My sister was extremely fussy about the state of her hair and became depressed if it was not dressed exactly as she liked it.

When I write to or counsel the terminally ill and the bereaved, I do it within the framework of their own religious beliefs. They are not interested or concerned with my personal beliefs, only with my psychic and spiritual perception which reveals to me knowledge and experiences denied to most other people to the same degree.

Life is for the greater part hard, cruel and bitter and none of us escape sorrow or suffering but it is all that we have until death releases us and most of us require a belief in a divine omnipotent Being in order to try to make sense of our pathetic situation, even if we only reach what D.H. Lawrence called 'the separate darkness of man's love for the present unknowable God'.

I long ago became impatient of any religion which claimed a monopoly of truth; truth is but a many-faceted diamond reflecting the heartfelt longings in all of us for security, peace and surety. What we believe is far less important than what we do, to ourselves and to each other. Our beliefs can change with time but our actions are the fruit of our belief or unbelief, and endure.

Krishnamurti maintained that 'the constant assertion of belief is an indication of fear' and most human beings fear death whether they acknowledge it or not; death is a taboo subject in our culture, we sensibly spend our lives and our energies in an effort to avoid this final, inevitable confrontation.

So what do I tell the terminally ill and the bereaved who seek me out for comfort and consolation? I relate to them my experiences with the dying and the so-called dead. I speak of my visions and of knowledge gleaned from the Ancient Wisdom, and that I am persuaded that nothing happens by chance, that all our days are numbered and that no one dies before their time on earth is completed.

There is a story in Islam concerning the Islamic Angel of Death, Azraïl,

> The Angel of Death passing once by Solomon in a visible shape, and looking at one who was sitting with him, the man asked who he was, and upon Solomon's acquainting him that it was the Angel of Death, said, 'He seems to want me; wherefore order the wind to carry me from hence into India', which being accordingly done, the angel said to Solomon, 'I looked so earnestly at the man out of wonder, because I was commanded to take his soul in India and found him with thee in Palestine'.

It is many years since my mother died, and a few months before her death when she was in apparent good health, she wrote and also spoke to me about several visitations she had experienced in her bedroom during the night. She referred to the spectre as an angel, of masculine appearance and dressed in a white robe. He appeared in a dazzling golden light of such intensity that it suffused the whole bedroom and caused her to awaken. During the first visit the angel simply stood by her bed and looked at her with a gaze of such infinite love and compassion that she was overcome with tears. 'My heart seemed to swell inside me,' she wrote, 'and I felt no fear at all.'

Ever the practical one I asked her, 'Why didn't you enquire who he is?'

On the second occasion she awoke to find the angel prosaically sitting on her bed, again he bestowed on her a look of utter tenderness, and mindful of my words this time she was constrained to ask in wondering tones 'Who are you?'

My mother was never one for wordy descriptions but she described his voice as 'deep and resonant' as he replied 'I am your guardian angel'. I asked her how he departed and she told me that he simply melted away into a mist which itself then disintegrated.

Once more in a practical way I told her, 'Ask him why he comes to you.' On the third occasion she told me that she woke to the sound of the most beautiful music she had ever heard. 'It is impossible to describe, it was not music of this world' and again the angel was standing by her bed smiling at her gently. He stretched out a hand to her as she asked him, 'What do you want with me.'

Incredibly he replied, 'You are almost at your journey's end, do not be fearful, I am coming to take you home.'

The average person would have been petrified to experience such night-time encounters but my mother was quite psychic and spiritually orientated and she was not in the least bit afraid, nor did the angel's information dismay her. She was in her seventies and weary of the effort of life and she looked forward with eager anticipation to a better world and reunion with all her lost loved ones.

'Lois,' she wrote to me, 'it seems that I am going to die soon, but I shall not be alone when I do and you must be happy for my release and not grieve or you'll hold me back in my progress, and when you die, be assured I will be the first one to greet you.'

I still have that letter, and she did die shortly afterwards, within three months to be exact. I have described her death and her promise to return to me and the fulfilment of that promise elsewhere in *Witch Amongst Us*.

So what are we to make of my mother's fulgent visitations, only a few months before her death? She was a very honest person, not given to flights of fancy or a vivid imagination; she was also a deeply religious woman, not in a churchy sense but inasmuch as she prayed a great deal for strength, help and healing, doubtless her prayers raised her consciousness and she was enabled to clearly perceive the spiritual presence which was sent to comfort her.

I have never doubted her veracity and in fact over the years since her death, reports of similar experiences from correspondents have reached me.

In *Witch Amongst Us*, I wrote of the sudden death of my eldest brother John due to a fall from a high building when I was four years old and my subsequent sighting of him in the garden which was the beginning of my psychic perception.

His wife Ellen survived him by many years and when she was confined to hospital during her final illness, nurses reported that she kept trying to get out of bed to follow someone. She told my mother that at times she could see John, he called her name and beckoned her to go with him. Another example of the so-called dead attending the death-bed of a loved one.

Many of the people who visit or write to me express fear concerning the actual moment of death, and I tell them that from the many communications I have received, and the spiritual contacts I have made, the moment of death is described as being quite painless and strangely pleasant.

Some years ago a close friend was killed in a motor-cycle accident when he crashed into a concrete bridge support on a slippery road. He died instantly, and when I heard the news I agonized over the pain he must have felt on impact, however transitory.

He communicated with me quite soon after his death and conveyed the words,

> I felt nothing, Lois, seconds before impact I was taken from my body. I was very puzzled to be looking down on my mangled flesh and yet there I was quite whole and unharmed. It took me a little while to realise I had not survived the crash, there was great activity and people rushing around, police and an ambulance and I could not understand what all the fuss was about until my father appeared beside me and took me away from the scene; believe me, I felt no physical pain.

Another friend who had suffered several heart attacks described to me an incident which occurred after the third. He was being nursed in the intensive care ward of his local hospital. He was resting on the bed and said that he felt quite well but rather sleepy, and he decided to close his eyes and have a quiet nod when suddenly there was a great disturbance and doctors and nurses came rushing in the ward and around his bed, ministering to him.

The nurse who had been in charge of the monitor in the next room had observed that from the screen, my friend's heart-beat was gradually slowing down and he reported, 'You were dying.' My friend opined that it was a very pleasant and peaceful sensation and that he would never again fear death.

18 When an Animal Dies

Many of the despairing letters I receive are from people who have been obliged to have an animal destroyed due to age or illness, and there can be few of us who, having loved and been owned by a pet, have not asked ourselves at the end of its too short life, whether animals survive death. I am persuaded that they do, although any evidence I can personally produce will be necessarily subjective and possibly regarded by some as slightly mawkish or whimsical. Nevertheless it is a subject upon which many people dwell.

Science teaches that matter cannot be destroyed it only changes form and although most orthodox religions scorn to consider the survival of animals Spiritualist literature has numerous examples of pets returning at direct voice séances and actually making their presence known vocally, and mediums often describe a deceased animal at public or private meetings. John Galsworthy wrote in *The Inn of Tranquillity*, 'If we have spirits that persist, they have; if we know after our departure who we were, they do'. We are apt to recoil before the magnitude of the vision, in the words of Milton, 'of millions of creatures walking the earth unseen both when we wake and when we sleep' but traditional ancient wisdom teaches that individual animals are redeemed by human love and survive as entities in their own right; the lower order of animals revert to a group soul of their species from which they are eventually reborn.

For fifteen years I had a very special friend. If she was not my familiar, she was most certainly my shadow. Nana was a mixture of various breeds with a distinct personality of her own, she was a gentle loving dog possessing a great deal of personal dignity and she was also a perfect lady, her manners were impeccable and it was never necessary to teach her anything. I always suspected that she was merely one step below a human being in evolution. She could be teased and would deign to be playful at times, but when she decided that she had pandered sufficiently to us she would bestow a withering look and stalk off purposefully in the direction of her basket. She considered it her natural entitlement and duty to accompany me everywhere, and if for some reason it was not possible, the reproach expressed with her eyes was almost unbearable.

We take so much that is precious in our lives for granted, and if I had ever even thought of it at all I suppose I considered Nana to be immortal and indestructible, and when inevitably the sad day came that we had to part, reminiscent of Elizabeth Barrett Browning's tribute to her dog:

> With my hand upon her head
> Is my benediction said
> Therefore and for ever

I stayed in the room whilst the vet administered a merciful injection to end her sufferings, and though I have known many griefs in my life, this was one of the deepest.

My husband buried her in the garden under the shade of an apple-tree, where in life she had liked to lie and sunbathe. That summer I was resting in the opposite corner to her grave when I heard the unmistakeable sound of a dog shaking itself. I sat up quickly, looking for Nana, forgetting for a moment that she was no longer alive, and by her grave I saw her fleeting shadow and then it was gone.

There is a door between my sitting-room and the kitchen and when I was cooking Sunday lunch Nana had a habit of pushing her nose against the door to peer round and see at what stage the cooking had reached and how long she would have to wait for titbits. One Sunday I was standing in the kitchen waiting for the vegetables to cook and looking sadly over the garden at her grave when the door opened slightly and then closed. My husband who is not in the least bit imaginative said simply, 'That was Nana.' There were no other doors or windows open which could have caused a draught.

I have often sensed and seen her briefly and on quite separate occasions when sitting reading quietly, both my husband and I have heard wheezy breathing and a creaking of her wickerwork basket coming from the corner which she occupied in life, its place now taken by a small table.

When some friends went on holiday, I took care of their dog Susie and one day, after some teasing play in the garden, as I walked into the house I heard a crash and discovered that a framed picture of Nana had fallen from a bookcase for no apparent reason. Not unnaturally, I took this as a sign of her disapproval of another dog being in the house.

The months passed and my home seemed cold and empty without an animal in it and I began to consider getting another dog. The opportunity presented itself when I encountered eight black Labrador puppies only four weeks old, they were very appealing and I decided to adopt one of the bitches. She was still very tiny, but as the mother had ceased feeding the puppies due to lack of milk and they could lap, I felt that the one I had chosen would benefit from individual care. I called her Güzel which is Turkish for beautiful and she quickly settled into her new home discovering where her food was to be found and tottering into the kitchen at frequent intervals on shaky legs.

Whilst shopping I met an old friend called Louise who had known and been very attached to Nana and distressed at her demise. I told her about Güzel and our odd experiences when Nana had appeared to manifest. She asked if she could see the new puppy and when she arrived one evening, Güzel bounded to the door.

Louise is a very psychic person but extremely down to earth and practical about such matters and as she walked through the door I heard her say to the puppy, 'I know that you are a lovely little dog because Nana told me so.' I looked at her quizzically as she sat down, my mind boggling somewhat at the prospect of what she was about to unfold.

She told me about a dream she had shortly after our last meeting. She had been walking along a seashore and in the distance could see Nana who looked much younger and more sprightly than she had been for many years. Nana bounded up to her, and it seemed, Louise said, that she was able to communicate with her telepathically. At that point it was not clear to Louise whether she was dreaming or having an out of the body experience, it was so real.

'What are you doing here Nana, don't you know that Lois has another dog?' she said.

Incredibly Nana apparently replied to her, 'Yes, I know, and I don't mind a bit, she is a lovely little puppy!'

'Is it possible,' I thought, my mind reeling, 'that Nana knew I had felt some misgivings about having another dog and she had been allowed to reassure me in this way?' Louise subsequently wrote to me and said that during her meditations she had seen herself back at my house and observed Nana quietly watching the new puppy at play, rather like an indulgent aunt.

I have never felt or seen Nana around the house since that time; she has obviously gone to her own place to wait for me. Spiritualist writings tell of an animal sphere where pets are cared for until their owners pass on, and in the 'Betty Books' by Stewart Edward White, his deceased wife communicated and told him that all her dogs were with her. I find it rather comforting to reflect that in that greater life, all the animals I have loved will be with me again.

Louise told me that she had once owned a canary to which she had been very attached. Its cage had been placed in an alcove in her sitting-room, and since its death both she and her husband had at times heard the tinkle of the bell which had been in the cage, the sound emanating from the alcove.

One of my neighbours reported that she had once owned a cat which insisted on weaving through her own and her husband's legs when they were kneeling in the garden doing some weeding. Since its death they had both felt the cat around their legs, still making a nuisance of itself.

A strange story was told to me by a friend Anita. Her sister Miriam had a dog called Beau which she loved dearly. Beau quite suddenly became very troublesome, barking at the television, at the telephone and displaying very aggressive tendencies when visitors called at the house. Miriam herself became quite ill at the time and found Beau's behaviour insupportable and she decided uncharacteristically to have him destroyed. Shortly afterwards, it was discovered that Miriam's illness was terminal, she was taken into hospital and nursed in a side ward. Anita and her mother went to visit at the hospital and as they walked into the side ward, Miriam looked up and said weakly, 'Oh, I see you have brought Beau with you, I didn't know that animals were allowed in the hospital ...', and then obviously remembered that Beau was dead. Miriam herself died a short time later.

The ancient wisdom teaches that during a long and protracted illness as the body weakens, the spirit gradually withdraws and the dying person begins to function in this world and the next; perhaps Miriam was able to see the dog waiting for her. During my nursing career when I cared for dying patients, I observed on numerous occasions that when on the point of death, many would call the name of some person with a beatific expression on their faces; some would stretch out their arms in greeting and I realized with the benefit of my own psychic vision that they were recognizing a loved one who had come to meet them.

When the late Duke of Windsor was dying, it is reported that his last words were, 'Mama, mama, mama!' and it was suggested that perhaps he was at the last seeking reconciliation for his abdication from the Throne. I suspect that his words had a more glorious intent, he was greeting his mother, the late Queen Mary, who had come to take him to his eternal home.

There is a general assumption in our culture that only human beings have souls and can anticipate immortal life, that once an animal dies it is gone for ever except as a memory lingering in the hearts of those who loved it. In the book *The Psychic Power of Animals*, the author Bill Schul reports the experience of a friend of his who was driving late on a narrow winding mountain road, when quite suddenly in the road ahead of him appeared his large collie Jeff who had died a year before. He braked, jumped out of the car and ran towards the dog calling his name; the dog turned and moved slowly ahead of him to the peak of the incline just ahead. As he reached the incline he saw a huge boulder in the road deposited by a landslide; had he been driving he would not have seen the boulder until it was too late and would have either hit the boulder, or in trying to avoid it, served over the cliff. When he searched for the dog it had disappeared.

The same book reports the story of a deceased dog scaring off a burglar. Food was being taken from refrigerators in a complex of apartments, and one night a woman was awakened from deep sleep by the sound of barking from her pet dog Jock. Hurried footsteps were heard from the room below, a door opened and sounds of someone running occurred, and investigation showed that a burglar had been raiding her refrigerator. The woman started to look for her dog and then suddenly remembered that it had died three months before.

If animals do survive death, what is their eventual purpose in the course of evolution? Regarding human experience, there is a growing movement of acceptance of the theory of reincarnation which holds that human beings return many times to physical life to learn and grow towards perfection. To many observers of animal qualities, it would seem unacceptable that their expressions of love, loyalty and dedication are only temporarily expressed in one lifetime without being given the opportunity to evolve towards higher states of awareness.

The great Sufi mystic and poet, founder of the Mevlevi dervishes in Turkey, Mevlana Jelalu'ddin Rumi, predated by many centuries Darwin's theory of evolution when he wrote:

> I died from minerality and became vegetable,
> And from vegetativeness I died and became animal.
> I died from animality and became man.
> Then why fear disappearance through death?
> Next time I shall die
> Bringing forth wings and feathers like angels
> After that, soaring higher than angels –
> What you cannot imagine,
> I shall be that.

Most traditions which accept reincarnation affirm it as a universal principle applying to all life forms. Life is seen as coming from a universal source and travels on a long evolutionary journey back to that source, evolving from the mineral kingdom to the plant, from the plant to the animal, and from animal to the human.

What does death represent to an animal? At present we have no way of knowing, and perhaps it is an individual experience, to be met by different animals in different ways. Some animals seem to be unaware of its approach, whilst others make preparations for the event as when certain dogs and cats search for places to be alone at the time of death, knowing it to be imminent. There is a story told to me by another friend which indicates that some animals are telepathically aware of the death of their friends. Two dogs, Rex and Sally were companions for many years and used to romp on walks together, Sally was apparently the only bitch that Rex never tried to seduce! One day Rex was lying in his basket at 5 p.m. when for no apparent reason he gave two long, piercing and heartrending howls which made his owner's hair stand on end.

At 7 p.m. the telephone rang, it was a call from the owner of Sally with the information that the vet had been to the house that afternoon to destroy Sally who had become very ill. Asked at what time the injection had been given, the answer was, 'At 5 p.m.'

There is evidence that some animals understand death as a physical occurrence. In an edition of the *Tomorrow* magazine published in 1953, there is a story of a farmer named Henry who owned many cattle near Trelawney. He cared a great deal for his cattle and when he died suddenly, his coffin was placed in a wagon for the journey to the cemetery. The distance was great and the route was lined with many mourners. During the procession the mourners were startled by the moaning and bellowing of cattle. Herds of animals gathered from the surrounding pastures and stood along the fence, tossing their heads, pawing the ground and lamenting in tones quite unlike their usual lowing.

Another story concerns John Gambill who founded the Gambill Wild Goose Reservation near Paris, Texas. He once nursed a wounded gander back to health and the following autumn the gander returned with twelve geese which became quite tame. Gambill died in 1962 and it was estimated that more than three thousand geese wintered in safety on the reservation. As Gambill died in a Paris hospital, hundreds of geese flew into the town and circled around and around the hospital honking a requiem. Somehow, and in some way, they knew.

In the land of Egypt in ancient times numerous animals were regarded as sacred and divine, the incarnations of gods. The dog was a particularly important animal and the cat the object of a mystical cult. Dr George Reisner, an archaeologist relates the story of an Egyptian dog buried with pomp and ceremony. On the inscription in stone relating to its burial was written that he was 'the Bodyguard of His Majesty', this was by order of the King (2600–2450 BC). He was so esteemed that he entered the after life as an honoured spirit before the Great God, to ensure the attendance of the spirit of the dog on the spirit of the King.

That animals have souls and the relationship of spirit incarnation in men and animals, of charity and affection and the obligations of kinship are shown in Hindu and Buddhist scriptures, in the religious teachings of ancient Persia and China, in Greek and Scandinavian mythology, in the famous Edicts of Asoka, Emperor of India. One of the characteristics of the saints of Christianity was their love and pity for animals. St Francis preached to the birds and encouraged the wolf to be good (why, if they have no souls?), St Roch was served in a time of trouble by his dog, St Jerome had a lion and St Columba a crane, St Cuthbert had otters and St Bernard a hare.

Sir Oliver Lodge with almost sixty years of psychic investigation once wrote,

> I have often been asked about the survival of animals. Well, affection is the most vital thing in life and like other vital realities, it continues. The universe is governed by love more than by anything else and no reality of that kind fades out of

existence. We have high authority for figurative statements emphasising this, such as that the hairs of our heads are numbered, and that not a sparrow falls to the ground without the knowledge of the Heavenly Father. Life itself does not go out of existence, but only leaves its association with matter. Ordinary plants and animals have not acquired individuality, and therefore for them there is no individual survival. The higher animals however, have developed some human qualities. They have attained a stage where there is individual memory which is the beginning of personality. Some of them have attained a stage where love for their human friends is dominant. The particular shape of the body matters little, it is the soul and the faculties that survive when they really and truly exist. Some four footed creatures seem to me to have attained that stage. The evidence or testimony is that survival in their case is a reality.

Sonya, 'my sister witch of the dark inclinations', told me an interesting story which she regards as evidence for animal survival of death with elements of reincarnation in it. She wrote.

Many years ago I had a young female cat called Broomstick to whom I was especially devoted (bearing in mind that I have for years had several cats). She was a pretty but otherwise unexceptional animal, a dark tabby with one distinguishing feature, her rear left hind paw was ginger. She died one day in my arms from a heart attack; it was her first birthday. I was devastated. I had mourned for cats before and since, but never as much as for Broomstick.

Some few weeks later I had a dream of Broomstick and in it she said quite clearly, 'I am lonely and want to return, please help me'. So I concentrated very hard for some days in trying to make this possible, I did not know how it could be done, but if sheer will-power could do it, then it would be so. Shortly after that I acquired a young black female cat and I called her Hallowe'en. She became pregnant, and definitely not by the sire of Broomstick, and in time produced three kittens, two as black as herself, and one tabby with a ginger rear paw, but this was the right one. A mirror image perhaps? This kitten grew up with all Broomstick's distinctive characteristics; she automatically sat in Broomstick's favourite place, ate in the same manner and followed me everywhere, so many things. On her first birthday, I found her dead. Perhaps it doesn't do to meddle; for all my efforts Broomstick was destined to die on her first birthday. I never dreamed of her again but did see her once, a friend who was with me also witnessed her apparition. Her ghost ran across the room and faded into a wall.

Psychic literature relates how a medium, Mrs Hewat McKenzie, along with other scientific investigators, all recorded at materialization séances careful impressions of the manifestation of an animal like a dog which fondled some of the sitters and pushed its nose into their pockets. Another incident reported was of a little boy who materialized, he looked about four years old and called out 'Doggie, doggie' and explained he had brought the dog to the séance and that he was looking after it on the Other Side. Whilst all this took place, the medium was in a deep trance in the 'cabinet' which is used at most materialization séances.

Tennyson seemed to be convinced of the survival of all life forms when he wrote:

> That nothing walks with aimless feet
> That not one life shall be destroyed
> Or cast as rubbish to the void
> When God hath made the pile complete.

Eastern philosophies laid greater emphasis on the essential unity of all creation, and Mohammed, the Prophet of Islam taught, 'There is no beast on earth nor bird which flieth with its wings, but the same is a people like unto you'. Mohammed was especially fond of cats, and it is recorded that rather than disturb his cat, he once cut off the sleeve of his robe on which it was sleeping. A state of greater awareness seems common to all illumined persons throughout history, a conviction of the oneness of life. Sri Ramakrishna drew the anger of the Brahmin priests when he gave offerings of food placed on an altar for the Divine Mother, to a hungry cat, and St Francis always referred to the animals surrounding him as his little brothers and sisters.

The certainty is that animals are related to us, they lack speech but their mental processes are similar to our own as are their fears, their pains and their affections. All their emotions in fact, although they may know them in a lesser degree than we. Perhaps they are like us, struggling on the long difficult road to perfection.

I remember many years ago, reading a poem about a dog

which died and in the classic Greek style was picked up by Charon who rowed the dead over the River Styx. Charon requested no obol or fare, and deposited the dog on a bank and the poem ended (with apologies to the unknown author for errors in recall):

> There shall you sniff his cargoes as they come
> And droop your head, and turn and still be dumb –
> Til one fine day, half joyful, half in fear,
> You run and prick a recognising ear
> At last, oh rapture, leaping to her hand
> Salute your mistress as she steps to land.

I hope that it may be so.

19 On Reincarnation

Voltaire wrote, 'It is not more surprising to be born twice than once; everything in nature is resurrection', and in *Witch Amongst Us*, I referred to the theory of reincarnation which is a basic tenet of the beliefs of most of the witches of my acquaintance; I made it clear that it is not a belief to which I totally subscribe; nevertheless, letters about reincarnation frequently appear in my post.

One woman wrote that she has a basic acceptance of the rules of karma and reincarnation.

> I know that you have trouble with these doctrines but you may still be able to supply the answer. The position as I see it is, 'As ye sow, shall ye reap'. The pattern of each person's life is set out according to his previous right actions or mistakes. The obstacles are put up. If you handle them correctly according to the eternal values of patience, courage, kindness, compassion, etc., they are overcome and pass away, if you get it wrong, the problems come back again to confront you for another try. The problems are predestined by your behaviour but you have free will in the way you choose to handle them. By meditation, prayer, devotion to God and kindness to others, you can hasten the process and learn to do better with your karmic trials. I differ from the understanding of karma in your book. Correctly understood, it should not engender feelings of helplessness and resignation, but present the ultimate challenge to rise above the present problems of birth, poverty, etc. It is the doctrine of Islam that is so dangerously fatalistic with its 'Will of Allah'. So each man's trials are important whether they be emotional, healthwise, poverty, etc. When witches perform beneficial magic to alleviate suffering, are they not interfering with the laws of Nature and setting someone back on an important test? Also there is a school of thought that it brings karma to the practitioner of

the magic. You say many witches believe in reincarnation and karma, how do they overcome this fundamental dilemma?

Not totally subscribing to the theory of rebirth, this has not been a problem which has exercised my mind. It is possible that I am sub-consciously guided towards what is permissible and what is not by the knowledge of what is practical, since I do not work magic for everyone who requests it. I do not, however, metaphorically envisage myself sitting on Mount Olympus and advising someone crippled with arthritis for instance, 'whilst I am sympathetic to your suffering, I feel this is your karma and I cannot interfere.' My instinct would be to heal them if I could. If the healing failed then perhaps that is karmic law in operation.

Alternatively, should my magical efforts result in someone avoiding an element of their karma, I consider it not beyond the bounds of possibility that the Law could instigate a further trial at a future date. As far as attracting adverse karma to myself is concerned, I feel that motive is an important element in any altruistic endeavour and I am more solicitous about other people's suffering today than my own karma tomorrow.

My friend June who communicates with me periodically through automatic writing and through clairvoyance, whilst not affirming rebirth has never categorically denied it, she just has very little knowledge of it in her present state of progress. She has asserted, however, that every individual has a relationship towards a 'group soul' and these vary in number from 100 to 1,000. When I questioned her about regression, she indicated that people who claim to recall previous lives with or without regression are really drawing on the memories of the lives of others who have passed to the next stage of existence and are members of their particular group soul.

In *Beyond Human Personality* by Geraldine Cummins, Frederick Myers who died in 1901 makes reference to group souls and relates that it is usually on the fourth plane of spirit life that individuals become aware of the group soul to which they are related and start to share the emotional and intellectual experiences of their comrade souls. Myers says some interesting things about the reincarnation of souls; where the soul is primitive or bound closely to the things of the earth, reincarnation is generally the rule. Such souls need to travel back, and in the earthly setting where their desire is centred, discover the necessity for something bigger. His own experience of the majority of people he has met leads him to suggest that two, three or four lives on earth are the usual number undertaken and for special circumstances there may be more, but the teaching of certain oriental religions that there is a long succession of lives until emancipation from the 'wheel' is attained is not confirmed by his experience. With the attainment of the fourth plane the power to enter subjectively into knowledge of the lives of comrades in the same group soul takes place and there can be gained breadth of experience and wisdom which would otherwise only be possible by many more lives in a physical body.

Myers says, 'Through our communal experience, I perceive and feel the drama in the earthly journey of a Buddhist priest, of an American merchant, of an Italian painter, and I am, if I assimilate the life thus lived, spared the living of it in the flesh. The soul perceives all the consequences of acts, moods, thoughts, in detail in this life of a kindred soul and so it may win the knowledge of all typical earth experiences.'

He also makes reference to the idea of karma and says that the relations at their deeper levels of the souls within a group are so close that the karma of one may sometimes considerably affect that of others. He states that on entering upon his last life on earth he inherited the karmic experience of another soul of his group who had died before he was born. He himself will not return to earth again, but the karmic framework that he left behind would be the inheritance of a younger soul of the same group. A human being is the meeting point of two streams of heredity, one is physical which he inherits from his parents and the other is the soul's heredity which is partly his own creation and partly that of his spiritual kindred whose evolution is closely linked with his own.

Whilst some individual souls attain the fifth plane of being, the group soul as a whole does not evolve until all the members of the lower plane attain the level of the fifth. Occasionally it happens that a soul is quite incapable of immortality and quite unworthy of it and in this case it will fall out of existence, but all that is of value in its experience is conserved for the benefit of others.

Myers also says that occasionally there is created by Divine Imagining a Spirit which remains in close contact with its source, it does not proceed along the evolutionary road but after death rises swiftly through the planes of being to resume immediate communion with God in the Divine Society; it seems clear that Jesus Christ was such a one.

Porphyry expounding Plotinus said, 'Particular souls are distinct without being separate; they are united to each other without being confused ...' which is close to the description of group souls of which Myers wrote.

In certain automatic writings, Myers makes some interesting observations on the idea of rebirth. He classifies human beings broadly according to their development, as animal men, soul men and spirit men, and although no definition of these classes is given it is clear that animal men are those whose interests are centred largely on sensation and the things of the body. Soul men have some appreciation of goodness, truth, beauty and love. Spirit men are rare beings who incarnate only once except for special reasons. Animal men apparently almost invariably reincarnate. He says of soul men,

> The majority of people only reincarnate two, three or four times, though if they had some human purpose or plan to achieve they may return as many as eight or nine times. No arbitrary figure can be named, and I do not write as one having authority, this little sketch of the soul's journey in relation to earth is written out of my own experience and knowledge.
>
> There is no set law concerning reincarnation, at a certain point in its progress, the soul reflects, weighs and considers the facts of its own nature in conjunction with its past life on earth. If you are primitive, this meditation is made through instinct, a kind of emotional thought, that stirs the depths of your being. Then you are helped to choose your future, you have complete free will, but your spirit indicates the path you should follow and you frequently obey that indication.

Such a view illumines much that is obscure in the inequalities of souls at birth, so that a Chopin or a Mozart at a young age demonstrates a degree of musical maturity which neither heredity nor environment can explain. Such gifts are also occasionally found in mathematics, spiritual maturity and aesthetic sensibility, and it is difficult to dismiss as delusions, the convictions of sensible people whose subjective experiences includes what they believe to be glimpses of former lives.

Another story I read in a Spanish newspaper outlined the story of a two-year-old child, Osel Iza Torres from Granada, who, according to Buddhist experts is the reincarnation of the Lama Yeshe. The child recently left Spain for a sanctuary in

Kopan where he will be formally invested as the late lama's reincarnation after being received in Bud Gaya by the Dalai Lama.

Osel, who holds tight to his feeding-bottle wears a lama's tunic, his father is the son of a Spanish peasant who emigrated to France, and is a Buddhist. His mother had a dream shortly before she became pregnant with Osel who was born in Bubion, a village in the Alpujarras, where his parents were two of the creators of a retreat. His mother relates, 'I had a dream where I was in a cathedral, Yeshe, the lama who had died two months before was in the centre of the cathedral, we walked in front of him and he laid his hands on us and I felt a sensation like a spring of water in the Alhambra, a feeling of joy and well being. A few days later I realized I was pregnant.' Tests by Buddhist monks who visited Los Alpujarras, convinced them that the child was the reincarnation of the Lama Yeshe and when Osel met people who had previously been his disciples, there was a high level of communication between them. Presented with a wide variety of objects, he chose the one which had belonged to the Lama Yeshe and this was the proof that he was indeed the reincarnation of the late master.

Dr Ian Stevenson who is the head of a research organization in America has made a special study of reincarnation and has produced some remarkable evidence to substantiate the theory. Many of the cases involved are in India, and other authorities have disputed his findings on these grounds, since interpreters are required for the various dialects, and misunderstandings can arise; also it is argued, orientals have a predilection for exaggeration.

Some years ago I dined with Dr Stevenson prior to his attendance at a lecture I gave at Cambridge University. I found him to be a charming, taciturn man and I was curious as to his own beliefs on the subject of rebirth, but he refused to be drawn and said he preferred to maintain an attitude of objectivity.

Ian Wilson, who wrote a book called *Mind Out of Time*, opined that many of the memories dredged up during regression are in fact unconscious absorption of information and events in this life. He quotes the case of a young woman who during regression began to speak in Middle English, the language of Chaucer, although in a normal state she had no conscious knowledge of this and denied any interest in it. She was regressed again, not to a past life but to the age of four or five in her present life and it was discovered that whilst in a reference library at this age accompanied by her mother who was researching some matter, the child had been idly flicking over pages of a book on Middle English whilst quietly singing to herself as a child would, and the Middle English had been unconsciously absorbed.

However, this does not explain how she gained the ability to actually speak Middle English which was the language of Chaucer. Few children of four or five would be able to read it, so one assumes that she had a photographic memory and what she observed casually was stored in her brain and released under hypnosis, but how did she know how to verbalize it?

In his book *The Psychic Detectives* published by Pan, Colin Wilson cites the case of an illiterate girl who, when in a fever, began to speak Greek, Latin and Hebrew. A young doctor was so intrigued by this that he investigated the girl's past life and discovered that at the age of nine she had lived with a Protestant pastor who used to walk around the house reading aloud in these languages. Consciously, the girl had not assimilated a single word but some hidden tape-recorder in the brain had preserved everything.

I have very little interest in any past life I might have enjoyed or otherwise, but certain friends claim to be able to read the Akashic Records, a Theosophical concept for an astral memory of all events, thoughts and emotions that have arisen since the world began. Psychics are said to be able to tune into this dimension and receive authentic impressions of past ages and learn of the previous incarnations of people. Some theosophical descriptions of Atlantis derive from this technique.

Whilst I was on a visit to the home of some friends in Istanbul, I was entertained by the family who each played a musical instrument, and I was entranced by the sacred music of the dervishes and the haunting ney, a reed flute about which Mevlana, the founder of the Mevlevi dervish order wrote at the beginning of his book, the Mathnawi:

> Hearken to this reed forlorn,
> Breathing even since 'twas torn
> From its rushy bed, a strain,
> Of impassioned love and pain.
>
> The secret of my song though near,
> None can see and none can hear,
> Oh, for a friend, to know the sign
> And mingle all his soul with mine.
>
> 'Tis the flame of love that fired me,

'Tis the wine of love inspired me,
Wouldst thou learn how lovers bleed,
Hearken, hearken to the Reed!

I remembered how I had seen dervishes cry because the beauty of God was almost too much to bear when they were completely absorbed in it.

One of my Turkish friends, Kaya, a divine healer who lived in England has asserted with confidence that I am more Turkish than himself, and he is quite convinced that in my last life I was a Turkish woman because the memory of that life is so near the surface.

I have an affection for many countries but it is true that Turkey is very close to my heart and there is within me a deep response to its history, its culture and its people. That night in Istanbul the music changed to a sinuous Middle-Eastern melody, and feeling very relaxed amongst the intimate company of my friends, I joined the wife of my host in a belly dance at the end of which one of the sons told me 'You do the belly dance very well, most English women do it as if they were making yoghurt!'

That event however fades into insignificance compared with an occasion which, as I recall it now, some years later, still makes me blush and squirm with deep embarrassment, for I made an exhibition of myself in public.

On another visit to Istanbul, I visited a nightclub with some Turkish friends and English people from my hotel and the wine flowed. I actually drink very little as I do not care for alcohol very much and, like the late Lady Astor, I like to know when I am enjoying myself so it was not intoxication. The orchestra started to play that undulating, alluring Middle-Eastern music and I walked onto the floor as if in a trance and started to dance like someone possessed.

I can recall even now, that as I danced I could hear in the far distance the sound of clapping and Turkish shouts of '*Huuuay!*', but the sounds hardly registered on my consciousness, the dance and the music were the only realities and my eyes were glazed with the fascination of the melody and the urgent need to express the sensuous, voluptuous rhythm.

When the orchestra stopped, the spell was broken and I looked with surprise and alarm at the sea of faces and clapping hands and wondered what on earth had come over me. 'Lois, you were away, it was marvellous!', my friends shouted at me over the noise, 'Your eyes were half-closed and you were out of this world!' Perhaps what took me over that night was what the Spaniards call the *'duende'*, the demon that sometimes takes over singers and dancers so that they seem to be possessed by a force greater than themselves.

It was for me a most unusual experience and one I hope never to repeat, and when the English people at the hotel crowded round me and demanded to know, 'Wherever did you learn to do the belly dance like that?', I could truthfully answer, 'I really have no idea!' Perhaps Kaya is correct, maybe I was a Turkish dancer in my last life.

In her book *Unfinished Symphonies*, Rosemary Brown who has spiritual links with deceased composers, questioned Liszt about reincarnation and he asserted that it is subtly different from the teachings of the subject on earth.

> What happens is rather like the putting out of a fresh shoot on a tree or a plant. On earth you think of yourselves as complete beings, but actually only a part of you has manifested through the physical body and brain, the rest is still in spirit but is linked and one with you.

This theory bears out the writings of Dr Paul Brunton in his various books on the significance of the Oversoul.

Liszt continued,

> Think of an atom, it is made of protons and neutrons which all go to make up the nucleus surrounded by electrons. That is what a soul is like. These separate parts are held together in the nucleus of the soul which can manifest as various personalities in your world. These are what the reincarnationalists call different incarnations, but they all belong to one soul which can choose which particular part of the soul it wishes to manifest.

Reincarnation has not, and can never really be proved this side of the grave, it can only ever, like religion be a matter of personal belief or faith, and iconoclasts of the theory opine that the revelations of people who are regressed are influenced by romantic fantasies induced by cryptoamnesia (the state of mind in which previously absorbed visual images, such as films seen in childhood or books read in teenage youth affect the subconscious memory). They may also be due to memories inherited from ancestors. Intimation of reincarnation in other states of consciousness could derive flashes of inspiration from the Universal Mind to which we all have access in periods of heightened awareness.

The views of Liszt are in accord with Spiritualist teachings when he declares that we are spirits with a body in order to experience the material world, not in a secondary connection, bodies with a spirit, and that this world is a preparation for the life to come. It follows therefore that if only parts of our soul are infused and manifest into new beings, our essential selves and our real home is already in the spiritual realms.

The seventeenth-century poet and mystic Henry Vaughan wrote:

> Man hath still either toyes or care;
> He hath no root, nor to one place is ty'd,
> But ever restless and irregular
> About this earth doth run and ride.
> He knows he hath a home, but scarce knows where;
> He says it is so far
> That he hath quite forgot how to go there.

The steady tramp of time will take us to our home.

20 *Communion*

Although I do not profess to be an authority on the world after death, I have gained over the years certain knowledge, made spiritual contacts and had experiences from which illations can be drawn. When the terminally ill and the bereaved seek me out and ask me to tell them what I know of the next world I share my experiences with them that they might draw comfort from them; the bereaved that they may find consolation in the thought that the one they have apparently lost is in a world of peace and beauty, the essence of which can hardly be imagined from our own world, and the dying that they may learn that there is really nothing to fear from the change called death which is as natural a process as birth, and merely a gateway into another and finer state of being.

If my informants are correct, it would appear that organized religions have misled us for centuries in their assertions that only by accepting certain beliefs shall we inherit the kingdom of Heaven, and that fires of Hell await those who do not subscribe to their own particular faith. What we believe seems to have little import on the immediate after-death state; a person is exactly the same five minutes after death as he was five minutes before, and no death-bed repentance or administration of extreme unction will make the slightest difference to his destination, which appears to have been automatically decided by his actions during the course of his life. It is a salutary thought that we are all, as we live from day to day, forming unknowingly, our future environment in the life beyond death.

Apart from the members of my family who have communicated with me, I have received a quantity of valuable information from a woman friend who died some fifteen years ago. June and I were very close, and when she died at the age of forty from a blood disease I was very grieved and greatly missed our intimate converse on a group of wide-ranging subjects. During her childhood she had contracted poliomyelitis as a result of which she lost the use of her left arm and hand, both of which became slightly withered, but she adapted well to this disability.

One day whilst meditating, I saw her clairvoyantly, she appeared in an effulgent light, and drawing my attention to her arm, clairaudiently said, 'Look at my arm, it's whole again'. (Clairaudience is the power of hearing things not normally present to the senses.) Apart from this she was almost the same as I remembered her. During her lifetime she had been slim to the point of thinness, and she appeared to be slightly more generously built with the same elfin face and short cropped hair.

From that time onwards she was often in touch with me. Her communications spanned a period of several months, sometimes I merely saw her clairvoyantly, on other occasions she utilized the medium of automatic writing, either by using my hand with a pen held lightly in my fingers, or by a method known as overshadowing when I would sit at my typewriter, and after a prayer for protection, place my fingers in a touch-typing position.

Automatic writing is strange and inexplicable, it can be seen and read but the source of its intelligence and the propellant which directs the pen or the typewriter keys is not perceivable by the five physical senses. Many books have been written totally by means of this directed force, including the Patience Worth series received by an American Midwestern housewife, and the fascinating New Testament stories dictated through Geraldine Cummins. The American author Ruth Montgomery also receives communications from her guides in the spirit world through her typewriter when she is overshadowed.

Those who doubt the existence of communication between the living and the dead argue that the thoughts originate within the subconscious where our memories are stored; others believe that the messages are imparted by a superconscious or higher self which has access to all knowledge through a type of all-pervading extra-sensory perception.

I do not subscribe to either of these theories and am persuaded that my communicator was the person she claimed to be, namely, my friend June, and whilst some of the intelligences imparted were at complete variance with my own personal cherished beliefs, I have nevertheless included them in the interests of honesty and the furtherance of knowledge and the hope that they will engage the attention of some of my readers.

I asked her many questions which she did her best to answer, always emphasizing that the information she gave me was based on her personal knowledge of her own environment and what she had gleaned from people around her. There were other disclosures which came to her from hearsay, and if it was within the confines of my question she would relate it with the proviso that she was not sure of the truth of it.

June's death had been preceded by that of her mother. During their lives their relationship had been somewhat strained and when I asked if she had seen her mother she replied

> Yes, I have, she met me when I made the passage to this life, together with my aunt and uncle and my mother's parents, my grandparents. I had been ill for some time as you know and my spirit body was very depleted. It was as if I just fell asleep and when I woke I couldn't think where I was. I found myself in a bright room filled with flowers, the windows were wide open and beyond them was a vista of beautiful landscape, right to the horizon. My mother and other relatives were sitting by my bed, I did not recognise them at first, they were so much younger than I remembered them. It dawned on me that mother was dead and I thought I must be dreaming. Apart from feeling a little weak, I had no pain and in fact felt better than I had for a long time. I was in the equivalent of a convalescent home, and I stayed there until I regained my strength. I must tell you that in this world everyone appears to be more or less of the same age. I know this sounds strange, but the fact is that when people come here in old age they gradually revert to what they considered to be their prime. In my case I died in my prime so I stayed the same.
>
> This is not to say that everyone looks the same age, its difficult to explain but the experience of the years spent on earth is apparent in people's features, it's a subtle thing and I can't explain it too well.

I asked her about babies and small children who die, those who are stillborn or aborted and she said, 'Once the spark of life has been ignited, a child possesses a spirit and it is received here by women who are trained for the purpose. Babies and children grow to maturity and because they have only briefly touched earth conditions they progress quickly through the spheres. They are schooled and educated and cared for with great love.'

I asked her, 'Where are you exactly in relation to the earth?'

'I have been told that there are seven spheres and I am on the second sphere from earth. I can visit the first sphere but not the ones above me until I have progressed sufficiently. There is no fence or gate barring my way, it is quite a natural barrier. We live in a world of harmony and I vibrate to the essence of this sphere where I am comfortable with people of similar outlook, attitude and tastes. People from higher spheres can descend to us and do. I am not up or down in relation to earth, our world's interpenetrate your world, we are all around you but we do not impinge on each other's world because we vibrate at different rates. You can see me and something of my world at times because you are on a higher vibration which makes you clairvoyant. If you can imagine a bicycle wheel revolving, you cannot see the spokes because they are rotating too quickly, but when the wheel slows you see the spokes clearly.'

There were so many questions I wanted to ask and I started with an obvious one, 'Where do you live?'

When June was alive she lived in a flat in London and loved to visit me because I was in the country and she replied,

> This sphere is a vast expanse, it is limitless and I have a cottage in the equivalent of the countryside. In your world I used to fantasise about a cottage in the country when I retired and when I arrived here I found my fantasy waiting for me. I have a little garden filled with beautiful flowers which never die, and because I carried the memory of my favourite pictures and ornaments I have these also and they are mine for as long as I continue to want them. I live alone but I can see my friends and relatives when I wish to, I was always a solitary person and enjoyed my own company and I have not changed in this respect. I must emphasise that this is a very natural world containing much that was familiar on earth but without earth's imperfections and our life here is also very natural, we do many of the things we were accustomed to do on earth. I have seen C. and he is as intense as ever but in his element since he now has access to ancient history and can confirm the truth of all his studies.

C. was an archaeologist and a mutual friend. He had no small talk and one discussed ancient Egyptian civilizations with him or nothing. June explained 'We have the equivalent of what we called museums on earth and it is possible to view the development of mankind since the beginning of time; we can watch the true history of every race unfold before our eyes, not as the history books record it, but as it actually happened.'

She continued, 'this sphere is still relatively near to earth and we still carry with us many earth habits and memories. As we progress higher, we gradually shed these, but here we have the ability to relive the happiest of our memories, not in a dreamlike state, but in a real sense and so we are able to experience again the happy times we spent with those we love who are still on earth.'

I asked how long it took an individual to progress to a higher sphere and June replied,

> I know this will be difficult to understand but time for us does not exist as it does for you and I have met people here who seem to have been on this sphere for the equivalent of a hundred years. They speak of earth as it was at that time, they have everything they want here, this is their idea truly of Heaven and they have no desire to go forward. We are allowed to grow at our own rate and no pressure is put on us. Eventually I gather a person begins to feel restless and the desire to move and progress arises and when this occurs the opportunity is presented.

I asked how it is presented and she said,

> There are spirits from higher realms who are in touch with us but not in an obtrusive way. We can send out a thought and there will be a response. This is a world of the mind, thoughts are living things, we speak to each other and at the same time telepathically receive the true essence of the communication; not as sometimes happens on earth, when speech does not adequately convey our thoughts and feelings. We also have to learn to discipline our thoughts because they can be read in their entirety!
>
> We are also very much aware of the thoughts of us which arise from earth, if they are kind and loving thoughts they warm us, but if unkind they can cause us hurt. 'Do not speak ill of the dead' is a true saying. We are also aware of the prayers of the living, it is essential to pray for us, it helps in our progress and we are comforted to know that we are not forgotten. I am always very conscious of your prayers for me.

I asked her about her activities and she replied,

As you know I always liked my own company and still do; there are vast libraries here containing the best of all the literature penned on earth. I read and I paint, better than I ever did on earth. I visit the art galleries and museums and compare my puny painting efforts with those of the great masters who continue to produce their work. This sphere also contains beautiful buildings which house vast lecture and concert halls and these are used for many activities. You once said to me that if you were to be happy in heaven there would have to be orchestral concerts and roses, you will find both here. For those who are interested there are lectures on any number of subjects given by experts in their field on earth, wonderful symphony concerts containing traditional music and compositions created in higher spheres.

My life is not all rest and relaxation, that may be sufficient for the present for some people but I was always an active person with an inquisitive mind and I am engaged in a learning process. I also have various duties to perform in settling new arrivals, this is a task which is endless and help is always needed.

There are also journeys to be made to other parts of this sphere which represents all the places and aspects of earth and I am constantly learning new things and meeting new people, as well as old friends. I have seen J. [another mutual friend] and this world was a great shock to him, as you know he was very irreligious and profane at times and did not believe in an after life. It has required a great effort on his part to come to terms with it but his mother and father who are here helped him a lot.

As you know, when on earth I loved to travel but did not have the opportunity to see as much as I would have liked. It is possible for us to reduce our vibration with practice and descend to the earth plane to visit the places which interest us. It is a great truism often expressed here that one does not see the whole of earth until one is dead! We have the advantage of doing it without aching feet, fatigue and other bodily discomforts. This is a wonderful sphere and at present it seems to me that there is sufficient here to occupy me for eternity but I am told I will change and eventually wish to move on.

I asked her what process was involved in order to visit the earth and she reminded me, 'this is a sphere of the mind, and though I am sure it will sound incredulous to you, when I wish to be in a certain place I merely wish it mentally and find that I am there. In this respect as you will see I needed training to discipline my mind and to concentrate on what I was doing at a particular time because if I allow my mind to wander to pleasant memories of another place I find myself perhaps inconveniently there.'

I said 'do you ever walk or do you always move in this instant fashion?'

'Yes,' she replied, 'I often walk, not to do so would mean that I would miss so many of the beauties of this place. I also swim. There are great and small lakes here, seas and oceans as on earth where people sail. The water is crystal clear, revitalizing and buoyant and when we step out from it, the water simply dissolves from us and we are quite dry without the necessity for towelling dry.'

'Do you have family celebrations?' I asked. She replied, 'If families are happy and harmonious together they do meet as a group frequently, sometimes for a celebration, more often to welcome a member who has just arrived. People not in harmony with each other do not meet, their very antipathy keeps them apart. Love is the deciding factor, if we love someone, we will always meet up with them and be with them for as long as we wish. Unhappily married couples are not together here unless they wish to make the effort towards a greater understanding of each other, otherwise they go their separate ways. One thing which will interest you,' she continued, 'is that during sleep some people are able to travel in spirit to these realms and fragments of dream memories are recall of this travel. In this way children who die prematurely are, I am told, able to meet their parents who travel here during sleep. Also children are sometimes taken by advanced spirits to the earth to see their parents so that when they are re-united, it is not as strangers.'

I questioned June about the Judgement beloved of orthodox religion and she told me surprisingly,

> As far as I am aware, and at least as far as this sphere is concerned, there is no Judgement, if you are referring to an appearance before the Almighty to confess your sins. My experience has been thus. A new arrival here is allowed to settle in and make the enormous adjustment necessary on leaving all that is familiar and finding himself still alive, with a perfect body relieved of all the blemishes of his earth body and feeling healthier than he ever did on earth.

Some people arrive here expecting to find themselves in the presence of God. Others expect to sprout wings and spend the time sitting on a cloud playing a harp. It is a great shock to many people to find themselves in a beautiful natural world very similar to earth in some respects, but containing some surprising aspects. They require time to adjust, and I use the word advisedly since there are no clocks here. As for myself, I neither believed nor did I disbelieve in a life hereafter, as you know, I was not particularly religiously inclined and whilst I was surprised to find that I had survived the change called death, I was also fairly delighted.

In this sphere there are higher spiritual beings who help, advise and instruct us, and when they decide that a suitable period has elapsed, a newcomer is gently approached concerning a review of his earth life; if it is mutually agreed that sufficient adjustment has been made, the review proceeds.

The memory of earth life is carried within the sub-conscious mind which survives the death of the body, this memory is vital and intense and contains every important aspect of a person's life. As I have explained, there are many more highly evolved spirits who minister to us, but there is always one who is closest to us. I suppose this spirit could be regarded as a loving reflection of ourselves being all that we would wish to aspire to in our better moments.

Certainly this spirit is drawn to us by love and a desire to serve, and I am told, has endeavoured to guide and help us during our incarnation on earth; it is with the assistance of this individual that we enter into a subjective review of our life on earth.

We are shown very clearly how our actions and words affected other people around us. We view opportunities given to us which were wasted, things we did which we should not have done, things we left undone. Every bad habit, every vice, every greedy, selfish inconsiderate act is presented to our gaze and it is a very sobering sight. Every kindness shown, every loving helpful act, every generous unselfish consideration shines like a jewel in this review and helps to balance and lighten the inevitable debit of our life.

The loving friend who guides us through this review makes no judgement to us. We judge ourselves, and oh, how harshly we judge ourselves when we see the heights to which we could have aspired. Every hurt and pain and grief we caused to another we experience ourselves, and it can be traumatising; every loving thought and gesture and helpful act is a healing balm to us and we experience the joy and happiness we caused to other people.

A great sorrow and weeping is not expected of us. It is enough to say quietly, 'Yes, I did or said this, and that was the sort of person I was.' An acceptance of our faults and our nature and our own judgement of our weakness is all that is required. If it is possible to make reparation or seek forgiveness, the way to do this is shown to us.

The average person who lives an ordinary decent life has nothing to fear from this judgement. I speak only of this sphere, there may be other judgements on other spheres, but I think not. We are not in a sadistic world where long drawn out repentance is expected of us. Earth is a schoolroom, and children often make mistakes.

One of the weaknesses I had to face personally was an element of selfishness in my nature. I was a solitary individual mainly and during my lifetime I was not overfond of humanity and preferred not to be too deeply involved with people. I saw that I had seriously neglected those who could have been helped by me.

Part of my learning process now is to be actively concerned with the well being of those of my family still on earth, and to help the newly arrived here. In this way I work towards my spiritual evolution.

21 *Further Communion*

The picture of life after death presented in June's communications sounded inspiring and comforting and when she referred to the average person who had lived an ordinary decent life encountering a gentle adaptation of being, I was curious regarding the fate of individuals who do not fall into this category.

> I am informed that there are lower realms where people who were deliberately evil and cruel are consigned. Malefactors, murderers, sadistic torturers and the like exist in a world created by their lives on earth. This sphere is dark and foetid and they continue to prey on each other like wild animals. They will exist there until they come to the realisation of the enormity of their offences and begin to feel repentance and desire to express it. There are beings from higher realms specially trained who visit these places seeking for a spark of spiritual regeneration amongst the inmates. Should one manifest, the individual is helped. It is necessary to understand that no one ever gets away with anything and inevitably the day of reckoning arrives, if not on earth, then in this world.

I asked her if there was an extension of our five senses when we pass to the next world and she wrote,

> In this world we have an extended vision which allows us to see into the future and into the past, something which you can also do to some extent because your vibrational level is higher. We can also see into the world we have left. As we continue to progress and move into spheres of other dimensions, these powers are further extended. In your world energy or vibration is lower than in our sphere and the spheres above are even higher in vibration. The world exists because man

exists to comprehend it, without man the Universe would be a void. The Creator is Mind and Will and has created beauty and form that we can appreciate through the senses. I am not sufficiently progressed to visit the spheres above me but I can tell you that they do not consist of ineffable holiness. Everything here is of a natural order with which we are familiar, there is mirth and humour. In higher spheres we learn more of spiritual values and do work suited to us which at present we cannot be capable of knowing and I am content to enjoy my present life on this sphere.

I asked how she would make the actual transition to a higher sphere and she wrote, 'It is, I am told, comparable to a second death but only in the sense that there is a momentary loss of consciousness and the body I now function through will dissolve and be replaced by one of higher vibration which will automatically ascend to the next sphere.'

'What can you tell me of the Creator?' I asked.

June replied, 'God is a Spirit which is everywhere present throughout the Universe, neither male nor female, this Spirit is an emanation which enters the hearts and minds of all who endeavour through love to lift the world from darkness into evolution towards perfection and thus help in the work of the Spirit'.

I asked June if she ate or slept and she replied, 'The etheric body which I now possess requires neither food nor rest. When people first come here they for a time continue old habits and like to eat and drink but eventually these habits are relinquished. I no longer require sleep but at regular periods I withdraw from activities and rest; it is a relaxation of mind and gives me the opportunity to reflect on what I have learned and experienced and I treasure these solitary periods.'

I was curious about what clothes were worn in the after-life. When I had seen her clairvoyantly she appeared to be wearing a long, simple dress which fell in folds and was waisted by a girdle. 'Because we live in more spiritual conditions we do not dress like Old Testament prophets, we wear whatever we find comfortable. There are certain colours available to us reflecting our degree of spiritual evolution and we would not be comfortable in a colour which represented a state to which we had not yet aspired.'

I asked her to describe her world and she told me, 'It is a world of tremendous beauty and harmony, everything found in the different regions of earth is here. The races gravitate to the equivalent of their own country because that is where familiarity lies. Imagine the most beautiful scenery you have ever seen and multiply it a thousand times. It is difficult to describe the wonders of this world in earthly terms.'

'Have you ever wished, even for a moment that you could return to earth?'

'Not for one moment,' she replied.

> I am completely happy and fulfilled here. It contains all I could desire. I have a perfect body which is never ailing, I am relieved of the necessity to earn a living, I can devote myself to what interests me but I no longer live for myself alone. I am taught to be of service to others in this world and am growing in knowledge and learning deep spiritual truths. It is not until we die that we really begin to live. I did not leave any deep emotional commitments and it is different for people who pass suddenly and leave loved ones behind. There is resentment at being cut off from life and a yearning for those left behind but such people are helped to come to terms with their new environment and are shown how they can assist and console those on earth. They are able to return under the guidance of a helper but are not always able to make their presence known. There is a great longing on this side for communication with the living but the channels are so few and sometimes debased by egotism.
>
> Of course there are some people who are overwhelmed to find themselves in this world, and they have no desire for communication with earth, they are just happy to be freed from its pain and sorrow, but for those who do grieve from this side there is a bureau where enquiries can be made as to the approximate date of the passing of a loved one on earth, and it helps to know how long it will be before re-union occurs. This world is not a haphazard place, we have organisation and order here.

I was mindful of the saying of Krishnamurti that, 'Constantly to seek the purpose of life is one of the odd escapes of man. If he finds what he seeks it will not be worth that pebble on the path'. Nevertheless I asked June if she could tell me what she had learned of the purpose of life.

There was no immediate response and I waited hopefully,

wondering if she had suddenly departed as she sometimes did, and then,

> You have asked me a very profound question and I am not at all sure that I have any qualification to answer it. I have not become all wise and all knowing because I have passed safely to the next stage of existence. From where I stand, it seems to me that the essence of life is progress, we must always attempt to increase our knowledge and learning and move ever upward and forward. The life on earth is a preparation for this world and if we do not successfully learn our lesson in your world, we have to learn it again in this world.
>
> On earth, the development of the spiritual side of our nature is hindered by misguided teachings which have diverted mankind throughout the ages. Great truths have been buried under obscure orthodox beliefs. The essential truth is, that whether we care for the idea or not, we all survive death and our place in this world is based on merit, how we lived in your world, and no vicarious atonement will save us from a place of correction if we have lived evil and selfish lives.
>
> Mankind is more concerned with the material world which he regards as the only reality, when in truth that world is but the reverse side of the spiritual. Your real self which will function in this life is already a part of you, hidden in its fleshly counterpart and is already in contact with the unseen world. The development of your spiritual nature should be a high priority whilst you still inhabit an earthly body.
>
> I have learned that the earth is but a small unit in a Universe so vast that we cannot comprehend it, but that Universe is insignificant compared with other Universes in space ruled by other Deities who have attained divinity by their attributes of purity and wisdom. All are however answerable to the Supreme Creator from whom they receive their creative energy.
>
> No one is born by chance, we all have a purpose in the infinite scheme as co-creators of a perfect plan. These things I have learned during my sojourn here, but even now the contemplation of the vastness and the implication of this knowledge is almost still beyond my comprehension.

Moved beyond measure by the profundity of these revelations, I nevertheless remembered a recent letter from a mother whose son had committed suicide and I asked June about the fate of those who take their own lives.

> Because they die by their own hand, no place is prepared for them, and often they wander in the mists which border the lower spheres, seeking a light and a way inside. There are helpers who patrol these areas and suicides are received with infinite compassion and cared for. Each case is judged on its merits. Some take their own lives because they have found the burden of life too great to bear and this is the real tragedy because the mere act of suicide does not resolve their problems, it merely robs them of the opportunity to find a solution. So many wish they could undo that act. Without the body of flesh their agony is compounded. Others kill themselves under the influence of drugs or mental derangement. They are considered to be not completely responsible and are cared for in the equivalent of hospitals which we have for that purpose.

I asked June about the fate of animals after death and she wrote,

> Animals do survive, we have cats, dogs and horses amongst us, animals such as elephants, tigers and lions etc. live in their own sphere quite happily. We have birds here too, a multitude of them, they are quite tame since cats no longer prey on them. I am told some animal life does reincarnate but pets are with us for as long as we want them, and they also evolve. We are able to communicate with them on a simple telepathic level here. When pets arrive before their owners they are cared for by relatives and friends. It is a great delight to see the expressions of joy on the faces of new arrivals when they are greeted by a loved animal they had thought was lost forever. Nothing that we have ever loved is lost to us, we will always find it, that is the Law.
> Love is a divine force in this world, it is an irresistible spiritual attraction drawing together all that is deepest and most enduring in humanity. When you pray for the dead, pray for our increase in knowledge and wisdom and that we may be surrounded by the love and the light of those illumined ones who seek only to serve and guide us. Do not grieve for us excessively but free us gently, great sorrow holds back our progress and we have many journeys to make;

neither make a shrine of our graves, they contain nothing but an old overcoat that we have discarded, we are more alive now than we ever were and we are only in the next room.

> Death is but an open door, we pass from room to room
> There is only just one life, no dying and no tomb.

This then is the message for the dying and the bereaved who write to me. It is a universal message of hope and joy, for one day we all have to pass through that door into another room, and perhaps the last words of Mary, Queen of Scots, 'In my end is my beginning', express the literal truth for everyone.

22 *Mediums and Mysticism*

Many of the letters I receive request personal interviews to discuss magic and witchcraft or just ask to meet me. Some require counselling on their problems, others are terminally ill and seek reassurance, yet others are bereaved and desire the use of my psychic ability on their behalf. It is a physical impossibility for me to give personal consultations to all who solicit them, and on occasions I recommend a friend locally because I am confident that her psychic work is genuine and honest having experienced it.

In the past I might have suggested the Spiritualist Association of Great Britain in Belgrave Square, London because I was personally acquainted with many of the mediums who worked there and was of the opinion that the cream of mediumship resided there, in particular one David Young whom I regard as the most outstanding medium of this generation. Over the years however, the familiar mediums have either retired, died or moved on; they are all strangers to me and a recent television programme illustrating the working of the SAGB was rather disappointing and mostly confirmed an experience related to me by a friend whom I shall call Anne.

Anne is a widow and a member of an organization which gives counsel and help to widows. She made the acquaintance there of another widow who desperately felt the need to make contact with her late husband through a medium, and as Anne was conversant with the activities of the SAGB since she subscribed to its teachings and beliefs, she undertook to make all the arrangements and requested an appointment with a medium of good repute for her friend. She told me, 'I prayed that she would be given a good medium and receive evidence which would comfort her.'

The widow in question (whose name I never knew) had no previous knowledge of psychic matters, she was a member of the Church of England and had never felt the need to take an interest in Spiritualism, this was to be her first experience with a medium and consequently she had no idea what to expect.

Subsequent to the appointment, she told Anne that after some stentorian breathing, the medium appeared to go into a trance and the supposed voice of her late husband addressed her through the medium. The voice was very aggressive and accused her of, amongst other things, keeping him alive by her ministrations and her will long after he should have been allowed to die, so that his sufferings were extended.

There was no evidence as such, which is really the purpose of mediumship and the widow was alarmed when the medium started moaning and groaning and clutching at her stomach in obvious agony. The widow knelt on the floor beside her and said in crisp tones, 'Can I help you? I am trained in first aid!'

When Anne told me this, I burst into inappropriate laughter. 'It's not funny, Lois,' she said severely, 'it's a tragedy, and it makes me feel so utterly disgusted that I feel like giving up any interest in Spiritualism.'

The late husband had died as a result of carcinoma of the stomach, and sometimes in trance, mediums 'take on' temporarily the symptoms of the terminal illness, but never, in my experience, with such exaggeration.

Why is it that often despite sincerity and prayer and a desperate need, mediumship proves so abysmal? I do not pretend to have an answer and can only hazard a guess. I suspect that the channel, i.e. the medium, is insufficiently trained and allowed to practise publicly before she is ready to do so. There is a lot of unnecessary mystique attached to mediumship, and whilst it engenders respect as does the ability to become a concert pianist or a portrait painter, it requires the same sort of dedication and practice, with the addition that the channel needs to be pure and clarified.

It should be remembered too that mediums, even the best, are human beings and they have their off days like everyone else, but they are expected to produce accurate information and evidence on every occasion like rabbits from a hat. People should not be discouraged if their first attempts at receiving communication are unsuccessful, another medium should be consulted at a later date. The evidence is available to any discerning person with the patience and application to pursue the search for it.

One of the complaints I sometimes receive in letters, is that my correspondent has witnessed a brilliant demonstration of clairvoyance at a public meeting and has decided to have a private consultation with the medium concerned, only to find that her performance was hardly even mediocre on a one-to-one basis.

The reason is, I think, that in a large gathering of people, a great deal of unconscious psychic energy is generated and the medium utilizes this and is probably quite unaware that she is doing so. In a private consultation she is dependent upon her own psychic capacity and any energy that the sitter is emitting is consumed by her anticipation.

Many of my correspondents seek my advice on personal psychic development, and the only truly safe way is under the auspices and guidance of a wise and experienced medium in a development circle. Such circles however are few and difficult to discover and need to be populated by people with a critical and sensible attitude towards the phenomena produced, trance and obsession should be firmly discouraged since they present very real dangers to a beginner in the search for knowledge.

Many of my correspondents complain of their inability to obtain completely convincing evidence of the survival of death of a loved one, and my help is sought in the securing of this.

Witches do not call up the dead, anymore than Spiritualists do, the dead communicate and correspond through ties of love, and if a particular person does not manifest, it may well be that they do not wish to communicate.

The accumulative evidence and experiences of my life have convinced me beyond any shadow of doubt that we all survive death, regardless of our race or our religion, but whilst my evidence satisfies me, it is no conviction or consolation to another person desperately bereaved and seeking comfort.

My friend June who communicated with me in such detail, emphasized that love is the great binding force of the Universe, and that nothing we have ever loved is lost to us, it all awaits to be rediscovered in the life beyond death.

Amongst the writings in my grimoire is the following:

Verily I say unto you, that if a soul cometh into Annurm, the Realms of Death the Mighty One, not knowing Love, then shall it abide even until it cometh by that knowledge. O you living ones on Earth, know you that each love you have for others bridges the many worlds between you and those long lost when you come into Annurm.

There is an ancient fable which runs in this wise. A certain rich and powerful Prince died and came into Annurm, but could of his own efforts in no wise succeed in passing beyond. Thereupon he importuned Death, the Mighty One, who thus replied, 'Thou mayest leave Annurm if thou wilt answer with truth this one question that I do put to thee, 'what is life?', and the soul of the Prince answered immediately as he had learned from the philosophers, 'Life is the will to live'. 'No', said the Mighty One, 'For that is naught but pride' and straightway the God vanished.

And time passed, and the soul thought more and more upon the question of the God. At length after a hundred years, the God appeared again unto the soul saying, 'Before thou goest hence, say what is life?', and the soul in fear lest it again answer in error replied, 'Great Lord, life is toleration for all men'. 'No', said the Mighty One, 'for that is naught but justice'. And straightway the God vanished from him.

And yet another hundred years passed before once again the soul stood in the presence of the God, whereupon it cried out. 'Great One, life is love'. Then said Death the Mighty One, 'O soul go upon thy ways and work, for thou hast learned the speech of the Gods'.

One of the things that I believe we have to understand and come to terms with is that we must attempt to release the dead and allow them to make progress and journeys through their new lives, confident and trusting that when it is our time to relinquish the earth, they will be waiting to greet us and we shall be reunited in that greater life.

One of my friends told me about her sister who was widowed in the last war at the age of twenty after only two years of marriage, and though she had remarried she still mourned her young soldier husband and lived in the past with him, feeding upon her memory of their brief time together. One night she had a dream in which he appeared and said to her, 'You have to let me go, you just have to let me go, you are holding me back.' The message of the dream was very clear and distressed her deeply, but she realized that she had at last to relinquish him and allow him to go forward towards the light of his spiritual life.

Carl Gustav Jung tells a story of his two friends William James and J.H. Hyslop who were both psychologists and who made a promise to each other that whoever died first, the other would, if there were individual life after death, do all that he could to give the survivor proof of it. James died first and Hyslop waited convinced that James lived on somewhere but the proof did not come. Years passed and Hyslop had almost despaired when one day he received a letter from Ireland, a country he had never visited. The letter was from a couple who apologized for intruding on him and wrote that they regularly used a planchette as a means of communication with the spirit world and for some months their experiments had been dominated by a person who purported to be one William James and who insisted they contact a Professor Hyslop of whom they had never heard. He was so insistent and demanding that they finally made inquiries about Hyslop's identity and address and delivered a message in the form of a question, 'Does he remember the red pyjamas?'

Hyslop's first reaction was one of utter consternation, he neither remembered any red pyjamas nor thought James had honoured their solemn pact by so banal and trivial a communication, but in the days that followed the more he thought about the message the more impressed he became and he realized that no channel of communication could have been more objective and protected against subjective elements than the one chosen. He recalled that as young men he and James had been on a grand tour of Europe and arriving in Paris one evening ahead of their luggage were compelled to shop for immediate necessities of which pyjamas were considered to be essential. The ones Hyslop bought were fancy red pyjamas and James had teased him about his dubious taste for some time.

What was significant about the communication was that even in that extraordinary transcendental state, nothing, however trivial, had not played its part or been overlooked, individual memory survived also.

Regarded in a symbolic manner and as imagery issuing from reality, the words made sense, connected as they were with an incident on a journey that James and Hyslop had taken to a part of the world they had not previously visited. They had arrived on a new stage of the journey ahead of their luggage which is an image of the impediments and inertia imposed on movement and changes of life in the here and now, and reflected the spirit of James who had arrived in advance of Hyslop on another stage of a journey, not so much died as gone on ahead.

Further symbolism was that in the message, the garments were pyjamas, and moreover red. Pyjamas were a man's personal sleeping-material, an image of the individual approach to the night, above all to sleep which always at all times and places symbolizes death and red was always the colour of vitality and life.

It is as if, in this recurrence of the imagery of red pyjamas, bought in advance of the baggage of physical existence in the present, James was saying to Hyslop, that in this sleep called death, he had only to look in the imagination they had called fancy and he would see that James lived on. Far from dismissing manifestations such as these as trivial, there was cause for humility of mind and spirit before such banalities, and inspiration to look deeper into their origin of meaning. Certainly for Hyslop the message of the red pyjamas was conclusive and his belief and interest never again wavered.

J.H. Hyslop was a former professor of ethics and logic at Columbia University and in his book *Science and a Future Life*, published in the early 1900s, he regretted that in his time, millions of dollars were being spent to explore the North Pole and the stars for deep-sea dredging and studies of protoplasm, all of which searched for the origin of man, but none was being spent on research to discover man's ultimate destiny, and yet this was the only question which really counted. He felt that the psychic field could serve as a bridge between religion and science and he questioned why, as the atom became scientifically known as being closer to energy than matter, and therefore more occult, it was less respectable to examine the possibilities of spirit and life after death. He wondered why some scientists considered it wrong to regard consciousness as not a function of the brain, but apart from it. With this in mind he went on to examine what evidence would satisfy the sceptic and stipulated two things, first it would have to be shown that an individual consciousness could be separated from its organism to prove an independent existence, and second, it must be established that communication with such an entity was possible, and personal identity of the deceased proved as far as possible. The facts must prove that the source of the phenomena is what it claims to be, and this personal identity of the discarnate means that the deceased person shall tell facts of personal knowledge in his earthly life, and tell them in such quantity and with such a quality that we should not doubt his existence any more than we would if we received the same incidents over a telephone or a telegraph wire. In this way alone can we show that the intelligence involved is outside the medium through which the facts come.

Professor Hyslop saw no reason why telepathy should be substituted as a theory for communication with the dead, because there was no reason to assume that the dead could not communicate by the same method, especially with a reliable and serious medium; he defined a medium as someone who claimed to communicate with the dead through trance, conscious state, automatic writing or the Ouija board, and examined some of the classic cases that fulfilled his strict criteria in detail.

Professor Hyslop died in 1920, and after his death his secretarial assistant documented dozens of séances with mediums which brought almost unassailable evidence that Hyslop himself was communicating through the medium and providing information that met his criteria for authenticity.

Before asserting that much of the information issuing from what we assume is the spiritual realms through mediums is banal and trivial, we would do well to consider the implications and difficulties involved in spirit communication.

Much of life generally is banal and trivial and if loved ones wish to prove their identity, they are likely to refer to insignificant matters known to both parties. When I receive a telephone call from a friend on earth, our conversation will be of everyday affairs in our lives, rather than an intellectual debate, and communications from the so-called dead recall shared memories in an effort to prove their survival.

The world of matter which we inhabit is slow and thick, it is so ponderous and heavy compared with the spiritual world that much of the inspiration in clairvoyance is lost in transmission, and in the attempt to slow down the higher and more subtle vibrations of spirit so that an impact can be made.

Communications are conveyed through the subconscious mind of the medium which in most cases is already trained through many years to think in certain directions, to express itself in certain ways, to use certain ideas. Communicators strive to bring their own thoughts and ideas and words, to attempt to make new tracks in the subconscious mind to get their message through.

During my mother's lifetime, I remember that we once had a discussion on the possibility that Joan of Arc was a witch, a follower of the Old Religion. Many years after her death, my mother communicated with me through another medium who told me, 'Your mother is here and she is showing me a statue of Joan of Arc, do you understand why?' I replied that I did, and I assumed that she was referring to our conversation so many years before. Alternatively, perhaps she had discovered in that greater world, that Joan of Arc had been a witch and this was her manner of informing me. Either way the message was evidential.

Sometimes people write to me and tell me in varying ways that the intense loneliness of their bereavement is destroying them, and they ask me how they can make themselves more receptive to those who have died. I asked this question of my friend June on an occasion when she was communicating and she told me,

> Those you love and who love you are never lost to you, they do not wander outside the radius of their love, they have not gone to some distant star, for as I told you, our world interpenetrates with yours, but sometimes they are closer than at others. They endeavour to influence you but you are receptive only when your mind is peaceful. When you are mentally enveloped in fearful thoughts, worried or anxious you create a barrier which makes it difficult for them to approach you, and when you are sad and shed tears you wash them away. If you would try to be calm and peaceful, full of brightness, hope, trust, faith and confidence you would always feel their presence.
>
> We strive to get close to you but our proximity is dependent on your atmosphere, your growth, your evolution, we cannot reach those whose souls are so dead to the things of the spirit that we have no area of contact. Where there is an awareness, a quickening of the soul we can make contact and forge links and bonds of unity.

I asked her on one occasion why some of my more profound questions had to remain unanswered and she told me that all communication between the two worlds is subject to certain rules and laws and that some things were not allowed to be revealed, mainly because until we actually experience conditions in the next world a lacuna exists in terms of reference, and this would only lead to confusion and misunderstanding.

This explains why in much spiritual and psychic endeavour there may seem to be a point beyond which we cannot go, an invisible barrier and which, according to June exists for our own protection.

During my travels in the Near and Middle East, I became interested in the teachings of the Sufis who are the mystical body of Islam. The faith of Islam is impatient of any speculation about God, for the Mohammedan Deity is an absolute Will who demands unquestioning obedience to the Law, as dictated in Heaven to his Prophet. His worship abounds with dogmas and rituals, Nature has no part in it and symbolism is unrecognized.

The Sufi extension of the main tenet of Mohammedism, the Unity of God, may be expressed in the maxim 'there is no real existence save Allah', all else being phenomenal and therefore non existent.

Sufis refuse to think of God as an arbitrary unlimited Will, separate and apart from everything, as one who reveals himself clearly only through the words of a Prophet, as a being before whom man is mere dust and ashes, and who demands no higher service than fear, unquestioning faith and outward obedience.

In their view God is immanent in all things and is the essence of every human soul. There is not only no God but God, but no being, life or spirit except the being, life and spirit of God and every man may be God's prophet and more even than his Prophet.

Sufism is generous to women, Muhyiddin Ibn Arabi, a twelfth-century Sufi saint and mystic wrote, 'God is never seen immaterially, and the vision of Him in woman is the most perfect of all'. My study of Islam and Sufism eventually centred on the writings of Mevlana Jalalu'ddin, the great Turkish philosopher, theosophist and poet, who was born in the city of Balh in Horasan in 1207. He settled in Anatolia at an early age and is renowned for being the founder of the Mevlevi (or 'whirling') dervishes. Amongst his writings is an invitation:

> Come, come again whatever you are,
> Come, whether you be Moslem, pagan or a lover of leaving,
> It does not matter,
> Ours is not a caravan of despair,
> Come, even if you have broken your vow a thousand times,
> Come, come yet again, come.

One of his observations was, 'Woman is God's holy light, not a beloved; as if she is the creator and not the created.' Mustafa Kemal Atatürk, the founder of the Turkish Republic who was not noted for his religious inclinations, and was responsible for closing the dervish *tekkes* (schools), and forbidding the veneration of the tombs of dervish saints in his attempts to modernize Turkey and rid it of superstition, turning its orientation from the East towards the West, nevertheless remarked about Mevlana, 'He made a great renewal in souls and beliefs, he is indeed very great. Whenever I visit Konya, Mevlana's spirituality envelops my whole person.' Konya, which is regarded as the 'holy city' of Turkey, never in its heart succumbed to Atatürk, and he was aware of this. His statue in Konya faces away from the city.

E.F.W. Tomlin, the British orientalist wrote of Mevlana:

> Although there is a lofty level of thought in Mevlana's beliefs, we see a concrete imagination; it has lost nothing in translation as the imagination is easily captured and it works itself into the soul. Man cannot attain the world of truth immediately, because as Mevlana mentions in the first book of the Mesnevi, 'God has set before us a ladder, we must climb it step by step,' and his following lines, 'There are many believers, but their belief is one,' expresses a universal reality to all of us, both to his fellow people and to all humanity, as he said, 'If you count the courtyards of all the buildings on which the sun shines, there are hundreds of houses, but if you remove the walls, all of these pieces of light are one and the same.'

Mevlana died on the 17 December 1273 in Konya, and the day is celebrated in Konya, not as the anniversary of his death, but as that of the 'return' as he saw death as 'returning to God', and said that the night on which the soul is parted from the body must be celebrated as a festival or wedding.

The *türbe* or Tomb of Mevlana lies in the dervish *tekke* in Konya which is now the Mevlana Mausoleum and a museum. To visit it is a feast for the eyes, for it abounds with colour, light and inexpressible richness and beauty which the poverty of words has no power to describe. The *türbe* is draped with a richly embroidered cloth of silver and gold, and at the head rests the high conical turban bound cap of the Mevlevi sheik. The mausoleum also contains the tombs of Mevlana's descendants, all equally richly draped. Over the entrance to the tomb are these words: 'This tomb, this station is the goal of the dervish's pilgrimage, his Ka'ba (the holy shrine at Mecca). He who enters lacking, leaves whole.'

The first time I visited Mevlana's tomb, steeped as I was in his writings, I was overcome by the sanctity and aura of his resting-place. I felt diffident, as if I were unworthy to be in the presence of this holy man. I only knew that his wisdom and his vision had inspired me and raised my consciousness to new heights, and I was grateful for all I had learned from him. I remember that I closed my eyes, and asked mentally that he would accept me as I was, a humble seeker of knowledge of the spirit, imperfect and insignificant.

As I stood there before his tomb, with the sound of the murmuring hum of a Muslim nearby telling his beads and praying to Mevlana, I felt a warm glow envelop me, as if I were standing before a fire. The feeling began in the area of my solar plexus from whence all my psychic and spiritual manifestations have their origin, it spread gently outwards, consuming all my body, and incredibly, I knew that he had heard me and had answered, and that the glow I felt was the warmth of his welcome to me.

I have since that time visited Mevlana's tomb on a number of occasions, and always, I am aware of this spiritual welcome. The most remarkable aspect of this story however, is that on an occasion when two friends were touring Turkey and I learned that their journey included Konya, I asked them if, when they visited Mevlana's tomb, they would give him a message from me. They were to simply concentrate on his *türbe* and say mentally, 'Lois sends her respectful love,' and they agreed to do it.

On their return I asked them if they had carried out my commission, and they told me that they had each done it separately without consultation, and when they had left the mausoleum, they said to each other, 'Did you remember to ...?' and they had compared notes. Each had been aware of an emanation which seemed to rise from the *türbe*, and both said, interrupting each other as they spoke, 'It was most odd, it was as if Mevlana heard and acknowledged the message and returned the love!'

I was not surprised, the dervishes call it *'baraka'*, the spirit of the presence, and it is still there after seven hundred years, but did he not write:

Come, come again, whatever you are ...

Every thoughtful person has a need to discover a philosophy of life, whether it is eclectic as mine is, or selective; for many it is a task which occupies a lifetime. To all of us there is an hour when we ache to understand the riddle of life and our place in it, why we exist and for what end we are bound, whether life is just a 'tale told by an idiot, full of sound and fury, signifying nothing', or whether it has meaning, a meaning of which we can grasp but a little. Some seek a meaning through a particular religion, others dispute that life has any meaning, and yet others involve themselves in distractions to negate the necessity of thinking at all.

The unconscious in man can only be observed through what is conscious, but the dreamers and the visionaries who are amongst us are a channel to the Goddess area of the unconscious, a last link to the sanity and love of the feminine principle so lacking in our present-day society.

D.H. Lawrence wrote that, '... in the dust where we have buried the silent races and their abominations, we have buried so much of the delicate magic of life', but I believe that in the Old Religion and in witchcraft of the beneficent kind, this magic of life is reborn, and that those who seek to unlock its secrets acknowledge the relationship between spirit and matter, and are more aware than most, of the claims of the eternal and the infinite which we ignore at our peril.

Despite the fake magicians, the ersatz witches, the silliness, the pretentiousness, and the inane posturing of many areas of the occult world, there is a hard core of dedicated practitioners whose aim is to establish a dialogue with the unseen world and make a celebration of life, and of the magic of life.

In his book *The Integration of the Personality*, Carl Gustav Jung wrote: 'We are in reality unable to borrow or absorb anything from outside, from the world or from history. What is essential to us can only grow out of ourselves.'

In some traditions of witchcraft is a Charge, and the words of the Goddess echo Jung:

> And thou who thinkest to seek for me, know thy seeking and yearning shall avail thee not, unless thou know the Mystery, that if that which thou seekest, thou findest not within thee, thou wilt never find it without thee.
>
> For behold, I have been with thee from the beginning, and I am that which is attained at the end of all desire.

> He who knows not, and knows not that he knows not,
>   is a fool – shun him.
> He who knows not, and knows that he knows not,
>   is a child – teach him.
> He who knows, and knows not that he knows,
>   is asleep – wake him.
> But he who knows, and knows that he knows,
>   is a wise man – follow him.
>
> Proverb

Bibliography

Anasteh, A. Reza, *Rumi, The Persian, The Sufi* (Routledge & Kegan Paul, 1974)
Barrow, Sir John, *Travels in China* (London, 1806)
Bourne, Lois, *Witch Amongst Us* (Robert Hale, 1985)
Briffault, Robert, *The Mothers* (New York and London, 1927)
Brown, Rosemary, *Unfinished Symphonies* (Souvenir Press, 1971)
Brunton, Dr Paul, *A Search in Secret Egypt* (Rider, 1969)
Brunton, Dr Paul, *A Search in Secret India* (Rider, 1934)
Chesterman, John, *An Index of Possibilities, Energy and Power* (Wildwood House, 1974)
Cummins, Geraldine, *The Road to Immortality* (Pilgrim Books, 1955)
Ehrenreich, Barbara and English, Deirdre, *Witches, Midwives and Nurses* (Writers and Readers Co-operative, 1976)
Frazer, J.G., *The Golden Bough* (Macmillan, 1911)
Gibran, Kahil, *The Prophet* (William Heinemann, 1926)
(trans. from Turkish) Holland, Muhtar, *The Unveiling of Love* by Sheikh Muzaffer Ozak Al-Jerrahi Al-Halveti (Inner Traditions International, New York, 1981)
Leland, Charles, *Aradia or The Gospel of the Witches* (David Nutt, 1899)
Neill, Robert, *Witchfire at Lammas* (Hutchinson, 1977)
(trans.) Nicholson, R.A., *The Mathnawī of Jalalu'ddin Rūmī* (Luzac, 1926)
Patai, Raphael, *The Hebrew Goddess* (Ktav, New York, 1967)
Peel, Edgar and Southern, Pat, *The Trials of the Lancashire Witches* (David and Charles, 1969)
Randles, Jenny, *Beyond Explanation* (Robert Hale, 1985)
Shah, Idries, *The Way of the Sufi* (Penguin, 1974)
Sheldrake, Dr Rupert, *The Presence of the Past* (Collins, 1988)
Strieber, Whitley, *Communion* (Century Hutchinson, 1987)
Summers, Montague, *Malleus Malficarium* (Dover, 1978)

Van der Post, Laurens, *Jung and the Story of Our Time* (Chatto & Windus, 1976)
Walker, Barbara G., *Women's Encyclopaedia of Myths and Secrets* (Harper & Row, 1983)